Developmental Psychopathology at School

Series Editors

Stephen E. Brock
California State University, Sacramento, CA, USA

Shane R. Jimerson
University of California, Santa Barbara, CA, USA

For further volumes:
http://www.springer.com/series/7495

Shelley R. Hart • Stephen E. Brock • Ida Jeltova

Identifying, Assessing, and Treating Bipolar Disorder at School

 Springer

Shelley R. Hart
Bloomberg School of Public Health
Department of Mental Health
Johns Hopkins University
Baltimore, MD, USA

Ida Jeltova
Graduate Center
City University of New York
New York, NY, USA

Stephen E. Brock
Department of Special Education,
  Rehabilitation
School Psychology and Deaf Studies
California State University, Sacramento
Sacramento, CA, USA

ISBN 978-1-4614-7584-2   ISBN 978-1-4614-7585-9 (eBook)
DOI 10.1007/978-1-4614-7585-9
Springer New York Heidelberg Dordrecht London

Library of Congress Control Number: 2013939186

To Bryant and Torynne Hart, as well as
everyone I love who has supported me
in this seemingly unending labor of love
Shelley R. Hart

To Dyana Christine and David Edward Brock
Stephen E. Brock

Acknowledgments

The authors wish to acknowledge the individuals and families who deal with the challenges this disorder presents and to commend their resilience in the face of adversity. We thank those who have participated in the research that propels knowledge and understanding forward and makes works such as this possible.

Contents

Chapter 1
Introduction and Overview

> Life means a lot of chaos. Grasping at coping strategies, constructive or otherwise, is all you can do. It reminds me of being out on a raft in the ocean riding the waves. All of a sudden a squall comes and the waves get really big and unpredictable. You are being tossed around and come crashing down only to be forced up again by the turbulent forces of the water. You have to do anything you can to stay connected and safe. You may cry, scream, try to swim, try to hold still and go with the swells, hold onto the raft for dear life, choose to let go of the raft and try to swim. You do whatever it takes to hold it together until the storm calms. It's survival—Olivia. (Anglada, 2006, p. 105).

Bipolar disorder is a condition that has interested physicians, scientists, and philosophers for centuries. Historically, it has experienced an evolution of terms and concepts, which continues to this day. Mention of the phenomenon can be traced back to 1845, in a textbook of "mental diseases" by German psychiatrist, Wilhelm Griesinger, who described a circular pattern of alternation between mania and depression in the same patient. Years later, Emil Kraepelin published several volumes dedicated to the disorder, termed "Manic-Depressive Insanity," to describe the condition, suggest biological origins, and distinguish it from schizophrenia in that there was believed to be complete recovery between episodes. In 1980, the diagnosis was first recognized as an entity separate from unipolar depression in the third edition of the American Psychiatric Association's (APA) *Diagnostic and Statistical Manual of Mental Disorders* (DSM), the diagnostic system used in the USA to classify mental health disorders (Pichot, 2006).

Typically characterized as a chronic and severe condition, a bipolar diagnosis is based on the presence of manic, hypomanic, and depressive symptoms. According to the most recent version of the *DSM* (*DSM-5*) there are three types of episodes (i.e., manic, hypomanic, and major depressive), which in conjunction with severity of symptoms and level of impairment result in seven possible bipolar diagnoses[1]: bipolar I disorder, bipolar II disorder, cyclothymia, substance-induced bipolar disorder, bipolar disorder associated with a known general medical condition, other

---

[1] Throughout the course of this book the term bipolar disorder is used to refer to this grouping of disorders unless otherwise specified.

S.R. Hart et al., *Identifying, Assessing, and Treating Bipolar Disorder at School*,
Developmental Psychopathology at School, DOI 10.1007/978-1-4614-7585-9_1,
© Springer Science+Business Media New York 2014

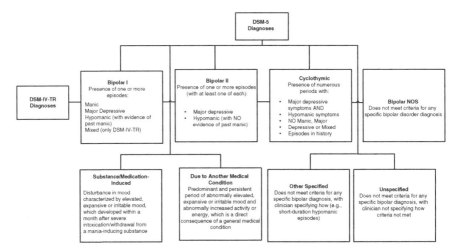

Fig. 1.1 This figure illustrates and briefly summarizes the four possible *DSM IV-TR* bipolar disorder diagnoses and the seven proposed diagnoses captured under the category of Bipolar and Related Disorders in the new *DSM-5*. *Note*. Adapted with permission from *The diagnostic and statistical manual of mental disorders: Fourth edition-text revision (DSM-IV-TR)* by the American Psychiatric Association, 2000, Author: Washington, DC. Proposed changes for *DSM-5* are available from www.dsm5.org

specified bipolar disorder and unspecified bipolar disorder (APA, 2013). DSM has recently been updated and there was speculation that new criteria would embrace the potentially different presentation in children, however, only minor changes were made from *DSM-IV-TR* (see Chapter 5). Briefly, the Mood Disorders category was divided and bipolar disorder included in its own chapter (i.e., Bipolar and Related Disorders), positioned between Depressive Disorders and Schizophrenia to emphasize its relationship to both, and several additional disorders were included (i.e., from four to seven). Figure 1.1 provides a brief breakdown. The essential feature of bipolar disorder has remained the same—the presence of a manic or hypomanic episode; major depressive episodes are often common, but not necessary for the diagnosis. Additionally, a new disorder Disruptive Mood Dysregulation Disorder (DMDD) was included to capture a more chronic, irritable presentation of mood disorder.

While believed to be a relatively low incidence disorder, current prevalence estimates vary considerably from less than 1 % to greater than 6 % of the general population, with differences typically attributed to methodology and research criteria. As milder forms of the "bipolar spectrum" are included in studies, the estimates increase substantially. For example, in a secondary analysis of national data from the 1999 National Institute of Mental Health's (NIMH) Epidemiological Catchment Area (ECA) database, Judd and Akiskal (2003) reported that when subsyndromal symptoms of mania (defined as two or more lifetime manic symptoms without meeting full criteria for a hypomanic or manic episode) were included, the lifetime prevalence rates of manic symptoms in the general population increased from 1.3 % to 6.4 %. This is important, as individuals affected by these subsyndromal symptoms evidence significantly more impairment than controls (i.e., significant increases in healthcare service use, a need for public assistance, and significantly more reported suicidal behaviors; Judd & Akiskal, 2003). Changes to DSM include in the Other Specified Bipolar Disorder diagnosis subcategories to codify subsyndromal episodes, providing further validation for the importance of understanding the entire bipolar spectrum (APA, 2013).

Even by a conservative definition, approximately 1.5 million American adults were estimated to be living with the disorder according to the original estimates of the 1999 ECA and the National Comorbidity Survey (NCS) data (Narrow, Rae, Robins, & Regier, 2002). Overall rates appear to be similar for women and men, although some differences may be evident in presenting episode and course of the disorder, as well as specific bipolar diagnosis (APA, 2000; Judd & Akiskal, 2003). Prevalence appears to be similar across race, ethnicity, and nationality in adult populations (Merikangas et al., 2011; Pini et al., 2005). The average age of onset reported in the *DSM-5* is 18-years-old (APA, 2000); however, retrospective reports indicate that symptom onset may occur much younger, in some cases with red flags, such as mood and sleep disturbances, hyperactivity, aggression and anxiety, evident in very early childhood (Faedda, Baldessarini, Glovinsky, & Austin, 2004).

Challenges to a Bipolar Disorder Diagnosis

Bipolar disorder is a complex diagnosis. It shares many symptoms and characteristics with other disorders, most notably for adults, unipolar depression. Recognition of bipolar disorder and differentiation among diagnoses are a challenging, but vital step in acquiring appropriate treatment. Misdiagnosis and underdiagnosis are important and unfortunately common themes. In a large survey sponsored by the Bipolar and Depression Support Alliance (BDSA), 69 % of respondents reported an initial misdiagnosis (Hirschfeld, Lewis, & Vornik, 2003). These respondents reported an average of almost 9-years before the disorder was appropriately diagnosed, with a mean of 3.5 other diagnoses received and 4 psychiatrists consulted before an accurate diagnosis was conferred. Working with a younger sample, Faedda and colleagues (2004) also indicated a delay of diagnosis, with a 7-year gap between onset of symptoms and first evaluation or treatment. In addition, bipolar disorder was initially considered in only 10 % of these cases, despite the presence of significant risk factors and warning signs (Faedda et al., 2004).

In the BDSA survey, 60 % of the individuals were originally diagnosed with a unipolar depression, with women more likely than men to have received this misdiagnosis (68 % vs. 43 %; Hirschfeld et al., 2003). Another recent, large, international study indicated that, upon further inquiry, approximately ½ of individuals originally diagnosed with unipolar depression presented with the core symptoms of bipolar disorder with observable changes in behavior (Angst et al., 2011). This implies that these important features were missed or overlooked in the initial assessment. Indicators of bipolarity included risk factors such as family history of bipolar disorder and comorbidity with substance use disorders.

While misdiagnosis is a concern, it may be that individuals with unipolar depression may also go on to develop bipolar disorder later in the course of their illness. In one 20-year longitudinal study, Angst, Sellaro, Stassen, and Gamma (2005) reported that the diagnostic conversion rate from unipolar depression to bipolar disorder was more than 1 % for each year, resulting in over ½ of the large sample diagnosed with unipolar depression at the start to have converted by the conclusion of the study. The risk of conversion remained constant throughout the course of the study, although with each recurring episode of major depression, the likelihood of conversion to bipolar disorder increased (Angst, Sellaro, et al., 2005).

Many researchers have speculated on the predicament of misdiagnosis and underdiagnosis. Shared diagnostic criteria and symptomatology (particularly with unipolar depression for adults, but also with schizophrenia), comorbidity with other disorders (e.g., substance abuse, anxiety disorders), the tendency for depressive episodes to precede episodes of mania or hypomania, poor diagnostic criteria for hypomanic episodes, lack of knowledge or awareness on the part of professionals, low rates of physician reimbursement for low-income health insured and/or not enough time spent with clients resulting in little inquiry about family history or hypomanic symptoms, lack of individual insight into symptoms and behaviors, and the tendency for individuals to seek help when depressed, but not manic, have all been presented as contributing to the current state of diagnosis (e.g., Benazzi, 2007; Emilien, Septien, Brisard, Corruble, & Bourin, 2007; Judd et al., 2003; McCombs, Ahn, Tencer, & Shi, 2007; Yen, Chen, Ko, Yen, & Huang, 2007).

Not recognizing a bipolar diagnosis carries with it important implications for an individual's life. Pharmacotherapy remains the primary treatment for bipolar disorder, primarily with mood stabilizers (e.g., lithium, valproate, lamotrigine; APA, 2002; Chou, 2004). Many studies regarding the benefits of introducing these medications to individuals with bipolar disorder have been conducted in recent years (see Hamrin & Iennaco, 2010; Nivoli et al., 2010 for reviews of these recent trials). Adjunct psychosocial therapy is highly recommended and the efficacy of certain forms of therapy has been highlighted in recent large, ongoing, national studies (e.g., Colom et al., 2003; Frank et al., 2005; Lam et al., 2003; Miklowitz, George, Richards, Simoneau, & Suddath, 2003; Miklowitz et al., 2007).

Individuals who are not diagnosed do not receive the benefit of these interventions, and given the high rate of suicide among this population (a frightening reality of this disorder to be discussed further later in this book) it may not be an understatement to suggest that obtaining these treatments can be a matter of life and death (e.g., Nery-Fernandes et al., 2012). Equally important, a misdiagnosis may result in crucial implications for the course of the disorder, as possible medications prescribed for competing disorders (e.g., antidepressants) may carry with them the burden of a possible switch for an individual with bipolar disorder into a manic episode (Mundo, Cattaneo, Russo, & Altamura, 2006).

Course and Outcomes Associated with Bipolar Disorder

Bipolar disorder is no longer thought to be an episodic illness with complete recovery to premorbid functioning between episodes. In one longitudinal study beginning in 1978 and continuing to this day, over 200 adults with bipolar disorder have been followed. While manic symptoms are believed to be the hallmark, and the cause of significant impairment for bipolar disorder, results from this study indicate that regardless of the type (i.e., predominantly manic pole in bipolar I or predominantly depressive pole in bipolar II), individuals spend considerably more time experiencing depressive symptoms, and demonstrate at the least subsyndromal depression (not quite meeting criteria for a major depressive episode) approximately 50 % of the time (Judd et al., 2003).

This indicates that individuals with bipolar disorder spend a significant amount of their lives experiencing symptoms of depression, which has important implications. First, depression is found to be associated with suicidal thoughts and behaviors, a prevalent issue for individuals with bipolar disorder. One recent meta-analysis reported that approximately ⅓ of individuals with bipolar I or II disorder will attempt suicide in their lifetime (Novick, Swartz, & Frank, 2010). Thoughts and plans of suicide are also unfortunately common among those with a bipolar diagnosis (Merikangas et al., 2011). Importantly, those with subthreshold and bipolar spectrum disorder are also at an increased risk of ideation and attempt (Merikangas et al., 2011).

The link between depression and suicidal thoughts and behaviors for individuals diagnosed with bipolar disorder is quite clear. In one study, clinically significant depressive symptoms were evident in 90 % of suicide attempters (Balázs et al., 2006). In another large study comparing the rates of attempts during each phase of bipolar illness, attempts were recorded to occur only during depressive, mixed, and depressive-mixed phases. Hopelessness and severity of depression were key indicators of risk. Whereas suicide attempts were associated with symptomatology, suicidal ideation was present throughout the population regardless of the current episode or type, although not as common in hypomanic or manic phases (Valtonen et al., 2007). Notably, studies have shown that individuals who receive treatment have a 2.5-fold lower suicide rate (Angst, Stassen, Clayton, & Angst, 2002).

Second, depressive symptoms have an important impact on functional outcome for individuals with bipolar disorder. Depressive symptoms have been shown to predict overall quality of social functioning, with even subsyndromal depressive symptoms adversely affecting the quality of social adjustment (Pope, Dudley, & Scott, 2007). Individuals with bipolar disorder report significantly more role impairment due to depression than mania (Merikangas et al., 2011), and severity of depressive symptoms has also shown to be associated with work impairment (Goetz, Tohen, Reed, Lorenzo, & Vieta, 2007).

Unfortunately, while severity of symptoms is associated with severity of impairment, poor functional outcome appears to be the rule, rather than the exception regardless of symptom severity; for example, one study indicated 72 % of subjects were receiving disability benefits (Brieger, Röttig, Röttig, Marneros, & Priebe, 2007), another reported that approximately 84 % were unemployed and 62 % indicated that at some point during their illness, they were unable to live independently (Levine, Chengappa, Brar, Gershon, & Kupfer, 2001). Similarly, Morgan, Mitchell, and Jablensky (2005) reported that 36 % of men and 15 % of the women studied had been under some form of legal guardianship over the previous year. Three-quarters of this study reported deterioration from their premorbid level of functioning, with 72 % living alone, 30–40 % not having ongoing contact with a close relative, and 15–30 % not having a close friend with whom to share thoughts or feelings or rely upon for support (Morgan, Mitchell, & Jablensky, 2005).

On a global level, bipolar disorder is reported to be the fifth leading cause of disability among individuals 15- to 44-years-old (World Health Organization, 2001). Clearly, the idea that bipolar disorder is a benign illness with episodic periods of dysfunction is a myth. In addition to the functional and clinical outcomes discussed above, bipolar often exists in conjunction with other disorders. Substance abuse and anxiety disorders are common comorbidities in adults. In addition, medical comorbidities are frequently seen to coexist with bipolar disorder. A study by Kilbourne et al. (2004) highlighted the prevalence of cardiovascular, endocrine, and pulmonary medical conditions, with increased rates of hypertension, hyperlipidemia, diabetes, and hepatitis C. The authors stated that the bipolar sample was younger on average than the control group, suggesting not only overall increased risk for these comorbid medical conditions, but that risk increases earlier in life for individuals with bipolar disorder (Kilbourne et al., 2004). Interestingly, with the concerns related to prescribing medications to youth with bipolar disorder, a recent study suggests that these rates of medical comorbidities are independent of medication; that is, that individuals with bipolar disorder are at increased risk regardless of the medications (or lack of) prescribed (Jerrell, McIntyre, & Tripathi, 2011).

Why School Professionals Should Read This Book

Once thought to occur only in adults, bipolar disorder is now being recognized with increasing prevalence among children and adolescents (NIMH, 2001). In two recent studies using large, nation-wide databases, changes in diagnostic patterns for children and adolescents were evaluated. Among admissions to inpatient psychiatric facilities, the likelihood of receiving a bipolar diagnosis had increased 90 % between 1995 and 2000 (Harpaz-Rotem, Leslie, Martin, & Rosenheck, 2005). Within the same time period, the likelihood of receiving a bipolar diagnosis had increased more than 65 % amongst privately insured children and adolescents. This increase was eclipsed only by the diagnosis of autism (Harpaz-Rotem & Rosenheck, 2004). It is anticipated that since 2000 the rates have increased even more.

While challenges exist in diagnosing adults, the issue is even more complex when attempting to diagnose children and adolescents. In 2001, the NIMH convened a

Table 1.1 Clinical phenotypes of early-onset bipolar disorder

Phenotype	Relation to DSM criteria	Proposed criteria/description
Narrow: (Hypo)Mania	Full-Duration Episodes, Hallmark Symptoms	Child exhibits clear episodes that meet full DSM-IV criteria, including duration of episodes (at least 1 week-mania or 4 days-hypomania or any duration if hospitalization is necessary) and hallmark symptoms of mania (e.g., elevated/expansive mood or grandiosity)
Intermediate: (Hypo) Mania Not Otherwise Specified	Short Episodes, Hallmark Symptoms	Child meets criteria for narrow phenotype of (hypo) mania except that episodes are between 1 and 3 days in duration
Intermediate: Irritable (Hypo)Mania	Full-Duration Episodes, No Hallmark Symptoms	Child meets criteria for (hypo)mania with irritable, not elevated or expansive, mood. Must occur in distinct episodes meeting duration criteria
Broad: Severe Mood and Behavioral Dysregulation		Child exhibits: • Abnormal mood (i.e., anger or sadness) present for at least half of the day most days and of sufficient severity to be noticeable by people in the environment • Hyperarousal defined by at least three of the symptoms of insomnia, agitation, distractibility, racing thoughts or flight of ideas, pressured speech, intrusiveness • Markedly increased reactivity to negative emotional stimuli manifest verbally or behaviorally Symptoms are present currently and have been present for at least 12 months without any symptom-free periods exceeding 2 months. Symptoms are severe in at least one setting and at least mild in a second

Note: Adapted from "Defining Clinical Phenotypes of Juvenile Mania," by E. Liebenluft, D. S. Charney, K. E. Towbin, R. K. Bhangoo, & D. S. Pine, 2003, *American Journal of Psychiatry, 160*, pp. 430–437

Research Roundtable, which acknowledged that a diagnosis of bipolar disorder was possible in children, however, tended to manifest differently in children than adults, for whom the criteria was written. The roundtable recommendations included assigning a bipolar disorder NOS diagnosis to those children with a more broad presentation of the disorder (NIMH, 2001). Leibenluft, Charney, Towbin, Bhangoo, and Pine (2003) expanded on this to describe four phenotypes, or presentations, of early-onset bipolar disorder.[2] These phenotypes are briefly outlined in Table 1.1. Understanding there are varying degrees and different presentations is important to the conceptualization of the "bipolar disorder spectrum," and will be useful not only when working

---

[2] While different terms are used in the field (e.g., pediatric, prepubertal, juvenile), we generally use the term early-onset to refer to bipolar disorder diagnosed prior to age 18-years, unless otherwise noted.

with youth with bipolar disorder, but also when consuming related research (e.g., attending to inclusion criteria).

Difficulties with diagnostic criteria are one challenge faced when attempting to recognize this disorder in children and adolescents. While the disorder may not present as classically defined bipolar disorder, there is also the issue of comorbidity, which may mask the symptoms and mislead practitioners. Behavioral disorders such as attention-deficit/hyperactivity disorder (ADHD), oppositional defiant disorder (ODD), and conduct disorder (CD) are often found to be comorbid with bipolar disorder in youth; also prevalent are anxiety disorders and substance abuse. Recent studies indicate that early-onset bipolar disorder seems to be associated with an even more chronic and debilitating course than that found among adults. As the remaining chapters of this book focus on these issues, briefly, relapse rates are higher, time to recovery is longer, percentage of time spent experiencing syndromal or subsyndromal symptoms is higher, rapid cycling (defined broadly as four episodes per year to more than 365 episodes per year) and mixed episodes are more prevalent, irritability and depression are the predominant characteristics (as compared to euphoria in adults), comorbidity with at least one disorder is the rule, and suicidality and psychosocial impairments are more common (e.g., Faedda et al., 2004; Geller et al., 2002; Jairam, Srinath, Girimaji, & Seshadri, 2004; Kowatch et al., 2005; Moor, Crowe, Luty, Carter, & Joyce, 2012).

In a recent report released by the Substance Abuse and Mental Health Services Administration (SAMHSA), 70–80 % of children with mental health conditions receive services from school-based providers (Sopko, 2006). Professionals based in the schools were reported to engage in the following types of mental health activities: assessment, behavior management consultation, case management, referrals, crisis intervention, individual counseling, group counseling, substance abuse counseling, medication for emotional or behavioral problems, referral for medication management, and family support services (Sopko, 2006). As more is learned about this disorder, these children will increasingly be found in the school system. School-based mental health personnel are uniquely positioned to spot the symptoms, attain a conglomeration of information from, and enhance communication between, students, parents, teachers, paraprofessionals, primary physicians, and psychiatrists, as well as to develop an educational environment that is supportive of students with bipolar disorder. Therefore, it is important for school professionals to be knowledgeable about the epidemiology, associated deficits and impairments, red flags which should lead to further investigation, current diagnostic criteria, and effective treatments for individuals with this disorder.

Bipolar Disorder and Special Education Eligibility

Unfortunately at present, there is a paucity of information regarding children with bipolar disorder and the educational realm. However, one can conclude from the available literature that these children at one time or another during the course of their education may be brought to the attention of the school-based mental health professional. This may happen in a variety of ways (e.g., teacher or staff consult, Student Study Team meeting, observation, parent contact). The student may or may not already be diagnosed, which will alter the professional's role.

While the US Department of Education Federal Regulations requires access to a free and appropriate public education (FAPE) for any student with a disability (US Department of Education, 2006), a diagnosis of bipolar disorder does not, in and of itself, constitute special education eligibility. However, it can alert psychologists, counselors, and teachers to the unique experiences, strengths, challenges, and needs the student may have. General knowledge about the disorder can guide accumulation of further pertinent information and assist significant others in learning how to work effectively with the student. To evaluate eligibility, a thorough and comprehensive assessment would address whether the student's disability was adversely impacting his or her education. Given a particular student's needs, a child with bipolar disorder may be eligible for special education in various categories, most commonly Emotional Disturbance (ED) or Other Health Impaired (OHI). Children with bipolar disorder may also meet eligibility requirements as a student with a Significant Learning Disability (SLD) or a Speech and Language Impairment (SLI).

Purpose and Plan of This Book

The purpose of this book is to provide professionals with the information necessary to assist in the identification, assessment, and treatment of bipolar disorder in the schools. To that end, Chapter 2 discusses the current research addressing the causes and etiology of bipolar disorder. Chapter 3 explores the epidemiology and complex and somewhat controversial issue of the comorbidities associated with this diagnosis. Chapters 4, 5, and 6 focus on the identification and assessment of the disorder, from the red flags that might prompt further evaluation to diagnostic and psycho-educational assessment. Chapter 7 offers a discussion regarding treatment options currently available. Finally, the Resource Appendix supplies the reader with opportunities to further explore areas of interest and resources to offer families and individuals affected by the disorder.

Chapter 2
Etiology

The exact cause, or rather the causes, of bipolar disorder are not known and most researchers now agree that there is no single etiological factor that accounts for all instances of the disorder. Rather it would appear that several factors combined lead to the behavioral manifestations, or symptoms, collectively referred to as bipolar disorder (National Institute of Mental Health [NIMH], 2008). As illustrated in Fig. 2.1, this disorder is thought to be a neurobiological disorder (associated with certain brain regions and the dysfunction of certain neurotransmitters). In turn, these brain differences are thought to be associated with genetic factors, external environmental stressors, and/or the interactions among these variables (Bressert, 2007).

Prior to considering the complexities of genetic, environmental, and neurobiological research on bipolar disorder in youth, we need to consider the bigger picture of conceptualization of mental health conditions in general. The diathesis-stress model is the dialectical model (the widely accepted nature vs. nurture model of thinking), which states that individuals possess predispositions and vulnerabilities for illnesses (e.g., Zuckerman, 1999). The number and degree of these vulnerabilities varies greatly in a population and is not known. It appears that this variability is determined by multiple genetic, neurobiological, and environmental factors. Vulnerability or predisposition is one's potential for having a disorder (referred to as genotype). Whether this potential is ever actualized into an illness (phenotype) depends on other various factors or *stresses* that also vary greatly. It is the interaction between one's predisposition and stresses that triggers the actualization of the illness. The more and the stronger predispositions that one has, the less amount of stress this person needs to experience an outbreak.

Applying this model to early-onset bipolar disorder, we can assume that a child begins developing the disorder when a critical amount of stress triggers the otherwise dormant predispositions. Importantly, the stressors that trigger the predispositions for early-onset bipolar disorder (e.g., stimulant medication leading to escalation of mania; Delbello et al., 2001; Reichart & Nolen, 2004) may not be the same stressors that keep it in place (e.g., high-level of conflict families; Birmaher,

S.R. Hart et al., *Identifying, Assessing, and Treating Bipolar Disorder at School*,
Developmental Psychopathology at School, DOI 10.1007/978-1-4614-7585-9_2,
© Springer Science+Business Media New York 2014

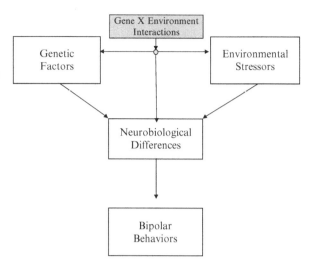

Fig. 2.1 Bipolar disorder is thought to be a neurobiological disorder. These brain differences are thought to be associated with genetic factors, external environmental stressors, and/or the interactions among these variables

Arbelaez, & Brent, 2002). Research is limited in identifying which stressors serve which function because of the tremendous heterogeneity of the early-onset bipolar disorder population.

There is evidence pointing to a biological basis for bipolar disorder (e.g., Pavuluri, Birmaher, & Nalor, 2005; Youngstrom, Birmaher, & Findling, 2008). Nonetheless, over the past two decades, mental health scientists and practitioners are shifting toward a systemic conceptualization and the above described diathesis-stress model. Scientists and practitioners are moving away from the medical model, which assumes that since the disease is present on a cellular level somewhere in the organism, the clinician's task is to locate the cells that are affected and administer treatment. According to this medical model (a) each cell is genetically programmed to progress according to a given trajectory; (b) diseases are fought via biological defense mechanisms; and (c) when and if the cell is assisted in fighting the disease with appropriate medical treatment, the cell utilizes medication to booster its natural arsenal and then gets back on genetic program. In case of mental health, psychosocial factors seem to play a very important role and psychological health is not as strongly influenced by genetic factors as is physical health. Therefore, as discussed in other books within this series (e.g., Brock, Jimerson, & Hansen, 2006, 2009), when discussing causes for mental health disorders it is imperative to attend to interactions between environment and genetic predisposition.

Again, even though research pinpoints various biochemical and neurophysiological factors in bipolar disorder, there is no biological or medical diagnostic test to reliably identify this disorder. Consequently, treatment protocols are highly dependent upon individual profiles. Multidisciplinary teams from biology, medicine, psychology, and other disciplines are continuously working to learn more about causes, triggers, and correlates of bipolar disorder in youth, find valid and reliable diagnostic tools, and establish empirically validated treatments (e.g., Faust, Walker, & Sands, 2006). The discussion that follows offers a brief review of what is currently known about the genetic, environmental, and neurobiological factors considered to play a causal role in bipolar disorder (with particular attention to early onset bipolar disorder).

Genetics

It has been suggested that the strongest biological factor to play a causal role in the development of bipolar disorder is genetics (Kato, 2008). Furthermore, the role of genetics may be particularly strong among individuals with early-onset bipolar disorder (Faraone, Glatt, Su, & Tsuang, 2004). Research that has examined the role of genetics in the development of bipolar disorder can be classified as family, twin, and molecular genetic studies.

Family Studies

Among the first studies conducted to establish the heritability of bipolar disorder were family studies. This research examined whether there is an increased incidence of bipolar disorder among the family members of bipolar patients. From their review of this research Althoff, Faraone, Rettew, Morley, and Hudziak's (2005) concluded that the "preponderance of evidence is that adult-onset bipolar disorder has clear familiality" (p. 599). Further, they conclude that the familiality of early-onset bipolar disorder may exceed that of adult-onset bipolar disorder. In other words, it is possible that genetics play a greater role in early-onset (vs. adult-onset) bipolar disorder.

Twin Studies

While family studies provide some evidence of the heritability of bipolar disorder, it is important to acknowledge that these findings could be related to a shared environment and not to shared genes. Thus, twin studies have been an important research methodology. Because twins share both a common environment and all (in the case of identical twins) or half (in the case of fraternal twins) of their genes, comparison of these sibling groups can help to determine the relative contribution of genetics and environment. Among adults Tsuang and Faraone's (1990) review suggested 60 % of bipolar disorder variance to be accounted for by genetic factors. However, more recent research has suggested an even more powerful role for genetics in the adult-onset of this disorder (with at least two studies reporting over 85 % of the bipolar disorder variance to be due to genetics; Althoff et al., 2005).

Twin studies of early-onset bipolar disorder are limited. However, Boomsma and colleagues (2006) have suggested that the heritability of early-onset bipolar disorder (as defined by Child Behavior Checklist profiles) increases with age (from 63 % at age 7 to 75 % at age 12). At the same time, this research suggested the environment to become less important as the child ages (or alternatively more important during the formative years of early-onset bipolar disorder).

Molecular Genetic Studies

While family and twin studies (as well as a limited number of adoption studies) have provided powerful evidence that bipolar disorder has a genetic component, they do not identify the specific genes implicated in the development of this disorder. Thus, researchers have employed molecular genetic studies, which have included linkage studies and candidate gene searches.

Linkage studies examine the genetic material of families that include individuals with bipolar disorder. Within these families, DNA sequences (or markers) along different chromosomes are examined for slight differences (or polymorphisms). Researchers then try to find differences that are consistently found among family members who have bipolar disorder, but not among those without the disorder. By determining how close the polymorphism, unique to the bipolar disorder family members are to a specific gene (done via statistical methods), the polymorphism can be "linked" to that gene. Hayden and Nurnberger's (2006) review suggested the best evidence for such linkages are areas on chromosomes 2p, 4p, 4q, 6q, 8q, 11p, 12q, 13q, 16p, 16q, 18p, 18q, 21a, 22q, and Xq. Study of early-onset bipolar disorder is limited and what research exists is not consistent with the findings of adult-onset research. For example, Faraone and colleagues (2004) found the age of onset of mania to be linked to chromosomes 12p, 14q, and 15q. From this finding Faraone and colleagues concluded "that individuals with an early onset of bipolar disorder are biologically different from those with a typical onset age and clinical presentation" (p. 628).

Candidate gene studies begin with the assumption that certain specific genes are likely to be associated with bipolar disorder. These prior assumptions are typically based upon clinical and empirical evidence (including linkage studies) that a specific gene is associated with the development of specific bipolar symptoms. Hayden and Nurnberger's (2006) review suggested a role for a number of different candidate genes including those listed in Table 2.1. Overall, findings from genetic and behavioral genetic research suggest that bipolar disorders are caused by many different genes working together. Identifying each one of the genes requires very careful investigations. Still, information about each separate gene contributes only a narrow window of insight into genetic mechanisms behind bipolar disorder.

Table 2.1 Specific genes thought to be associated with bipolar disorder

Gene[a]	Abbreviation[a]	Chromosome location[a]	Function
Catechol-*O*-methyltransferase	COMT	22q11.21-23	Breaks-down catecholamines and may modify the course of BPD, by increasing predisposition to rapid cycling[b]
Solute carrier family 6 (neurotransmitter, dopamine), member 3	SLC6A3 (AKA DAT)	5p13.3	Removes dopamine from synaptic cleft[c]
5-hydroxytryptamine (serotonin) receptor 4	HTR4	5q32	Modulates the release of various neurotransmitters[a]
Dopamine D4 receptor	DRD4	11p15.5	Mutations in this gene have been associated with various behavioral phenotypes[a]
Dopamine receptor D2	DRD2	11q23	Encodes the D2 subtype of the dopamine receptor, inhibits adenylyl cyclase activity[a]
5-hydroxytryptamine (serotonin) receptor 2A	HTR2A	13q14	A receptor for serotonin[a]
Solute carrier family 6 (neurotransmitter transporter, serotonin), member 4	SLC6A4	17q11.1-12	Encodes a membrane protein that transports serotonin from synaptic spaces into presynaptic neurons. Terminates the action of serotonin and recycles it in a sodium-dependent manner. A repeat length polymorphism in the promoter of this gene has been shown to affect the rate of serotonin uptake and may play a role in depression-susceptibility in people experiencing emotional trauma[a]
D-amino acid oxidase activator/G30 complex	DAOA or G72/G30	13q33	Polymorphisms in this gene have been implicated in susceptibility to schizophrenia and bipolar affective disorder, possibly due to decreased levels of D-serine and decreased NMDA receptor functioning[a]
Disrupted-in-schizophrenia 1	DISC1	1q42.1	This gene is disrupted in a translocation which segregates with schizophrenia and related psychiatric disorders in a large Scottish family[a]
Purinergic receptor P2X, ligand-gated ion channel 7	P2RX7	12q24	An ATP receptor[a]

(continued)

Table 2.1 (continued)

Gene[a]	Abbreviation[a]	Chromosome location[a]	Function
Monoamine oxidase A	MAOA	Xp11.3	Encodes monoamine oxidase A, an enzyme that degrades amine neurotransmitters, such as dopamine, norepinephrine, and serotonin[a]
Brain-derived neuro-trophic factor	BDNF	11p13-15	The protein encoded by this gene is a member of the nerve growth factor family. It is induced by cortical neurons, and is necessary for survival of striatal neurons in the brain. This gene may play a role in the in the biology of mood disorders[a]

[a]Entrez Gene (http://www.ncbi.nlm.nih.gov/sites/entrez?Db=gene)
[b]Lachman et al. (1996)
[c]Greenwood et al. (2001)

Environment

While bipolar disorder appears to have a strong genetic component (McGuffin et al., 2003), it is likely that the environment plays a role (NIMH, 2008) and may interact with genes to cause this disorder (Serretti & Mandelli, 2008). There is emerging evidence that psychosocial stressors may contribute to the onset (and recurrence) of bipolar disorder (Leahy, 2007). For example, in their literature review, Alloy and colleagues (2005) report:

> Overall, studies of life events have found that bipolar individuals experience increased stressful events prior to the first onset and recurrences of mood episodes. Moreover, most studies have found that negative life events precede the manic/hypomanic as well as the depressive episodes of bipolar individuals. (p. 1048)

Post and Leverich (2006) have suggested that psychosocial stress plays an important role in the onset (as well as the course) of bipolar disorder. In other words, childhood adversity may be a risk factor that increases the chances of early onset bipolar disorder.

Jones and Bentall's (2008) review of the literature examining the children of bipolar parents reveals that there has been limited study of the relationship between early onset bipolar disorder and negative life events. However, they conclude that given the evidence obtained from the study of adult bipolar disorder suggesting that different events influence manic and depressed episodes and that life events have consistently been associated with the first onset of this disorder, these environmental variables warrant additional study. The Jones and Bentall review also observed that the family functioning as a risk factor for early onset bipolar disorder has been the subject of limited empirical investigations. Again, however, they conclude that the evidence obtained from the study of adult bipolar disorder suggests that critical comments, hostility, or emotional over-involvement among relatives has been associated with risk of relapse among adults with bipolar disorder; these environmental variables also warrant additional study.

Most recently, the role of stressful life events has been studied among youth already diagnosed with bipolar disorder. Romero and colleagues (2009), in a study of over 400 children and adolescents with bipolar disorder, reported that 20 % had experienced physical and/or sexual abuse. While not associated with an early onset of the disorder, when compared to individuals without bipolar disorder, the presence of child abuse was reported to be associated with a longer duration of bipolar disorder.

Neurobiology

When linking bipolar disorder to brain functioning, contemporary research examines possible abnormalities in (a) brain structure or neuroanatomy (various regions of the brain, such as fronto-limbic regions), and (b) brain chemical agents that regulate its activity (e.g., neurotransmitters) or neurochemistry (e.g., Sublette, Oquendo, & Mann, 2006).

The building blocks of our nervous system are a highly specialized group of cells. Identified as "neurons," these cells are connected to one another via branches. In between any two connected neurons is a small space—a synapse. Neurons emit neurotransmitters as a chemical message via the synapse so that the next neuron receives the signal by accepting the neurotransmitter. The message is then transmitted in this way from one neuron to the next until it reaches its destination in the brain or any other region of the body. The route of the neurotransmitter in this message delivery is called a neuropathway. There are many different neuropathways that the brain is "wired" with and that we use to function. For example, when we logically solve a problem, it is mainly the neuropathways located in the frontal lobes that are activated. Emitting neurotransmitters into the synapse is the only way in which neurons relay signals. If the neuropathway and/or neurotransmitter release is altered in some way it will effect brain functioning. Many of the functions that are central to bipolar disorder, such as mood regulation and impulse control, are dependent on neuropathways and governed by various neurotransmitters (Lacerda et al., 2004). In fact, many of the symptoms of bipolar disorder have been found to be related to dysfunction of brain circuitry and neurobiological abnormalities (e.g., Chang, Adleman, Wagner, Barnea-Goraly, & Garrett, 2006; Gogtay et al., 2007). Neuroimaging research is expected to provide insight into neurophysiological correlates or markers for pediatric bipolar disorder.

Brain Structure and Activity

Among the commonly used brain or neuroimaging techniques are Computerized
Axial Tomography (CAT) and Magnetic Resonance Imaging (MRI). CAT is
similar to digital photography where a series of X-rays or photos are taken to
scan the brain and create a three-dimensional image. MRI produces a multitude
of digital photos of the brain from different angles to yield a rather precise
three-dimensional image of the brain. Research studies that employ CAT and
MRI techniques have helped uncover structural changes that are present in the
brain of individuals diagnosed with bipolar disorder. Across all age groups,
lateral ventricle enlargement and increased rates of deep white matter hyperin-
tensities have been associated with bipolar disorder (Kempton, Geddes, Ettinger,
Williams, & Grasby, 2008).[1] Perhaps helping us to understand the different presentations of adult vs. early onset bipolar disorder, a recent meta-analysis found
children and adolescents to have significantly smaller amygdalas (located in the
medial temporal lobe and a part of the brain that regulates emotional valence)
when compared to a control group (a difference that was not found when bipolar
adults were compared to controls; Pfeifer, Welge, Strakowski, Adler, & Delbello,
2008).

Gogtay et al. (2007) conducted one of the few dynamic investigations of cortical
brain development in early-onset bipolar disorder. Cortical growth was evaluated
both before and after onset of first manic episode, allowing researchers to detect
changes over time. The changes observed in individuals with bipolar disorder were
significantly different from changes observed in individuals with childhood-onset
schizophrenia. These findings are significant because it provides a clear basis for
differentiating bipolar disorder from schizophrenia. Individuals with schizophrenia
demonstrated an overall loss of grey matter volume. In individuals with an early-
onset of bipolar disorder, cortical, or grey matter (the clay for neural pathways)
growth was asymmetrical with greater mass concentration on the left side. However,
these changes were seen only after the onset of first manic episode, not at the beginning of the study. This research provides insight into the deficits in motor inhibition
(e.g., Leibenluft et al., 2007), spatial working memory, visual sequencing and scan-
ning, abstract problem solving, and verbal fluency (e.g., Bearden et al., 2007)
observed in individuals with bipolar disorder.

It is important to note that, while they help us to understand the possible etiology
of bipolar disorder, at this point in time routine neuroimaging should not be used as
a diagnostic tool in cases of mood disorders. For example, Serene, Ashrari, Szeszko,
and Kumra (2007) reviewed empirical investigations of brain development via neuroimaging and concluded that some of the reported abnormalities found in children
diagnosed with mood disorders were also observed in healthy children. A majority
of neuroimaging studies tend to be correlational in nature, include heterogeneous

---

[1] See Kempton (2008) for the meta-analysis database used in this study.

cases of bipolar disorder, and only take a snapshot of the individual's functioning. It is a burgeoning area of research and practice that holds great promise, but at present does not offer definitive answers.

Brain Chemistry

In addition to structural differences between relatively healthy and bipolar brains, neurochemical differences have been established. Research has identified several key neurotransmitters that seem to play an important role in bipolar disorder: dopamine (McTavish et al., 2001; Powell, Young, Ong, Caron, & Geyer, 2008; Silverstone, 1985; Yatham et al., 2002), GABA (Benes & Berretta, 2001; Cotter et al., 2002; Fatemi et al., 2005; Sakai et al., 2008), glutamate (Öngür et al., 2008), and norepinephrine and serotonin (Wiste, Arango, Ellis, Mann, & Underwood, 2008). When studying neurochemical functioning of the brain, researchers examine neurotransmitters' chemical variants, locations, and roles. Whether the presence, absence, or change in these chemicals is a cause or outcome of bipolar disorder remains to be determined, but the importance of neurochemicals in bipolar disease is indisputable. The relevancy of these findings to overall brain functioning in bipolar and normal individuals is not yet understood (e.g., Singh, Pfeifer, Barzman, Kowatch, & DelBello, 2007). Psychopharmacological treatment targets these chemical imbalances.

Concluding Comments

In summary, clinical research and practice on bipolar disorder in adults and children pinpoints the need to consider complex multidimensional nature of bipolar disorder. Current data are limited and mostly correlational in nature. At this point in time we can discuss possible triggers and co-occurring changes in bodily functioning, but not the exact *causes* of bipolar disorder. Establishing causal effects will require extensive longitudinal research. Available information suggests that the diathesis-stress model is highly relevant to early-onset bipolar disorder. It is plausible that it is the synergy of environmental stress causing disruptions in multiple systems (e.g., nervous, endocrine, and immune) with genetic predisposition for bipolar disorder that results in the manifestation of bipolar symptoms.

Chapter 3
Prevalence and Associated Conditions

As indicated in previous chapters, a complete understanding of bipolar disorder remains elusive, particularly with an early-onset of the disorder. As such, an accurate accounting of how common this disorder is in the general population also remains to be unequivocally made. However, a recent meta-analysis of epidemiologic, community-based studies has estimated the prevalence of an early-onset bipolar disorder to be approximately 1.8 % (Van Meter, Moreira, & Youngstrom, 2011). As subthreshold cases are included, estimates increase to 6–7 % (see Van Meter, Moreira, et al., 2011 for studies included in this meta-analysis). These subthreshold cases are particularly important as research has demonstrated that a substantial majority—almost half—of these individuals will convert to a bipolar I or bipolar II diagnosis in their youth (Axelson et al., 2011).

Among more specific populations (e.g., clinic-based) the rates of individuals treated for an early-onset of bipolar disorder are even higher. For example, Blader and Carlson (2007) reported diagnoses at discharge from a psychiatric facility and demonstrated that 34 % of the children and adolescents included in the study (i.e., admitted to a psychiatric facility) were diagnosed with bipolar disorder. In a similar evaluation, Lasky, Krieger, Elixhauser, and Vitiello (2011) demonstrated that amongst adolescents, a diagnosis of bipolar disorder accounted for almost half the mood-related admissions; that is, bipolar disorder was almost equally as prevalent as unipolar depression.

In comparison to those with an onset in adulthood, for those individuals with an early-onset of bipolar disorder, the course tends to be more chronic and persistent, characterized by even more substantial treatment delays, significantly more comorbidity with other psychiatric disorders, more suicidal thoughts and behaviors, more psychotic symptoms, less time euthymic and more rapid cycling/mood changes (Jerrell & Prewette, 2008; Moor, Crowe, Luty, Carter, & Joyce, 2012; Post et al., 2010). There appear to be differences within an early-onset of the disorder as well, in terms of chronicity, comorbidities, course, and functional outcomes (Meyer & Carlson, 2010). This chapter will briefly explore issues related to the prevalence of early-onset bipolar disorder and then focus on the common correlates associated with such a diagnosis.

S.R. Hart et al., *Identifying, Assessing, and Treating Bipolar Disorder at School*,
Developmental Psychopathology at School, DOI 10.1007/978-1-4614-7585-9_3,
© Springer Science+Business Media New York 2014

Changes in Prevalence in the General Population

In recent years, much speculation has occurred regarding potential increases in the prevalence of bipolar disorder. This is particularly relevant for an early onset of the disorder. Much evidence for this increase comes from studies investigating insurance or discharge claims. For example, Moreno et al. (2007) found that the number of visits to a doctor's office (i.e., outpatient visits) that resulted in an early-onset bipolar diagnosis (under the age of 19) had increased 40 times over the last decade. This study found that youth visits resulting in a bipolar diagnosis increased from 25 out of every 100,000 in the year 1994–1995 to 1,003 in the year 2002–2003.

Investigating the National Hospital Discharge Survey, Blader (2011) found striking increases in the annual rates of general psychiatric hospitalizations for children and adolescents, including those for a bipolar disorder diagnosis between the years 1996 and 2007. Similarly, Lasky et al. (2011) found that while the rates for hospitalization of an adolescent due to a mood disorder were fairly stable between 2000 and 2006, the rates for hospitalization due to a depressive disorder decreased from 9.1 to 6.4 per 10,000 but the rates due to a bipolar disorder increased from 3.3 to 5.7. Finally, Blader and Carlson (2007) demonstrated an increase in the proportion of bipolar disorder diagnoses at discharge from 10 % in 1996 to 34 % in 2004. Differences were evident in rates for children and adolescents, with 7.3 per 10,000 discharges for children and 20.4 per 10,000 discharges for adolescents with a bipolar diagnosis.

Interestingly, when examining epidemiological studies, a slightly more complex picture emerges. For example, in their meta-analysis of studies including individuals from ages 7 through 21 and spanning from 1985 through 2007, Van Meter, Moreira, et al. (2011) determined there was no evidence of an increase in the rates of bipolar disorder over time. This seemingly contradictory information may be interpreted several ways. First, it may be that bipolar disorder is being over-diagnosed in these more impaired populations. Second, it may be that while true increases of the disorder are not occurring in the general population, individuals with this condition are now more readily accessing treatment resulting in an increase in diagnoses. Third, it may be that clients and care providers are more aware of the risk factors and warning signs of bipolar disorder, resulting in more accurate or explicit report and better querying of symptoms and appropriate diagnoses. Whatever the reasons, the rates of youth receiving a bipolar diagnosis in treatment is undoubtedly increasing and understanding the correlates of this disorder while increasing effective treatment for these students should be a crucial element of any research paradigm and a focus of school-based mental health professionals.

International Rates of Early Onset Bipolar Disorder

Given the strong biological foundation of bipolar disorder illuminated in Chapter 2, it would be expected to find few differences internationally. The meta-analysis of epidemiological studies conducted by Van Meter, Moreira, et al. (2011) provides some evidence for this claim. Half of the studies included in the analysis were from countries other than the USA (e.g., the Netherlands, the UK). Researchers concluded that there were no differences between rates reported by US and non-US studies, although there was a wider range of rates reported in the US studies depending on whether subthreshold cases were included. This may suggest that non-US researchers are less likely to diverge from strict DSM criteria.

Another review of non-US studies demonstrated estimates of epidemiological studies fairly consistent with the Van Meter, Moreira, et al. (2011) meta-analysis (Soutullo et al., 2005). Interestingly, it may be that while the disorder is as common internationally in the community, other countries may experience differences in patterns of diagnosis. For example, one large study examining a large mental health trust providing outpatient and inpatient services in the UK demonstrated the prevalence of bipolar disorder in youth was low (1.0 %) and it was extremely unlikely for an individual under the age of 13 to receive this diagnosis (Chan, Stringaris, & Ford, 2010). Soutullo et al. (2005) found much more variability internationally in these more specific populations vs. epidemiological studies (centering around 1.8 %); that is, in outpatient clinics reported rates ranged from 0 % (the UK) to 4 % (Spain) and in psychiatric hospitals from 0 % (Finland) to 4.2 % (India).

One important consideration when examining international rates is differences between the International Classification of Diseases (ICD) system (World Health Organization, 1992) and the DSM. The ICD tends to be more restrictive; for example, two episodes of mania are necessary for a bipolar diagnosis vs. one in the DSM. Therefore, it would be expected to find lower rates in studies/countries utilizing strict ICD criteria.

Prevalence of Students with Bipolar Disorder Served Under IDEA

While no studies to date have been conducted to specifically investigate the prevalence of students with bipolar disorder in special education, several have reported on the number of individuals in their sample who report receiving special education services. Biederman et al. (2004) reported that approximately 41 % of their sample indicated placement in a special class. Additionally, approximately 22 % of these individuals reported being retained. Henin, Mick, et al. (2007) reported slightly lower rates of special education service utilization (approximately 23 %), although the sample consisted of those diagnosed with comorbid bipolar and attention deficit hyperactivity disorder (ADHD). This group (bipolar plus ADHD), as well as the group of youth with only an ADHD diagnosis (18 %), was significantly more likely to require special education services than the control group without either disorder (5 %), despite no differences in assessed cognitive abilities and after controlling for variables such as socioeconomic status and comorbidity. Pavuluri, O'Connor, Harral, Moss, and Sweeney (2006) reported that of the children and adolescents with bipolar only (18 %) or bipolar plus ADHD (19 %) who were receiving special education services, 45 % demonstrated reading difficulties, while 29 % were reported to have challenges with math. Half of the children with reading problems also had math difficulties, while 81 % of those with math difficulties also had problems with reading.

While population-based studies examining the rates of special education service use have not been conducted (i.e., studies indicating how many students in special education have a bipolar disorder), evidence available indicates that approximately ¼ to ½ of students with the diagnosis are accessing these services. Additionally, as will be evident from the following discussion of the negative correlates associated with bipolar disorder, it can be assumed that a significant proportion of youth with this diagnosis will require additional services and support in the educational arena.

Gender Issues in Early-Onset Bipolar Disorder

In a recent review of the literature, Diflorio and Jones (2010) investigated gender issues relevant to a bipolar diagnosis. While their review discussed research conducted with adult samples, a brief exploration here is appropriate. In general, it appears that there are not significant differences in the prevalence, clinical presentation (e.g., age of onset), or treatment response among males and females. However, there may be differences in the rates of subtypes or episode frequency. For example, there is substantial evidence that females have an increased risk of having a bipolar II disorder, experiencing hypomanic and mixed episodes, and more frequently demonstrate a rapid cycling course. In addition, there is some evidence that there may be differences between the genders in patterns of comorbidity. For example, alcohol disorders appear to be more prevalent for males, while eating disorders and post-traumatic stress disorder (PTSD) appear to be more prevalent with females.

Research examining these issues in youth tends to confirm these results. For example, Biederman et al. (2004) demonstrated no differences in prevalence, clinical presentation, course, educational deficits, or severity of family/interpersonal impairment. Males were more likely to have an earlier onset (although both genders were more likely to have a prepubertal vs. adolescent onset) and to have a comorbid ADHD diagnosis, while females were more likely to have comorbid anxiety diagnoses. Similarly, Duax, Youngstrom, Calabrese, and Findling (2007) found no gender differences in overall prevalence or within subtypes; however, they also illuminated several differences related to presentation. Females were more likely to experience depressed mood and to report greater severity of depressive symptoms. Males were more likely to experience mania, although the severity of the manic symptoms experienced was commensurate with females' experience of mania. Finally, Staton, Volness, and Beatty (2008) demonstrated similar rates for several of the cardinal symptoms of mania (i.e., grandiosity, elation, racing thoughts) as well as problematic distractibility-inattention; however, an interaction between the presence of rage and gender did emerge. That is, for females the presence of rage decreased with age, but for males the presence of rage increased with age.

Correlates and Association with Other Conditions

Unfortunately, a number of negative correlates often accompany a diagnosis of bipolar disorder. As a result of this constellation of challenges, individuals with this diagnosis in youth report a significantly lower quality of life (i.e., satisfaction and well being in a variety of domains such as physical, emotional, social, and occupational) in comparison to healthy controls, as well as those with other psychiatric or medical diagnoses (Freeman et al., 2009). In a review of the literature from 1970 to 2003, Krishnan (2005) explored the most common medical and psychiatric comorbidities in adults with a bipolar diagnosis (see Table 3.1). Although less well established, research is beginning to identify negative correlates for those with an early onset (i.e., for youth with a bipolar diagnosis). These correlates often serve as risk or protective factors (Miklowitz & Johnson, 2009). The sections that follow will discuss the psychosocial, neuropsychological, and medical correlates associated with an early onset of bipolar disorder. The chapter will conclude with a discussion of the prevalent psychiatric disorders that co-occur (i.e., comorbidity). While these issues are broken into sections and discussed for the most part in isolation, it should be emphasized that these challenges act interactively and influence each other. As a very simplistic example, verbal memory dysfunction may cause problems in the family if the child has challenges remembering instructions (e.g., to pick up clothes) given orally.

Table 3.1 Common psychiatric and medical comorbidities in adults with bipolar disorder

Comorbid condition	Mean rate of comorbidity (%)
Overweight	58
Substance use disorder	56
Anxiety disorder	71
Social phobia	47
Post-traumatic stress disorder (PTSD)	39
Personality disorder	36
Migraine	28
Obesity	21
Binge-eating disorder	13
Panic disorder	11
Obsessive-compulsive disorder (OCD)	10
Type 2 diabetes	10
Hypothyroidism	9

Note. Adapted from "Psychiatric and Medical Comorbidities of Bipolar Disorder," by K. R. R. Krishnan, 2005, *Psychosomatic Medicine, 67*, p. 2. [permission pending]

Psychosocial Correlates

Several psychological and social areas of development tend to present challenges and can result in substantial functional impairment for individuals with an early-onset of bipolar disorder. Due to the developmental processes occurring at these crucial ages, depending on the age of onset, different patterns of problematic behaviors may occur (McClure-Tone, 2010). Research has indicated that individuals currently experiencing any affective (either depressive or manic) episode evidence more impairment in important psychosocial domains (Goldstein et al., 2009), although depressive symptoms appear to be more impairing than mania on psychosocial functioning (Judd et al., 2005). There is evidence that more severe symptoms are associated with more significant impairment (e.g., Freeman et al., 2009; Judd et al., 2005). However, it has also been demonstrated that individuals who are euthymic or in partial remission from their illness continue to evidence significant impairment in these domains (Goldstein et al., 2009). Additionally, those at most risk of developing bipolar disorder (i.e., those with a bipolar parent) also demonstrate significant psychosocial impairment (Bella et al., 2011). The following section will address issues specific to a discussion of bipolar disorder in youth regarding interpersonal functioning, sleep problems, psychotic features, incarceration, trauma, and suicidal behaviors.

Interpersonal Functioning

The interpersonal functioning of youth with an early-onset of bipolar disorder is important developmentally to understand. These areas are also key when developing interventions in the schools. Challenges in the areas of family functioning and peer relationships will be explored followed by a discussion of social cognitive deficits. Interested readers are encouraged to access Keenan-Miller and Miklowitz's (2011) review of this area for further exploration.

Family Functioning

Perhaps the most researched interpersonal domain investigated to date is the family. There appears to be consensus that these families are typically characterized by chaotic environments and highly conflict-laden relationships, with both parent–child and sibling dynamics demonstrating significant impairment (Keenan-Miller & Miklowitz, 2011). An early study on the psychosocial functioning of children and adolescents with an early-onset bipolar disorder found that in these families, mothers were significantly less likely to engage in frequent activities and set consistent limits and more likely to express frequent hostility and utilize corporal punishment with her child, than were mothers of healthy controls (i.e., no psychiatric diagnoses) or those with an ADHD diagnosis (Geller et al., 2000). Fathers in these families were more likely to express frequent hostility and utilize corporal punishment. Both parents reported their child was less likely to confide in them and there was less warmth characterizing their relationships with this child. These parents were also less likely to agree on child-rearing or to demonstrate effective problem-solving as a unit. Finally, the children with bipolar disorder reported that their relationships with siblings were significantly poorer than healthy controls.

There is an important interaction between the youth's symptoms and the experience of functioning of the family. Sullivan and Miklowitz (2010) reported that more severe depressive symptoms were associated with lower parent-reported family cohesion, while more severe manic symptoms were associated with lower adolescent-reported cohesion. Esposito-Smythers et al. (2006) found that if the child with bipolar disorder also had a comorbid externalizing disorder, the parents reported lower family cohesion and higher family conflict, while the presence of an internalizing disorder affected the child's report of family functioning. Hua et al. (2010) found that the presence of psychotic features predicted lower family cohesion.

The family can play either a risk or protective role in the course of the disorder, depending primarily on when the disorder is diagnosed, whether the family is intact, if the parent has a mood disorder, or how the family unit resolves conflict (Miklowitz & Johnson, 2009). For example when family conflict is high or family problem solving is poor, youth report higher levels of symptomatology (e.g., Esposito-Smythers et al., 2006; Townsend, Demeter, Youngstrom, Drotar, & Findling, 2007) and pharmacological treatment outcomes are impaired (i.e., adherence to medications is low; Townsend et al., 2007), lower maternal warmth has been shown to predict less time in remission from symptoms (Geller et al., 2002), and two parent families have been shown to predict faster time to recovery and less psychosocial impairment (Geller et al., 2002; Goldstein et al., 2009).

Peer Relationships

Less well-studied are peer relationships for youth with bipolar disorder. Considering the increasing importance of peer relationships during the childhood and adolescent periods, this area of development cannot be overlooked. Geller et al. (2000) found that in comparison to healthy controls (i.e., no psychiatric diagnoses) or those with an ADHD diagnosis, children and adolescents with an early-onset of bipolar disorder were significantly more likely to report having few to no friends, to experience frequent teasing by peers and to have poor social skills. Freeman et al. (2009) reported that youths with bipolar disorder reported significantly lower quality of life regarding peer relationships than healthy controls (i.e., no psychiatric or medical diseases) or youth with asthma, obesity, atopic dermatitis, arthritis, or those who had had heart surgery as infants or were currently on oxygen.

Interestingly, there is some indication that these challenges with peer relationships may correspond with onset and course of the disease. For example, in adults, social rhythm regularity (i.e., regularity and frequency in social life events) was found to be associated with time to first onset and length of time euthymic between affective episodes (Shen, Alloy, Abramson, & Sylvia, 2008). Impaired peer relationships in childhood and adolescence have been shown to be predictive of later adult functioning (i.e., substance abuse or dependence, worse symptomatic course, and increased suicide attempts; Goldberg & Ernst, 2004). Kutcher, Robertson, and Bird (1998) indicated that premorbid peer relationships (as evaluated by parent report and school record review) were either expected/average or excellent in 90 % of their sample. It is important to note that this was an adolescent-onset sample and there may be differences in the presentation and course of the disease based on the developmental period of onset. Additionally, replication of these results is necessary.

Social Cognition

Crick and Dodge's (1994) widely accepted model of social cognition (also termed social-information processing) breaks the processes essential to social behavior into three general categories: (a) perception and interpretation, (b) clarification of interpersonal goals, and (c) development and implementation of behavioral responses. As highlighted by Keenan-Miller and Miklowitz (2011) in their review, there are multiple opportunities for deficits to impact social cognition in these areas for children and adolescents with an early-onset of bipolar disorder.

Regarding deficits in the area of perception and interpretation, much of the work has focused on the processing of facial emotions/expressions. For example, youth with an early-onset of bipolar disorder are more likely to view neutral faces as more threatening (Rich et al., 2006) and to make the most mistakes labeling expressions in comparison to those with ADHD, CD, anxiety, or major depressive disorders (Guyer et al., 2007). Important work in this area is being conducted that links neuropsychological deficits with psychosocial impairments. For example, there is evidence that amygdala volume and functional connectivity abnormalities are implicated in impairments in social signal processing and emotion/behavior regulation, which are likely to result in many of the social deficits observed. Rich et al. (2006) demonstrated that youth with bipolar disorder have increased left amygdala activity when rating their fear of, or the hostility perceived on, neutral faces. To follow up on these findings, the connectivity in networks shown to be critical to processing faces and emotional stimuli (i.e., amygdala and temporal association cortical regions) were examined (Rich et al., 2008). Youth with bipolar disorder demonstrated deficient connectivity in these networks. These deficits were not correlated with mood and could not be explained by comorbidity with ADHD, Oppositional Defiant Disorder (ODD), or anxiety disorders. It can be concluded that these deficits are important in understanding the challenges youth with bipolar disorder demonstrate in processing and understanding social and emotional stimuli, as well as regulating their emotions and behaviors in relation to responding to these stimuli. Therefore, these findings provide evidence of deficits at two places in the social cognitive model.

Little is known regarding the perception and interpretation of other areas of social stimuli (i.e., aside from facial emotion processing). Researchers have started investigating the ability of youth with bipolar disorder to identify nonverbal emotional cues through the tone of verbal speech (i.e., prosody). Deveney, Brotman, Decker, Pine, and Leibenluft (2012) found that overall, both individuals with bipolar disorder and severe mood dysregulation made more errors labeling emotions than did their healthy control counterparts. Current symptoms were not related to the number of errors for these groups. All children made more errors labeling adult voices than children's and there were no differences found regarding the emotion being labeled (e.g., an equal number of errors were made labeling happy vs. angry toned neutral content sentences). Interestingly, youth with bipolar disorder who were not medicated did not differ from the control sample, implying that this effect may be influenced by medications (i.e., medicated youth with bipolar disorder did make more errors than healthy controls). Clearly, more research in this area is needed.

Finally, the interpretation of social cues may be influenced by deficits in theory of mind (Schenkel, Marlow-O'Connor, Moss, Sweeney, & Pavuluri, 2008). A relatively new area of research regarding an early onset of bipolar disorder, theory of mind refers to the ability of an individual to understand what another is thinking or feeling (i.e., take another's perspective) based on the verbal and nonverbal cues given in a situation. Schenkel et al. (2008) demonstrated that youth with bipolar disorder demonstrate deficits in theory of mind concepts (i.e., measures of false belief and social inference). These deficits appeared to be particularly impaired in negatively valenced contexts and when the individual was more acutely manic. Additionally, an earlier age of onset was associated with greater impairment. Again, more research in this area is warranted.

Within the social cognitive model, the majority of research for an early-onset of bipolar disorder has been conducted in the perception and interpretation of social cues. Some research has been conducted regarding behavioral responses in social contexts. This research indicates that while youth with bipolar disorder may not display deficits in social skills knowledge, they may have poorer overall social skills performance (i.e., more inappropriately assertive, more impulsive, more jealous and withdrawn, and more overconfident; Goldstein, Miklowitz, & Mullen, 2006), deficits in expressive pragmatic language and the formulation of socially appropriate responses (McClure et al., 2005). These deficits have been found to be present regardless of mood state or severity of symptoms, comorbidity, or age of onset.

Sleep Problems

Sleep problems are a common experience for individuals with an early-onset of bipolar disorder, although causality cannot be inferred from these associations (i.e., are sleep problems the cause, consequence or both of bipolar disorder). In one, large, Internet-based survey, nearly all parents of youth with bipolar disorder reported some type of sleep disturbance occurring from two to seven times per week

(Lofthouse, Fristad, Splaingard, & Kelleher, 2007). The following five disturbances were reported by over 90 % of respondents: daytime sleepiness (98 %; e.g., wakes up in a negative mood; hard time getting out of bed); parasomnias (97 %; e.g., restless and moves a lot, talks during sleep); night wakings (96 %; awakes once during the night, moves to other's bed at night); bedtime resistance (94 %; e.g., struggles at bedtime, does not go to bed at same time); and sleep anxiety (91 %; e.g., afraid of sleeping in the dark, needs parent in the room to sleep). Significant impairments at home, in school, and with peers were associated with these disturbances.

Roybal et al. (2011) also investigated sleep patterns in adolescents with a bipolar diagnosis compared with controls (i.e., those with no Axis I diagnoses). These researchers found that there was a distinct pattern characterized by prolonged sleep onset latency (i.e., difficulty falling asleep), frequent nighttime awakenings, and more time spent awake during these awakenings for youth diagnosed with bipolar disorder. Mood symptoms (e.g., total time awake correlated with a decreased need for sleep, an increase in goal-directed activity, and increased productivity; depressed mood was associated with increased sleep length) and reports of worsening mood in the evenings were associated with these sleep disturbances. The majority of the sample of youth diagnosed with bipolar disorder was currently medicated. Despite an adverse effect of the medications typically prescribed for bipolar disorder being somnolence (i.e., sleepiness or drowsiness), there was no difference in the amount of sleep reported by medicated vs. non-medicated youth.

Preservation of sleep and regulation of the circadian cycle has been indicated as an important prevention activity for future manic episodes (APA, 2002). In their review, Plante and Winkelman (2008) summarize the literature noting that while disruptions in the sleep cycle (also captured under the term "social rhythm disruption") result in more manic symptoms/episodes, treating the sleep disorders resulted in better outcomes, such as fewer hypo/manic symptoms, speedier response to the advent of a manic episode (e.g., recognizing one might become manic and taking preventive measures), quicker discharge times when hospitalized, lower doses of mood stabilizers, and more cooperation and less irritability reported in treatment.

Psychotic Features

Psychotic features, or psychosis, are indicated if the individual presents with a significant disturbance in reality-testing in the form of delusions, hallucinations, or thought disorders (Pavuluri, Herbener, & Sweeney, 2004). In a recent meta-analysis, Kowatch, Youngstrom, Danielyan, and Findling (2005) reported a weighted average rate of 42 % of children and adolescents with an early onset of bipolar disorder who experienced psychotic features. There was significant variability in the rates reported with a large 95 % confidence interval of 24–62 %. As described by Hua et al. (2010) one possible explanation for the wide variation in rates reported by researchers may be due to different definitions. For example, grandiosity may be viewed as a symptom of psychosis (i.e., feelings/delusions about the self that are not reality-based or age appropriate, action on, and impairment resulting from, the thoughts; Pavuluri, Herbener, et al., 2004) and flight of ideas can be seen as a symptom of disordered thinking (i.e., thought disorder). Depending on how researchers interpret the presentation of these symptoms will influence the prevalence of these features. Regardless, psychotic features are most commonly associated with schizophrenia, and it is important for individuals recognizing these symptoms in youth to be aware that they can be quite frequent in the presentation of an early-onset of bipolar disorder as well.

Unfortunately, the presence of psychotic features presages a more impaired course. For example, Hua et al. (2010) reported that youth with psychotic features experienced more affective episodes, hospitalizations and comorbidities and poorer overall global functioning. Additionally, these individuals demonstrated more neuropsychological (i.e., slower processing speed) and academic impairment (i.e., math achievement) and lived in more dysfunctional families (i.e., more likely to have a family history of psychosis and lower reports of family cohesion). The most common psychotic feature reported was auditory hallucinations. Pavuluri, Herbener, et al.'s (2004) review of the literature supports those findings. These researchers also discussed the differences between a prepubertal and adolescent-onset, mentioning that the prepubertal group tended to have higher rates of mixed episodes and more grandiose and paranoid delusions, while the adolescent-onset group presented with more thought disorders and severe behavioral disturbances. Finally, this group suggested that significant differences exist in the psychotic features present for an individual with early-onset schizophrenia vs. bipolar disorder. For example, perhaps most importantly, in an early-onset bipolar disorder, delusions (typically grandiosity) tend to be mood congruent (i.e., to be affectively charged and present during affective episodes) while with schizophrenia, delusions tend to be more stable and consistent, regardless of mood. Grandiosity itself is far less frequent in schizophrenia than bipolar disorder, while hallucinations and loosening of associations are more frequent in schizophrenia. Making the distinction between these two disorders can be critical to inform prognosis, course, and treatment.

Incarceration

It has been indicated that a substantial amount of offenders suffer from some type of mental illness (Grisso, 2008). Stoddard-Dare, Mallett, and Boitel (2011) examined a large random sample of juvenile court data from an urban, US county. These researchers indicated that while youth with an ADHD or conduct disorder (CD) diagnosis were significantly less likely, individuals with a bipolar disorder were significantly more likely to be locked in a detention center for a personal crime. These results are somewhat surprising, given the established relationship with CD and delinquent behavior.

Quanbeck et al. (2004) investigated correlates of adults with bipolar disorder who were incarcerated. They found that these individuals were most likely experiencing manic and/or psychotic symptoms upon arrest, to be arrested for a violent offense (although the most frequent crime was "terrorist threat" which included verbal threats rather than actual physical violence), to have had at least one prior misdemeanor conviction, to have been recently discharged from a psychiatric hospital, and to have failed to enter any outpatient treatment. This study implies that there may be a group of individuals with bipolar disorder at particular risk for offending and that without treatment, these individuals may decompensate in their illness and re-offend. Childhood trauma (discussed next) appears to be a particular risk factor for offending behaviors. For example, Conus et al. (2010) found that those with a history of sexual or physical abuse in childhood were more likely to have a forensic history and to disengage from treatment, and less likely to live with family during treatment. Perhaps including treatment for trauma into an individual's treatment program may increase treatment adherence ultimately decreasing offending behaviors. Additionally, school-based professionals who interface with the juvenile justice system are well placed to assist in the appropriate identification, assessment, and treatment programs for youth with a bipolar disorder.

Trauma

It seems that traumatic experiences, including childhood physical or sexual abuse and neglect, are fairly common in individuals with bipolar disorder. For example, Assion et al. (2009) reported that 50 % of their adult sample had experienced childhood trauma with approximately 20 % of the sample significantly affected by these traumas generating PTSD diagnoses. Conus et al. (2010) reported 80 % of their sample had been exposed to stressful life events during their youth with 25 % experiencing physical or sexual abuse. Krishnan's (2005) review suggested a PTSD comorbidity in 39 % of adults with a bipolar disorder.

A recent latent class analysis of the National Comorbidity Survey highlighted the vulnerability of this population in comparison to individuals without any or with other psychiatric diagnoses (Houston, Shevlin, Adamson, & Murphy, 2011). In comparison to the identified latent class demonstrating low probabilities of experiencing any of the traumatic events, individuals with bipolar disorder were almost 38 times more likely to be found in the class demonstrating the highest probability of experiencing *all* the traumatic events (i.e., the high-risk class) and 9 times more likely to be found in the class characterized by exposure to nonsexual adult interpersonal violence (e.g., life-threatening accident) and non-interpersonal trauma (e.g., witnessing a fire). In the high-risk class, bipolar disorder demonstrated the highest adjusted odds ratio (AOR = 37.64) when compared to those with psychosis (AOR = 31.75), drug dependence (AOR = 14.81), alcohol dependence (AOR = 4.11), and depression (AOR = 4.61), indicating extreme vulnerability to experiencing these events. Odds of being in the non-interpersonal trauma/interpersonal violence class were similar for those with bipolar, psychosis, and drug dependence, yet significantly less for those with alcohol dependence or depression.

Frequently assessed retrospectively in adults, few studies have focused on the topic of trauma in younger samples. Strawn et al. (2010) reported 66 % of their adolescent sample had been exposed to traumatic events. Interestingly, while exposure in this sample was high, severity of post-traumatic stress symptoms was much lower, with 14 % meeting the threshold for clinically significant symptoms, and only 3 % meeting criteria for PTSD. The researchers posit that it is possible that bipolar disorder may serve as a risk factor for the development of PTSD later in life (e.g., following more affective episodes). Romero et al. (2009) also investigated trauma in children and adolescents with bipolar disorder, specifically regarding physical and sexual abuse. They found approximately 20 % of their large sample had experienced either physical or sexual abuse (or both). Compared to those individuals in the sample without an abuse history, those with this history were more likely to be from lower socioeconomic status homes and to live in non-intact families. Males and females were equally likely to report such a history, although females were more likely to report sexual abuse. In addition to living in a non-intact family constellation, the most robust correlates of any abuse included PTSD, CD, psychosis, and a family history (first-degree relative) of mood disorder.

This history is likely predictive of several negative outcomes. As discussed in the previous section, individuals with this history frequently have a forensic history (Conus et al., 2010). In their study of the clinical impact of childhood trauma in clients with severe mental disorders, Alvarez et al. (2011) found that in those with a history of childhood abuse, onset of the disorder was approximately 3 years earlier, and rates of hospitalization and the number of suicide attempts were significantly higher. While an uncomfortable topic for many school-based professionals, this discussion clearly indicates the importance of assessing for abuse and trauma when working with students diagnosed with bipolar disorder. Additionally, this research should lead care providers to incorporate components of intervention related to this topic as well as to address opportunities to prevent these types of experiences into any treatment protocol.

Suicidal Thoughts and Behaviors

A diagnosis of bipolar disorder is recognized as a significant risk factor for suicidal thoughts and behaviors. It has been reported that between ¼ and ½ of youth diagnosed will attempt suicide (Bhangoo et al., 2003; Geller et al., 2002; Goldstein et al., 2005; Lewinsohn, Seeley, & Klein, 2003). Risk of attempt has been shown to be significantly higher for bipolar youth in comparison with unipolar depressed youth, a group acknowledged to be at an increased risk for suicidal behaviors (Lewinsohn et al., 2003). Youth with bipolar disorder who attempt suicide also tend to be younger at first attempt, make more lethal attempts, and are more likely to make multiple attempts (Goldstein et al., 2005; Lewinsohn et al., 2003). Alarmingly, Lewinsohn et al. (2003) found that almost 90 % of youth with bipolar disorder who reported an attempt had multiple attempts vs. approximately 52 % of youth with unipolar depression. A prepubertal onset and delay of medication confer even greater risk of suicidal behaviors (Moor et al., 2012; Nery-Fernandes et al., 2012). Also significantly higher in youth with bipolar disorder in comparison to youth with unipolar depression are rates of suicidal ideation (Axelson et al., 2006; Goldstein et al., 2005). The connection between ideation and attempt is an important one; the majority of attempters report a lifetime history of frequent and intense ideation (Goldstein et al., 2005). As ideation represents a potential opportunity for prevention of suicidal behaviors, assessing for these thoughts, feelings, and beliefs is crucial. Risk factors associated with an early-onset of bipolar disorder will be explored in more detail in Chapter 4.

Neuropsychological Correlates

It is possible that neurocognitive functioning may play as important a role as affective symptoms in producing functional impairment and also may predict recovery (Jaeger, Berns, Loftus, Gonzalez, & Czobor, 2007). There has been substantial attention regarding the neuropsychological impairments associated with bipolar disorder, although some domains have received more research than others. Several reviews and meta-analyses have been conducted in recent years that indicate deficits in important neurocognitive domains for youth with bipolar disorder in comparison to healthy controls (see Table 3.2; Horn, Roessner, & Holtmann, 2011; Joseph, Frazier, Youngstrom, & Soares, 2008; Nieto & Castellanos, 2011).

Perhaps the most consistent, stable, and substantial differences are in the domains of verbal learning/memory and processing speed. Less well established are areas such as visual memory, verbal fluency, and motor speed; while these still represent areas of impairment in comparison to healthy controls, the effect sizes tend to be smaller. Deficits in the domains of attention, executive function, verbal memory, and working memory (as a set) have been shown to be predictive of reading problems, while attention (alone) is predictive of mathematics problems (Pavuluri, O'Connor, et al., 2006). It is important to highlight that the general cognitive abilities of youth with bipolar disorder, while lower than the healthy controls (i.e., small to medium effect sizes), were reportedly still in the average range (Nieto & Castellanos, 2011). Additionally, methodology may play a role in the results, in that studies with larger samples produced lower effect sizes (particularly with general cognitive ability, verbal memory, and working memory; Joseph et al., 2008) and the inclusion criteria used influenced findings (e.g., high rates of comorbid ADHD produced larger effect sizes in certain domains; Joseph et al., 2008; Nieto & Castellanos, 2011).

Results regarding the impact of medication on abilities have varied. In their meta-analysis, Nieto and Castellanos (2011) reported that in the domains of processing speed, attention, executive control and working memory, smaller effect sizes were evident in studies where there was a lower percentage of the sample medicated. However, there may be differences based on the type of medication prescribed. In the review conducted by Horn et al. (2011), they concluded that mood stabilizers, neuroleptics, stimulants, or selective serotonin reuptake inhibitors

Table 3.2 Neuropsychological impairments in early-onset bipolar disorder

Domain	Effect size
Verbal learning/memory	Large
Processing speed	Large
Working memory	Medium–large
Attention	Medium–large
Executive function/control	Medium
Visuospatial/visual-perceptual skills	Medium
Visual memory	Medium
Verbal fluency	Small–medium
General cognitive ability	Small–medium
Motor speed	Small

Note. Adapted from "A quantitative and qualitative review of neurocognitive performance in pediatric bipolar disorder" by M. F. Joseph, T. W. Frazier, E. A. Youngstrom, J. C. Soares, 2008, *Journal of Child and Adolescent Psychopharmacology, 18,* 595–605 and "A meta-analysis of neuropsychological functioning in patients with early onset schizophrenia and pediatric bipolar disorder" by R. G. Nieto and F. X. Castellanos, 2011, *Journal of Clinical Child & Adolescent Psychology, 40,* 266–280

(SSRI's) did not produce any effects on abilities based on the studies examined. Lithium, antiepileptics, or atypical antipsychotics were found to result in slower processing speed.

Finally, in addition to comparisons between healthy controls and youth with bipolar disorder, comparisons have also been made for those with other psychiatric comorbidities. In general, youth with bipolar disorder or schizophrenia appear to demonstrate similar patterns of neuropsychological impairment, although those with schizophrenia demonstrate more marked impairment in these domains (Nieto & Castellanos, 2011). The exception to this is in the case of verbal memory, where these deficits are similar in magnitude between the two groups. Studies comparing the effects of ADHD on neuropsychological impairment typically found that in the case of processing speed, general cognitive abilities, and attention, effect sizes were smaller in studies with lower comorbidity (Joseph et al., 2008; Nieto & Castellanos, 2011). Henin, Mick et al. (2007) demonstrated that besides processing speed, youth with bipolar disorder and those with comorbid ADHD had no differences in neuropsychological impairments and concluded that many of the deficit areas can be attributed to the significant amount of ADHD comorbidity typically present in youth with bipolar disorder. Lastly, impairments in motor speed and working memory are similar to those found in ADHD, CD, and ODD, and impairments in executive function and attention seem to be similar to those with unipolar depression, psychotic disorders, and autism (Joseph et al., 2008).

Medical Correlates

A recent, large, cohort study identified several medical conditions that were more prevalent in youth with a bipolar diagnosis (see Table 3.3; Jerrell, McIntyre, & Tripathi, 2010). Within the youth diagnosed with bipolar disorder, females were more likely to demonstrate obesity while males were more likely to demonstrate organic brain disorders/mental retardation. Over ¼ of these individuals were diagnosed with two or more chronic medical conditions. Similarly, Evans-Lacko, Zeber, Gonzalez, and Olvera (2009) found that in comparison to youth with other psychiatric diagnoses, youth with bipolar disorder were more likely to have two or more chronic health conditions (i.e., 8 % vs. 36 %, respectively). These researchers investigated medical claims of a national sample of youth and found several medical conditions that were more prevalent in those with a bipolar diagnosis (see Table 3.3). In addition, toxic effects and adverse events, including effects from nonmedicinal agents and complications to medical surgery or mechanical devices, were also significantly higher in youth with bipolar disorder. This may indicate vulnerability in these individuals above and beyond that evident in others with psychiatric diagnoses (e.g., those also prescribed psychotropic medications).

One of the concerns regarding an early onset of bipolar disorder is related to the psychotropic medications that typically accompany this diagnosis and the effect these medications can have on the health and wellbeing of a developing individual. Adverse effects such as weight gain can be significant (Maayan & Correll, 2011). Interestingly, a recent study investigating the effects of these medications on medical conditions in youth with bipolar disorder suggest that while the medications may worsen certain adverse effects (e.g., weight gain/obesity), these medical conditions do occur in the absence of medications (Jerrell et al., 2011), perhaps indicating a predisposition for medical challenges for those individuals with a bipolar illness. Chapter 7 will provide a more expanded discussion about the topic of the adverse effects associated with frequently prescribed medications.

Comorbidities

Having at least one other psychiatric diagnosis in addition to an early onset of bipolar disorder seems to be the rule rather than the exception. This pattern continues over the lifetime, with 90 % of adults reporting at least one additional psychiatric diagnosis and 70 % of those individuals reporting a history of three or more diagnoses (Merikangas & Pato, 2009). Comorbidity can be important in understanding the course, correlates, prognosis, and functional and treatment outcomes (Joshi & Wilens, 2009). In general, comorbid disorders tend to precede and typically indicate an earlier onset of bipolar disorder (Henin, Beiderman, et al., 2007). There may be evidence of gender differences in the comorbidities; that is externalizing disorders such as ADHD and CD occurring more frequently in males (Masi, Perugi,

Table 3.3 Comorbid medical conditions more common in individuals with an early-onset bipolar disorder

Condition	Odds ratio[a] (95 % confidence interval)	Odds ratio[b] (95 % confidence interval)
Obesity	1.92 (1.53–2.40)	
Type 2 diabetes mellitus	1.59 (1.08–2.35)	
Endocrine disorders	2.06 (1.49–2.85)	
Migraine headaches	1.84 (1.37–2.48)	
Central nervous system disorder/epilepsy	3.38 (2.48–4.59)	
Organic brain disorders/mental retardation	1.81 (1.47–2.23)	
Cardiovascular disorders[c]	1.38 (1.06–1.79)	1.95 (1.59–2.38)
Asthma	1.43 (1.21–1.68)	
Gastrointestinal/hepatic		1.46 (1.23–1.72)
Neurologic		1.55 (1.34–1.80)
Musculoskeletal		1.21 (1.05–1.39)
Female reproductive		1.94 (1.56–2.41)
Respiratory		1.24 (1.08–1.42)
Toxic effects/adverse events		3.45 (2.82–4.21)

Note. Adapted from "A cohort study of the prevalence and impact of comorbid medical conditions in pediatric bipolar disorder" by J. M. Jerrell, R. S. McIntyre, and A. Tripathi, 2010, *Journal of Clinical Psychiatry, 71*, 1518–1525, and "Medical comorbidity among youth diagnosed with bipolar disorder in the United States" by S. E. Evans-Lacko, J. E. Zeber, J. M. Gonzalez, and R. L. Olvera, 2009, *Journal of Clinical Psychiatry, 70*, 1461–1466. While there is obvious overlap in the conditions listed in the table (e.g., asthma would be considered a respiratory condition), due to differences in classification between the studies and for the purpose of clarification, the conditions are typically listed separately

[a]Odds ratios listed in this column refer to the Jerrell et al. (2010) article and indicate the increased likelihood of an individual with a bipolar diagnosis evidencing the medical condition in comparison to an individual in the control cohort—i.e., those without a psychiatric diagnosis or prescribed any psychotropic medications. The only conditions listed here are the ones that demonstrated significant ($p \leq 0.01$) differences between the bipolar and control cohorts

[b]Odds ratios listed in this column refer to the Evans-Lacko et al. (2009) article and indicate the increased likelihood of an individual with a bipolar diagnosis demonstrating the medical condition in comparison to an individual with another psychiatric diagnosis. The conditions listed here are significant at the $p \leq 0.05$ level

[c]Most common cardiovascular disorders included arrhythmias, congestive heart failure, and ischemic/pulmonary heart disease (Jerrell et al., 2010). Evans-Lacko et al. (2009) do not list specific disorders, but categorize this simply as "cardiology"

Millepiedi, et al., 2006) and internalizing disorders such as anxiety occurring more frequently in females (McIntyre et al., 2006).

As symptoms of bipolar disorder may mask as symptoms of another psychiatric disorder and development may influence the presentation of various symptoms in children and adolescents, comorbidity has been a complicated and controversial topic. Researchers have utilized several methods to parse out the issue, with results typically supporting the reality of such high frequency of comorbidities. However, as most studies rely on cross-sectional data, to truly understand the intersection of these disorders, more longitudinal data is needed (Joshi & Wilens, 2009).

Table 3.4 Rates of psychiatric comorbidity in early-onset bipolar disorder

Disorder	Weighted rate (95 % confidence interval)
ADHD	62 % (29–87 %)
ODD	53 % (25–79 %)
Anxiety	27 % (15–43 %)
CD	19 % (11–30 %)
Substance use disorder	12 % (5–29 %)

Note. Adapted from "Review and meta-analysis of the phenomenology and clinical characteristics of mania in children and adolescents," by R. A. Kowatch, E. A. Youngstrom, A. Danielyan, and R. L. Findling, 2005, *Bipolar Disorders, 7*, p. 490

One recent meta-analysis of youth 5- to 18-years-old examined the clinical characteristics, including comorbidity, of a bipolar diagnosis in youth (see Table 3.4 for the rates of psychiatric comorbidity; Kowatch et al., 2005). As is evident from this analysis, externalizing disorders appear to be the most common comorbidities with an early onset of bipolar disorder. An important component of this table to attend to is the confidence interval. There is wide variation in the rates reported for each of these disorders within the studies investigated. A partial explanation for this is likely developmental. For example, ADHD tends to be more prevalent in a younger sample (or those with an onset in childhood), while substance abuse is more common in an adolescent sample (Joshi & Wilens, 2009). Therefore, the age of the sample will influence the rates of comorbid disorders seen.

Externalizing Disorders

Perhaps the most studied comorbidities for an early onset of bipolar disorder include externalizing disorders; that is, ADHD, the disruptive behavior disorders (CD and ODD), and substance abuse. The relationship between ADHD, CD/ODD and bipolar disorder has been of particular interest to researchers. Carlson and Glovinsky (2009) offered possible explanations for this relationship, including: (a) ADHD/CD/ODD are a prodrome or subsyndromal form of mania asked by developmental factors (e.g., pre-puberty) that will look more obvious later in life (e.g., post-puberty), (b) the comorbidity marks a particularly malicious form of bipolar disorder (hence early age of onset of bipolar disorder is a risk factor), and (c) mania occurs following, and is likely precipitated by, organic factors, medications, seizures, central nervous systems infections, metabolic disturbances, tumors or other pathology. Regardless, as these children may be more noticeable due to their patterns of symptoms, they are the most likely to be brought to the attention of school-based professionals.

Attention Deficit Hyperactivity Disorder

Perhaps the most controversial comorbidity is ADHD. Substantial overlap exists in symptoms (e.g., distractibility, hyperactivity, restless, talkativeness; Galanter &

Leibenluft, 2008); however, when controlling for this overlap, the diagnoses typically still remain appropriate for both disorders (Kim & Miklowitz, 2002). While in children with bipolar disorder, it is common to see comorbid ADHD, in children with ADHD, bipolar disorder is far less frequent (Biederman et al., 1996). However, evidence exists to suggest that each disorder serves as a risk factor for the other, in that people with bipolar disorder are more likely to have comorbid ADHD and individuals with ADHD more likely to have comorbid bipolar disorder than those without either of these disorders (Lewinsohn, Klein, & Seeley, 1995; Kessler et al., 2006).

As ADHD typically precedes bipolar disorder, longitudinal studies examining the rates of individuals with ADHD to develop bipolar disorder are important. Tillman and Geller (2006) found that approximately 29 % of youth with ADHD developed bipolar disorder over a 6-year follow-up. The progression to comorbidity was predicted by more impaired functioning, paternal history of a mood disorder, and *less* stimulant medication use. Similarly, Biederman et al. (2009) reported that 28 % of individuals with ADHD and unipolar depression switched to bipolar depression over their 7-year follow-up. This switch rate was significantly higher than controls without ADHD, and was predicted by baseline CD, school behavioral problems, and a positive history of family mood disorder. While family history of bipolar disorder is one of the most important risk factors for development of bipolar disorder (see Chapter 4 for a more elaborate discussion of this topic), for children with ADHD it appears to substantially increase the risk (Sachs, Baldassano, Truman, & Guille, 2000). Additionally, when a parent had the bipolar-ADHD comorbidity, their children were significantly more likely to have a child with bipolar disorder, but *not* ADHD (Chang, Steiner, & Ketter, 2000).

A more noxious course of bipolar disorder is associated with an ADHD comorbidity. Individuals with the comorbidity tend to experience a more chronic (vs. episodic) course with irritable mood more common than euphoria/elation, more frequent depressive episodes, and more rapid cycling with mixed episodes (Diler, Uguz, Seydaoglu, Erol, & Avci, 2007; Masi, Perugi, Toni, et al., 2006). When comorbid, the symptoms of either disorder appear to be more impairing in that the comorbid group demonstrates more severe inattentive and hyperactive-impulsive symptoms than the ADHD-alone group and more severe manic symptoms than the bipolar-alone group (Arnold et al., 2011). Additionally, those with the comorbidity appear to be at increased risk for other psychiatric disorders, including ODD/CD and anxiety disorders, have more severe mania symptoms, significantly more internalizing, aggressive and externalizing behaviors, have higher rates of hospitalization, and present with greater psychosocial impairments (Biederman et al., 2005; Diler et al., 2007; Masi, Perugi, Toni, et al., 2006).

A crucial element of the discussion regarding ADHD and bipolar disorder is differentiation vs. comorbidity. Geller et al. (1998) determined that five hallmark symptoms of mania were capable of differentiating between the two disorders, including: (a) elated mood, (b) grandiosity, (c) hypersexuality, (d) decreased need for sleep, and (e) racing thoughts. These symptoms were significantly more likely to present in individuals with bipolar disorder in comparison to those with ADHD.

Luckenbaugh, Findling, Leverich, Pizzarello, and Post (2009) found that youth with bipolar disorder demonstrated significantly more irritability, decreased need for sleep, and inappropriate sexual behaviors. When present, periods of mood elevation (either brief or extended) were highly discriminatory as well. However, neither of these samples included those with comorbid bipolar disorder and ADHD. Diler et al. (2007) found that the five characteristics identified by Geller et al. (1998) were most elevated in those with the comorbidity vs. those with bipolar disorder alone. Therefore, evidence of these symptoms may indicate the presence of bipolar disorder, while the issue of comorbidity vs. differentiation still remains unclear.

Disruptive Behavior Disorders

As an early onset of bipolar disorder is frequently associated with a chronic course characterized by irritable mood and aggressive outbursts, it is not surprising that the disruptive behavior disorders are also among the most frequent comorbidities (Joshi & Wilens, 2009). Youth with bipolar disorder have been shown to engage in serious acting out behaviors, including behaviors indicative of ODD and CD (e.g., arguing with adults, defiance, intentionally annoying others, stealing, burglary, skipping school; Kovacs & Pollack, 1995); however, it is difficult to ascertain if this is due to the willful defiance associated with the disruptive behavior disorders or the behavioral disinhibition and emotion dysregulation of bipolar disorder.

It is proposed that this comorbidity may confuse the clinical presentation (e.g., children with the comorbidity are often diagnosed with comorbid ADHD and CD) and may account for some of the reason that early onset bipolar disorder is often unrecognized (Kovacs & Pollack, 1995). Again, family history is an important factor in differentiation, as youth with bipolar disorder are more likely to have relatives with bipolar disorder but not CD, youth with CD more likely to have relatives with CD but not bipolar disorder, and youth with the comorbidity more likely to have relatives with the comorbidity (Wozniak, Biederman, Faraone, Blier, & Monuteaux, 2001). Additionally, it has been suggested that the aggression when bipolar disorder is present is more disorganized and impulsive (Joshi & Wilens, 2009).

There are similarities and differences between ODD and CD comorbidities with bipolar disorder. Like ADHD, ODD appears to be more frequent in younger individuals and the inverse comorbidity is not as frequent (i.e., bipolar disorder is not found as frequently in individuals with ODD; Greene & Doyle, 1999; Masi, Perugi, Millepiedi, et al., 2006). CD, on the other hand, appears to be found as often in children as adolescents, and the overlap in disorders is similar (Biederman, Faraone, Chu, & Wozniak, 1999; Masi, Perugi, Millepiedi, et al., 2006). There is evidence that as the severity of CD increases, an individual is at increased risk for the development of bipolar disorder (Robins & Price, 1991). Individuals with bipolar disorder and a substance abuse disorder are at an increased risk of CD (Carlson & Kelly, 1998). The presence of an ODD/CD comorbidity with bipolar disorder results in poorer baseline functioning, as well as less improvement over the course of treatment (West, Weinstein, Celio, Henry, & Pavuluri, 2011).

Both ODD and CD symptoms, particularly aggression, appear to be impacted by medications typically prescribed for bipolar disorder. The primary medications that have been investigated with some evidence of efficacy include: risperidone, quetiapine, olanzapine, lithium, ziprasidone, and aripiprazole (see Joshi & Wilens, 2009 for a review of this literature). Recent research has suggested that the comorbidity may warrant different treatment regimens as one study demonstrated that risperidone was more effective than divalproex on manic symptoms in youth with the comorbidity (West et al., 2011).

Substance Use/Abuse Disorders

Substance use/abuse is quite frequent in youth with bipolar disorder. Particularly at risk are youth with an adolescent-onset (interestingly, a prepubertal onset appears protective in later substance use/abuse disorders (SUD) comorbidity; Wilens et al., 2008), and the comorbidity is associated with poorer overall functioning, including legal problems, academic difficulties, pregnancy, suicidality, and higher rates of additional comorbidities (Goldstein et al., 2008; Wilens et al., 2008).

Several theories have been proposed to account for the high rates of this comorbidity. Current research indicates that there may be shared genetic risk (Goldstein et al., 2008; Kerner, Lambert, & Muthén, 2011). Other research has supported the theory of "self-medication," or the attempt of individuals with bipolar disorder to manage their affective symptoms through substances (Lorberg, Wilens, Martelon, Wong, & Parcell, 2010).

In relation to onset, SUD's are the one comorbidity that bipolar disorder appears to precede (Goldstein & Bukstein, 2010). As such, prevention of substance use/abuse should be made a priority in treatment for youth with bipolar disorder. To that end, Goldstein and Bukstein (2010) recommend screening for substance use in individuals with bipolar disorder as young as 10-years-old in order to curtail this comorbidity. For those with the comorbidity, it is recommended that a simultaneous approach is taken (i.e., concurrent medication and psychosocial interventions; Joshi & Wilens, 2009). While the data is limited, several medications (i.e., lithium and valproic acid) have been shown to reduce substance use (see Joshi & Wilens, 2009, for a brief review of these studies).

Internalizing Disorders

It is perhaps counterintuitive to examine bipolar disorder, characterized by disinhibition or under-regulation of emotion, as comorbid with internalizing disorders, which are characterized by inhibition or over-regulation of emotion; however, these disorders also tend to co-occur quite frequently (Joshi & Wilens, 2009). Although understudied in relation to the externalizing disorders, anxiety has received the most attention by researchers of any internalizing disorders, and will be the sole focus of this section. Eating disorders have received limited attention in adult populations, indicating high rates of comorbidity (see McElroy, Kotwal, & Keck, 2006 for a review), but research in youth is unfortunately lacking.

Anxiety Disorders

Anxiety disorders are among the most frequent comorbidities with an early onset of bipolar disorder; some studies report higher rates than with ADHD (see Jolin, Weller, & Weller, 2008a for a review). There tends to be subtype differences, in that individuals with bipolar II disorder are more likely to have this comorbidity (Jolin et al., 2008a). While there are eight anxiety disorders listed in the *DSM-IV-TR* (APA, 2000), many studies compile them resulting in a less specific understanding of these relationships. Sala et al. (2010) outlined the prevalence of anxiety disorders in their community sample of youth with bipolar disorder indicating the most common was separation (24 %) and generalized anxiety disorders (GAD; 16 %), followed by obsessive compulsive disorder (OCD; 7 %), PTSD (6 %), social phobia (6 %), panic disorder (6 %), and agoraphobia (2 %). Many individuals with bipolar disorder meet criteria for more than one anxiety disorder and presence of the comorbidity indicates poorer outcomes including longer duration of mood symptoms, more severe depressive symptoms, less time euthymic, and increased risk of substance abuse, suicidal thoughts and behaviors, and psychiatric hospitalizations (Jolin et al., 2008a; Joshi & Wilens, 2009; Sala et al., 2010).

Due to the significant overlap for youth with bipolar disorder and anxiety, the Juvenile Bipolar Research Foundation has characterized a fear of harm phenotype for early onset bipolar disorder. The phenotype includes significant symptoms of anxiety and obsessiveness (i.e., likely the youth with the anxiety/bipolar comorbidity) and may represent a particularly inherited form of the disorder (Papolos, Hennen, Cockerham, & Lachman, 2007; Papolos, Mattis, Golshan, & Molay, 2009). Youth with higher levels of the fear of harm traits tended to have an earlier age of onset of bipolar disorder, have more severe mania and depression, more social impairment, and more reported severe injury to self and others (Papolos, Hennen, & Cockerham, 2005; Papolos et al., 2009). These traits are important considerations for school-based mental health professionals in the treatment planning for students with bipolar disorder.

Concluding Comments

While a relatively rare disorder, an early onset of bipolar disorder heralds many challenges for children and youth throughout life. This chapter has focused on several issues regarding prevalence as well as the correlates associated with the disorder. The chapter concluded with comorbidity, which is the rule rather than the exception in youth with early onset bipolar disorder, complicating the diagnosis and course of the disease. While most of the issues discussed in this chapter may be viewed as negative, there is some evidence that bipolar disorder is also associated with positive outcomes, such as increased creativity. Unfortunately, most of this research has focused on adult populations and, as such, is not expanded on in this volume. Hopefully, future research will explore these more positive correlates of an early onset of bipolar disorder.

Chapter 4
Case Finding, Screening, and Referral

As indicated in Chapters 1 and 3, the rates of bipolar diagnoses in children and adolescents are dramatically increasing. However, many individuals report a delay of an appropriate diagnosis, with an average of 7–9 years between the onset of symptoms and a bipolar diagnosis (Faedda, Baldessarini, Glovinsky, & Austin, 2004; Hirschfeld, Lewis, & Vornik, 2003). Unfortunately, bipolar disorder is not often considered initially (i.e., around 10 % of the time), despite recurrent affective symptoms (including mania) and a positive family history of affective and/or substance use disorders (Faedda et al., 2004).

So, what is happening in that time between onset of symptoms and appropriate diagnosis? For the large sample surveyed by the BDSA, an average of 3.5 other diagnoses was assigned by an average of four psychiatrists before an accurate diagnosis was appointed. The most commonly assigned initial diagnosis was Major Depressive Disorder (MDD) or unipolar depression (Hirschfeld et al., 2003). Individuals with an early-onset of the disorder are most often initially diagnosed with Attention-Deficit/Hyperactivity Disorder (ADHD), disruptive behavior disorders (Oppositional Defiant Disorder [ODD], or Conduct Disorder [CD]), and anxiety disorders (including Obsessive Compulsive Disorder [OCD]; Faedda et al., 2004). These disorders often have accompanying psychopharmacological treatment and there is evidence that these medications (particularly stimulants or antidepressants) may cause destabilization of mood in individuals with bipolar disorder (Mundo, Cattaneo, Russo, & Altamura, 2006).

Even in the absence of an inappropriate medication regimen, there are possible deleterious effects to misdiagnosis. Post (1992) proposed a sensitization model, also known as "kindling," whereby pathways inside the brain become kindled or sensitized; that is, cells once activated are reinforced and easier to activate again. While initial episodes of depression, mania, or hypomania tend to be triggered by external stimuli (i.e., stressors), if the disorder is allowed to progress unchecked, future episodes will occur by themselves (i.e., independent of an outside stimulus), with greater frequency, more severity, and less treatment responsiveness. Clearly, this hypothesis emphasized the importance of early identification and proper intervention.

S.R. Hart et al., *Identifying, Assessing, and Treating Bipolar Disorder at School*,
Developmental Psychopathology at School, DOI 10.1007/978-1-4614-7585-9_4,
© Springer Science+Business Media New York 2014

In addition, as described earlier, suicidal ideation and behaviors are commonplace among individuals with bipolar disorder. In the 34–38 year longitudinal study conducted by Angst, Stassen, Clayton, Angst (2002) individuals diagnosed with bipolar disorder had a 20- to 30-fold increase in suicide mortality over same-aged, same-sex controls. Individuals left untreated were 2½ times more likely to die by suicide than matched controls. Psychopharmacological treatment has implications for suicidal behaviors, as antidepressants in the presence of an undetected bipolar disorder have been shown not only to increase the risk for destabilization of mood, but possibly to increase the risk of suicide and suicidal behaviors, even when coupled with mood stabilizers (Yerevanian, Koek, Mintz, & Akiskal, 2007). Conversely, medications typically used in the treatment of bipolar disorder (particularly lithium, divalproex, and carbamazepine) have been reported to offer protective effects against suicidal thoughts and behaviors (Yerevanian, Koek, & Mintz, 2007). Delay of the advent of these medications has been shown to increase the risk of suicide attempts (Nery-Fernandes et al., 2012).

Case Finding

Early identification of bipolar disorder is not only important for appropriate and timely treatment, but might also be considered mandated by the federal government through Child Find legislation of the *Individuals with Disabilities Education Improvement Act* (IDEA; U.S. Department of Education, 2006). Child Find mandates require school districts to identify, locate, and evaluate all children with disabilities, regardless of severity. While a goal of Child Find is the early identification of children with disabilities, the law requires school districts to continually monitor students for the development of disabilities and is therefore important for school psychologists working with youth of any age.

Case finding refers to those activities consistent with Child Find mandates designed to assist in the identification of individuals with atypical developmental patterns. Case finding efforts are not designed to diagnose disorders, but rather to alert professionals to risk factors (which when present increase the odds of bipolar disorder) and/or warning signs (which are the early manifestations of bipolar disorder) in order to consider the need for further screening and evaluation (Brock, Jimerson, & Hansen, 2006). The risk factors of and warning signs for bipolar disorder are listed in Table 4.1. School-based mental health professionals are uniquely positioned to recognize these risk factors and warning signs.

Risk Factors

There appear to be several risk factors for bipolar disorder in children. The presence of these factors should signal to the school-based mental health professional the need to be especially vigilant for the warning signs of a disorder (Brock et al., 2006).

Table 4.1 Risk factors and warning signs of bipolar disorder

Risk factors	Warning signs
Family history	Bipolar symptoms
Particular diagnoses	Treatment response
Suicidal ideation/behaviors	Emotionality
Personality type	
Perinatal trauma	

Family History

Bipolar disorder rivals schizophrenia in terms of its tendency to run in families and is among the most heritable of human illnesses. For example, it has been shown to be similar to height and type I diabetes and more heritable than breast cancer, coronary heart disease in males, and type II diabetes (see Craddock, O'Donovan, & Owen, 2005 for a review of these findings). A family history of bipolar disorder appears to be the most robust risk factor for developing bipolar disorder (Goldstein, 2012). Children of a bipolar parent are at an increased risk of developing psychopathology, with more than one-half typically retaining a psychiatric diagnosis. In addition to bipolar disorder, these diagnoses include ADHD and other disruptive disorders, unipolar depression, anxiety disorders, psychosis, and substance use disorder (Chang, Steiner, & Ketter, 2000; Duffy, Alda, Hajek, Sherry, & Grof, 2010).

It has been shown that children with one bipolar parent have a 15–30 % increased risk for developing bipolar disorder, while individuals with two bipolar parents have a 40–75 % increased risk (Chang et al., 2000; Gottesman, Laursen, Bertelsen, & Mortensen, 2010; Hauser et al., 2007). When the bipolar parent reports a lifetime diagnosis of ADHD, the risk to the child of developing bipolar disorder increases substantially, but interestingly, the child is not at greater risk of developing ADHD (Chang et al., 2000). Age of onset for parental bipolar disorder also appears to be related to development of a child's bipolar disorder, in that parents with an earlier onset of the disorder have been shown to be more likely to have a child diagnosed with bipolar disorder (Chang et al., 2000; Somanath, Jain, & Reddy, 2002).

"Bottom up" studies of bipolar disorder (i.e., starting with a bipolar child and looking at family history) also indicate psychopathology in relatives. In addition to an increase in the rates of bipolar disorder in the relatives of a bipolar individual, there are also elevated rates of unipolar depression, schizophrenia, schizoaffective, anxiety, substance use, ADHD, and disruptive behavior disorders (CD and ODD; Mortensen, Pederson, Melbye, Mors, & Ewald, 2003; Somanath et al., 2002; Wozniak et al., 2004).

While family history is one of the strongest risk factors for bipolar disorder, it is important to note that many children with a bipolar relative (or more than one) do not go on to develop bipolar disorder. Therefore, while it should prompt awareness and further questioning (e.g., into symptoms of mania), it is not, in and of itself, sufficient to warrant further screening and/or diagnostic assessment. On the other hand, lack of a reported family history of psychiatric challenges is not sufficient to rule out bipolar disorder (Youngstrom, Findling, Youngstrom, & Calabrese, 2005).

Table 4.2 *DSM-5* psychiatric diagnoses that suggest the need for evaluation of bipolar disorder

Depressive disorders
• 296.xx Major depressive disorder (unipolar depression)
• 296.99 Disruptive Mood Dysregulation Disorder
• 300.4 Dysthymia
• 291.xx-292.xx Substance/Medication-Induced Depressive Disorder
• 293.83 Depressive Disorder Due to Another Medical Condition (particularly if mixed features are indicated as a specifier)
• 311.xx Other Specified and Unspecified Depressive Disorders
Attention-deficit and disruptive behavior disorders
• 314.xx Attention-deficit/hyperactivity disorder (ADHD)
• 313.81 Oppositional defiant disorder (ODD)
• 312.xx Conduct disorder
Anxiety disorders
• 300.02 Generalized anxiety disorder
• 300.23 Social phobia
• 300.3 Obsessive compulsive disorder
• 309.21 Separation anxiety disorder
Substance related disorders

Families often have complex constellations that may make gathering an accurate history very difficult, or parents may be reluctant to report prior (or current) symptoms and/or disorders.

Presence of Psychiatric Diagnoses

The presence of certain psychiatric diagnoses should also prompt further investigation for several reasons, including: (a) when undetected, bipolar disorder is frequently initially diagnosed with another psychiatric disorder, (b) bipolar disorder is more often than not comorbid with other disorders, and (c) in most cases, the comorbid disorder presents initially (e.g., anxiety symptoms exist prior to bipolar symptoms). Therefore, it is recommended that bipolar disorder be a "rule out" diagnosis when conducting an evaluation of the disorders listed in Table 4.2, and family history and information regarding the presence of additional risk factors or warning signs should be obtained. Chapter 5 will discuss differentiation of several of these disorders with bipolar disorder more fully.

Suicidal Ideation/Behaviors

As indicated in Chapter 3, suicidal ideation and behaviors are unfortunately quite common in individuals with bipolar disorder. Therefore, screening for these behaviors in youth diagnosed with bipolar disorder is imperative. In addition, as youth with bipolar disorder may not yet be identified and the tendency of individuals with bipolar disorder to be overrepresented among suicide completers, it is also recommended that a psychologist inquire about additional risk factors or warning signs of

Table 4.3 Risk factors for suicidality in bipolar population

Clinical/illness history variables	Comorbid diagnostic conditions
Previous attempts	Presence of psychotic features
Presence of suicidal thoughts and feelings	Substance use disorder
Presence of mixed episodes or depressive episodes with hypomanic symptoms	Panic disorder
Early-onset of disorder	
Psychiatric hospitalizations	
Presence of self-injurious behaviors	
Presence of sexual or physical abuse or trauma	
Rapid cycling	
Presence of impulsivity and aggression	
Family history of suicidality	

Note. These are particular for early-onset bipolar disorder, although many of the predictors are robust for late-onset as well

bipolar disorder during a suicide risk assessment with individuals who do not currently have a diagnosis of bipolar disorder. Table 4.3 illuminates the particular risk factors for suicidal thoughts and behaviors associated with this diagnosis.

The highest levels of ideation are reported to occur during mixed episodes, and attempts are most common in the presence of depressive and mixed symptoms. Ideation is positively correlated with levels of anxiety, hopelessness, and depression (Valtonen et al., 2007). Early-onset attempters are more likely to be female, have an early age of bipolar disorder symptom onset, exhibit rapid cycling, experience more mixed episodes, and have a history of psychiatric hospitalizations and/or psychotic features (Coryell et al., 2003; Goldstein et al., 2005; Levine, Chengappa, Brar, Gershon, & Kupfer, 2001). In addition to these characteristics, research specifically addressing suicidal ideation and behaviors in children and adolescents indicates a positive correlation with age, elevated rates of family history of suicide attempts, more non-suicidal self-injurious behaviors, increased rates of physical and sexual abuse, more panic and substance use disorders, and more parent reports of impulsive/aggressive indicators (Goldstein et al., 2005; Papolos, Hennen, & Cockerham, 2005).

Interested readers are encouraged to access Goldstein (2009) for a review of these factors as well as a discussion regarding assessment and intervention. Briefly, as with any suicide assessment, professionals are encouraged to engage in direct questioning regarding suicidal thoughts and behaviors, such as "Are you having thoughts of suicide?". While these questions may feel uncomfortable for adults, it is very important to be direct and clear when inquiring. Table 4.4 illuminates the primary elements important for a suicide assessment. Readers are also referred to Brock, Sandoval, and Hart (2006) for general guidance regarding understanding, assessing, and intervening with students with suicidal thoughts and behaviors.

Personality Type

While hypomania is a specific episode in the diagnosis of bipolar disorder, it has also been characterized as a personality style (e.g., dimensions of sociability,

Table 4.4 Elements of a suicide assessment

Suicidal intent: the extent to which an individual wishes to die. Four aspects of intent should be investigated

1. Belief about intent—the extent an individual wishes to die
2. Preparatory behaviors—steps taken towards the attempt, such as giving away possessions, saying goodbye to friends, etc.
3. Prevention of discovery—careful planning so that the attempt is not likely to be aborted
4. Communication of intent—who, if anyone, the individual has confided in about his/her thoughts, feelings, or behaviors

Suicide plan: what specific plans have been thought out? How developed is the plan?

Access to means: does the individual have access to means for the suicide (e.g., gun)? Has the individual made an effort to secure the means?

Recent precipitants: most common precipitants include interpersonal conflict or loss (e.g., fight with parent, break-up with girl/boyfriend). Disciplinary actions or legal troubles (e.g., being suspended from school, being arrested) are also common. Trauma history and recent experiences are also important to inquire about

Motivation: what is the motivation behind the attempt? Is it to die or escape a painful situation? Or does the individual want to communicate pain or anger to others? Does s/he want to make others hurt the way they have hurt her/him?

Environmental contingencies: are there naturally occurring factors in the environment that might reinforce (e.g., friends who support suicidal behaviors, family history of suicidal thoughts and behaviors) or dissuade from suicidal behaviors (e.g., strong religious family)?

Note. Adapted from "Suicidality in pediatric bipolar disorder", by T. R. Goldstein, 2009, *Child and Adolescent Psychiatric Clinics of North America, 18,* 339–352

ambitiousness, speeded mood, increased energy, and perceived uniqueness). Longitudinal studies have indicated that individuals identified in late adolescence or early adulthood with elevated scores on the Hypomanic Personality Scale (HPS; Eckblad & Chapman, 1986) were at heightened risk for bipolar and unipolar disorders and reported higher rates of substance use disorders in adulthood. In addition, individuals who endorsed HPS impulsive, antisocial traits reported higher rates of bipolar disorder and arrests, and more severe ratings of alcohol use than other participants (Kwapil et al., 2000). Interestingly, a more recent investigation of this scale indicated that high scores on the HPS were only indicative of a bipolar disorder when combined with high levels of, and more fluctuation with, negative affect and negative coping styles (i.e., rumination and risk-taking; Bentall et al., 2011).

Perinatal Trauma

There is some evidence to suggest that children diagnosed with bipolar disorder display more perinatal risk factors (e.g., intrauterine exposure to prescribed medications, intrauterine exposure to illegal drugs, birth complications) than healthy controls (Pavuluri, Henry, Nadimpalli, O'Connor, & Sweeney, 2006; Singh, Pfeifer, Barzman, Kowatch, & DelBello, 2007). It should be noted that perinatal trauma is linked to many developmental complications and evidence of trauma would not indicate bipolar disorder (or other disorders) in the absence of additional concerns and information.

Warning Signs

While risk factors suggest the need to be vigilant for further signs of a disorder, warning signs provide more concrete evidence of its presence (Brock et al., 2006). In addition to the warning signs that bipolar disorder is present, researchers have been attempting to define a bipolar prodrome (i.e., a clinical picture of an individual who will later develop a full-blown bipolar disorder). These warning signs are often identified as indications of that prodrome.

Symptoms of Bipolar Episodes

Obviously, evidence of hypomanic or manic symptoms should signal further evaluation, monitoring, and/or intervention. In addition, it is proposed that symptoms of depression should also warrant careful investigation due to the following: (a) the conversion rate from unipolar to bipolar disorder is high, (b) the first episode typically reported in bipolar disorder is depression, and (c) individuals with bipolar disorder spend a significant amount of their life experiencing depressive symptoms. Symptoms of (hypo)mania or depression may be apparent in a subthreshold manner (i.e., not meeting full criteria for a diagnosis), may not appear in the classic sense of the disorder (e.g., mania as irritability not euphoria), often occur in mixed states (i.e., symptoms of mania and depression at the same time), and typically exist in a chronic pattern (i.e., not presenting discrete episodes) making awareness and/or diagnosis difficult.

While Chapter 5 discusses symptoms of bipolar episodes in greater detail, a brief discussion is offered here. Irritability, qualitatively distinct in its intensity, frequency, and aggressive out-of-control behavior, is the most often-reported early-onset bipolar disorder symptom (Biederman et al., 2005; Kowatch, Youngstrom, Danielyan, & Findling, 2005). Irritability is a predominant symptom in both manic and depressive episodes. When aggression is separated from irritability in descriptions, both symptoms are often the most commonly reported, present in over 80 % of children (Danielyan, Pathak, Kowatch, Arszman, & Johns, 2007; Pavuluri, Henry, Devineni, Carbray, & Birmaher, 2006). These symptoms, while prominent in children with bipolar disorder, may also indicate other disorders. Therefore, even though they should prompt further investigation, they are not sufficient to indicate bipolar disorder. Sleep disturbances and increased energy are also frequently reported, present in 50–80 % of children diagnosed with early-onset bipolar disorder (Danielyan et al., 2007; Kowatch et al., 2005; Lofthouse, Fristad, Splaingard, & Kelleher, 2007). The more classic symptoms of mania (e.g., euphoria, grandiosity, racing thoughts) present more conflicting results in the literature; however, if present they should also warrant further screening, as these symptoms are specific to bipolar disorder and have been reported among children with the disorder. The behaviors assessed for in the screeners listed later in this chapter identify the most significant symptomatic warning signs of the disorder.

Treatment Response

While antidepressant- or stimulant-associated switch to hypomania or mania were not sufficient criteria for a bipolar diagnosis according to the *DSM-IV-TR*, it had previously been recommended that such medication responses should prompt further consideration and screening for bipolar disorder (Emilien, Septien, Brisard, Corruble, & Bourin, 2007). In *DSM-5* substance-induced bipolar disorder is a diagnosis, with the mood disturbance (i.e., elevated, expansive, or irritable mood) prompted by a substance or medication and lasting a "substantial period of time "e.g., about 1 month)" (APA, 2013, p. 142). It is recommended that if risk factors or warning signs of bipolar disorder are present, psychologists inquire about previous response to medication trials.

Emotionality

Children with bipolar disorder are often described as extremely emotional. The degree of their emotion seems to be out of context with the external environment and they can swing from extreme happiness to extreme sadness very quickly (sometimes they may do so many times within the same day!). They may rage for extended periods of time, and often feel out of control of their behavior, apologetic, guilty, and confused afterwards. They tend to have difficulties calming themselves or being calmed by others when they become upset. They may perceive the world as hostile and act uninhibited, impulsive, and at times bizarrely (e.g., a fifth grader who crawls around on the floor of her classroom during a lesson meowing like a cat and attempting to aggressively "snuggle" on the feet of her classmates, despite the lack of acceptance and encouragement of her classmates and attempts to redirect by her teacher). These children are described as having difficulties with mood regulation (i.e., the ability to control one's own mood state), mood reactivity (i.e., to what degree and how quickly the mood state is able to resolve with external consoling), mood lability (i.e., the tendency to experience differing moods rapidly), and rejection sensitivity (i.e., perceiving rejection from external sources; Chang et al., 2000; Faedda et al., 2004). Again, the presence of these symptoms in and of themselves do not "diagnose" bipolar disorder, and it is vital to differentiate bipolar from other disorders that may manifest in similar challenges with mood (e.g., autism, early-onset schizophrenia).

Developmental Screening

When warranted, specific inquiry regarding risk factors and warning signs will assist in the identification of individuals with bipolar disorder. Routine developmental screening by school districts should bring children to the awareness of school-based mental health professionals so that further inquiry can occur. Parents of children diagnosed with bipolar disorder report symptomatic onset as early as age 3, with irritability, moodiness, sleep disturbance, hyperactivity, aggressiveness, and

Table 4.5 Social–emotional development screening tools

Instrument	Age range	Brief description	Administration time (min)
Ages and stages question-naires—social–emotional (ASQ-SE; Squires, Bricker, & Twombly, 2002)	Birth to 5 years	Domains: • Social–emotional problems • Behavioral problems • Social competencies Available in English and Spanish	10–15
Infant-toddler social and emotional assessment (ITSEA; Carter & Briggs-Gowan, 2000)	1–3 years	Domains: • Externalizing • Internalizing • Dysregulation • Competencies • Maladaptive behavior • Atypical behavior • Social relatedness Available in English, Spanish, French, Dutch, and Hebrew	30
Devereux early childhood assessment (DECA; LeBuffe & Naglieri, 2003)	2–5 years	Strength-based approach Domains: • Initiative • Self control • Attachment Available in English and Spanish	5–10
Eyberg child behavior inventory (Eyberg & Colvin, 1978)	2½–11 years	Domains: • Conduct problems • Aggression • Inattention Items are also rated whether or not behaviors are problematic Available in English	5

Note. Adapted from "Assessment of young children's social-emotional development and psycho-pathology: Recent advances and recommendations for practice" by A. S. Carter, M. J. Briggs-Gowan, & N. O. Davis, 2004, *Journal of Child Psychology and Psychiatry, 45*, pp. 109–134

anxiety the most frequent initial symptoms (Faedda et al., 2004). Other reports indicate diagnosis as early as the age of 5- to 7-years (Danielyan et al., 2007; Wozniak et al., 2004). The early-onset of bipolar disorder and bipolar symptoms indicates that inquiry into preschool feelings and behaviors is a necessity.

While developmental screenings may assist in the identification of other types of disorders, such as autism (Brock et al., 2006), the psychologist would want to pay particular attention to social–emotional development when investigating screening results for risk factors or warning signs of bipolar disorder. Research documents that challenges with social–emotional development (i.e., problems characterized by abnormal intensity of, or deviance from, typical behaviors) often persist throughout life (Carter, Briggs-Gowan, & Davis, 2004). Research is increasing in this area, and several screening instruments have recently been validated for use. Table 4.5 presents several brief tools a district may choose to utilize.

Staff Development

It is likely that a student with bipolar disorder will come to the attention of the school-based mental health professional through referral from staff members. These staff members may include paraprofessionals (e.g., yard duties, cafeteria workers, bus drivers, aides) as well as professionals (e.g., school psychologists, counselors, teachers, vice principals, principals, reading specialists). It is therefore imperative that these staff members are aware of the risk factors and warning signs as identified in this section in order to assist in case finding efforts.

Screening

Screening efforts are expected to bring early awareness to children experiencing challenges. It has been argued that valid and reliable screening tools are more useful in predicting a bipolar diagnosis than identifying a family history (i.e., changes in odds of 8–9 yielding probabilities of around 30 % in settings with a prevalence of 5 %). It has also been demonstrated that screeners are more useful in *decreasing* the odds a child has bipolar disorder (i.e., ruling bipolar disorder out) with low scores than ruling it in, although high scores should indicate further assessment (Youngstrom, Findling, et al., 2005).

When considering screening tools, the psychologist is concerned with several issues: expense, time to complete and score, and technical properties. Sensitivity and specificity are important technical issues to consider when discussing screening.[1] Sensitivity refers to whether a test correctly identifies a condition (i.e., true positive) such as bipolar disorder, and high sensitivity is required when early identification is necessary. Specificity is whether a test correctly finds a condition is not present when it is not, in actuality, present (i.e., true negative). As screenings are not looking for diagnosis, but rather to identify children that *may* have bipolar disorder in order to indicate the need for further assessment, it is preferred to have high sensitivity with adequate specificity. In other words, it is better to identify children that do not have bipolar disorder and follow up with additional assessment than to miss potential children that do have bipolar disorder. However, in the interest of preserving resources (i.e., the time, effort, and energy to engage in further assessment with a child that is not truly bipolar), it is important that specificity not be too low. It is a challenge of developers then, to balance both sensitivity and specificity of the measures (Carter et al., 2004).

Carter et al. (2004) recommend a multistage process to screen large numbers of children for developmental delays and behavior or social–emotional problems. The first stage would include a brief and inexpensive screening assessment tool

---

[1]The companion properties of positive predictive value and negative predictive value are also important properties in regards to screening; however, they will not be discussed here.

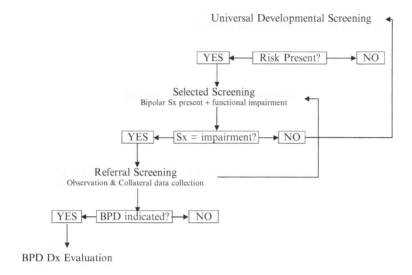

Fig. 4.1 An illustration of Carter and colleagues (2004) recommended multistage process to screen large numbers of children for social–emotional challenges such as bipolar disorder

administered to all children. Children identified as at-risk in this first stage would then be referred for a more comprehensive screening. This second stage might include a somewhat longer screening instrument and questions regarding (a) degree of concern regarding behaviors; and (b) presence of social, academic, and/or functional impairment as a result of the behaviors. When concern is heightened and significant impairment identified, the child would continue to the third stage of screening. Children with a moderate level of concern and impairment would continue to be monitored and interventions addressing the student's challenges proposed and implemented. The third stage would include an even more comprehensive screening instrument, observations, information from collateral informants, and possible referral for a more thorough diagnostic evaluation. This multistage screening process is illustrated in Fig. 4.1. Universal and selected screenings are activities school psychologists can expect to be involved in. Universal screenings can be thought of as the first stage of Carter and colleagues' model, and selected screenings a part of the second and third stages.

Universal Screening

Universal screenings are administered to all students or caregivers. Developmental screenings are one example of these. An effective and efficient universal screening tool specifically addressing behavior and emotion is the *BASC-2 Behavioral and Emotional Screening System* (BESS; Kamphaus & Reynolds, 2007). The *BESS* is available in teacher, parent, and child forms, can be completed in approximately 5 min, and is appropriate for preschool- to high school-aged children (with the exception of the child form, which does not have a preschool version). The child and parent forms are available in English and Spanish. The computerized scoring software program (ASSIST) provides T scores, percentile ranks, and qualitative risk labels (normal, elevated, extremely elevated). One intriguing feature of the *ASSIST* is the possibility of customizing reports in order to utilize local norms (as one might wish with a Response to Intervention [RtI] model). The *BESS* can also be hand-scored.

The *BESS* was developed using items selected from the *BASC-2*. While the technical properties are outlined in the manual, briefly, it was standardized on over 12,000 individuals, ranging from 3- to 18-years-old and closely matched to the population by geographic region. Split-half reliability estimates were consistently above the criterion of 0.90 established for screening instruments (Kamphaus & Reynolds, 2007). Test–retest and interrater reliability were demonstrated to be high for all forms and levels (from 0.80 to 0.91, and from 0.71 to 0.83, respectively). The *BESS* was strongly correlated with other general measures of behavior and emotion problems (e.g., the Achenbach Scales), and moderately to strongly correlated with narrow measures (e.g., ADHD, anxiety, depression, adaptive behavior). Several predictive studies have been conducted to demonstrate correlations with disciplinary infractions, special education placement, pre-referral interventions, reading and math scores (Kamphaus et al., 2007).

Selected Screening

While universal screenings are administered to all students or caregivers to identify a variety of academic and behavioral/emotional concerns, selected screenings are administered to address specific concerns, in this case, manic and/or depressive symptoms. Recently, several measures have been validated for use with juvenile populations to screen for symptoms of mania. The presence of mania is what defines bipolar disorder; therefore the importance of accurate screening for these symptoms is paramount. Determining who to administer the screening instruments to (e.g., child/adolescent, parent, teacher) has been a question for researchers. In many cases, these self- and other-reports are compared to a more "gold standard" clinician rating or clinician-conducted interview to determine their usefulness in accurately identifying youth with bipolar disorder. Youngstrom, Findling, and colleagues (2004) recently compared screening instruments developed to identify bipolar disorder in children and adolescents. This study demonstrated that parent reports have better diagnostic accuracy than either teacher- or self-reports of symptoms; therefore parent-rating scales are included in the discussion below. Again, diagnosis is not the purpose of these evaluations, but utilizing these tools should assist in determining if a diagnostic assessment is warranted. All school psychologists should be prepared to participate in this level of screening for bipolar disorder.

Child Mania Rating Scale-Parent Version

The child mania rating scale-parent version (*CMRS-P*) is presented in Fig. 4.2 (Pavuluri, Henry, Devineni, et al., 2006). The full version of the *CMRS-P* is 21-items and is appropriate for use with children 5- to 17-years-old to screen for current manic symptoms. It was initially validated on a sample of over 150 children demonstrating excellent internal consistency and test–retest reliability statistics (0.96 for each). Content, construct, criterion-related, and convergent validity have been demonstrated. Strong correlations were apparent with other clinical and research scales assessing manic symptoms. The scale was shown to differentiate children with bipolar disorder from children with ADHD or healthy controls, between bipolar disorder and bipolar disorder with comorbid ADHD from ADHD alone, as well as bipolar disorder I from bipolar disorder II (with higher scores demonstrated for bipolar I children); however it did not discriminate between bipolar disorder and bipolar disorder with comorbid ADHD or between ADHD and healthy controls (Pavuluri, Henry, Devineni, et al., 2006).

The authors report that the full version of the *CMRS-P* can be completed in 10–15 min. A cut score of 20 on the scale demonstrated good sensitivity (0.84) and excellent specificity (0.98) in the identification of bipolar disorder (i.e., differentiating individuals with bipolar disorder from healthy controls) and good sensitivity (0.82) and excellent specificity (0.94) differentiating bipolar from ADHD. A brief version of the scale has also been developed (items marked with an asterisk in Fig. 4.2 identify these items; Henry, Pavuluri, Youngstrom, & Birmaher, 2008). Validity and reliability were excellent for this form as well. A cut score of 10 on these items provided excellent sensitivity (0.92) and good specificity (0.82) differentiating bipolar disorder from healthy controls, and good sensitivity (0.84) and specificity (0.83) differentiating bipolar disorder from ADHD. Therefore, it appears that a score of 20 or above on the full version, or 10 or above on the brief version, should prompt further investigation into additional risk factors and warning signs of bipolar disorder and may indicate the need for a diagnostic evaluation.

Parent General Behavior Inventory: Short Form 10 (P-GBI: SF10)

The *PGBI: SF10* (see Fig. 4.3; Youngstrom, Frazier, Demeter, Calabrese, & Findling, 2008) is an adaptation of the *Parent General Behavior Inventory* (Youngstrom, Findling, Danielson, & Calabrese, 2001), a tool appropriate for use with children 5- to 17-years-old. The *P-GBI* has demonstrated strong construct validity and excellent internal consistency (0.94–0.97; Youngstrom et al., 2001). In several studies including over 900 children, the *P-GBI* performed the best among six tools used in the screening for symptoms of mania (Youngstrom et al., 2004; Youngstrom, Meyers, et al., 2005). The *P-GBI* demonstrated significant ability to discriminate bipolar disorder from non-bipolar children in both academic/research as well as community health settings, and across a range of ages, gender, ethnicity, and demographic variables.

One strong limitation to the *P-GBI* is the length (76 items). The *P-GBI: SF10* was developed to address this shortcoming. The initial study including over 600 youth demonstrated the *P-GBI: SF10* to be strongly correlated with the *P-GBI* ($r=0.95$) and to perform significantly better in identifying bipolar disorder than the full scale (AUROC of 0.86 vs. 0.83). This study further demonstrated the scale to have good reliability ($\alpha=0.92$), and to effectively discriminate bipolar disorder

---

CMRS, PARENT VERSION

_____   ___ ___ ___   _____
Child's name   Date of Birth   Case # / ID #
                                     (mm/dd/yy)
INSTRUCTIONS

The following questions concern your child's mood and behavior in the **past month**. Please place a check mark or an 'x' in a box for each item. Please consider it a problem if it is **causing trouble** and is beyond what is normal for your child's age. Otherwise, check 'rare or never' if the behavior is not causing trouble.

Does your child . . .	NEVER/ RARELY	SOMETIMES	OFTEN	VERY OFTEN
1. **Have periods of feeling super happy for hours or days at a time, extremely wound up and excited, such as feeling "on top of the world"**	0	1	2	3 _____
2. **Feel irritable, cranky, or mad for hours or days at a time**	0	1	2	3 _____
3. Think that he or she can be anything or do anything (e.g., leader, best basket ball player, rap singer, millionaire, princess) beyond what is usual for that age	0	1	2	3 _____
4. **Believe that he or she has unrealistic abilities or powers that are unusual, and may try to act upon them, which causes trouble**	0	1	2	3 _____
5. **Need less sleep than usual; yet does not feel tired the next day**	0	1	2	3 _____
6. **Have periods of too much energy**	0	1	2	3 _____
7. Have periods when she or he talks too much or too loud or talks a mile-a-minute	0	1	2	3 _____
8. **Have periods of racing thoughts that his or her mind cannot slow down , and it seems that your child's mouth cannot keep up with his or her mind**	0	1	2	3 _____
9. **Talk so fast that he or she jumps from topic to topic**	0	1	2	3 _____

Fig. 4.2 The Child Mania Rating Scale-Parent Version. *Note*: Reprinted with permission from "Child mania rating scale: Development, reliability, and validity" by M. N. Pavuluri, D. B. Henry, B. Devineni, J. A. Carbray, & B. Birmaher, 2006, *Journal of the American Academy of Child and Adolescent Psychiatry, 45*, 550–560

	NEVER	SOMETIMES	OFTEN	VERY OFTEN	
10. Rush around doing things nonstop	0	1	2	3	___
11. Have trouble staying on track and is easily drawn to what is happening around him or her	0	1	2	3	___
12. Do many more things than usual, or is unusually productive or highly creative	0	1	2	3	___
13. **Behave in a sexually inappropriate way (e.g., talks dirty, exposing, playing with private parts, masturbating, making sex phone calls, humping on dogs, playing sex games, touches others sexually)	0	1	2	3	___
14. Go and talk to strangers inappropriately, is more socially outgoing than usual	0	1	2	3	___

Does your child . . .

	NEVER	SOMETIMES	OFTEN	VERY OFTEN	
15. Do things that are unusual for him or her that are foolish or risky (e.g., jumping off heights, ordering CDs with your credit cards, giving things away)	0	1	2	3	___
16. **Have rage attacks, intense and prolonged temper tantrums	0	1	2	3	___
17. Crack jokes or pun more than usual, laugh loud, or act silly in a way that is out of the ordinary	0	1	2	3	___
18. Experience rapid mood swings	0	1	2	3	___
19. Have any suspicious or strange thoughts	0	1	2	3	___
20. **Hear voices that nobody else can hear	0	1	2	3	___
21. See things that nobody else can see	0	1	2	3	___

TOTAL SCORE _____

Please send comments to:
Mpavuluri@psych.uic.edu

**Items included in the Brief CMRS-P.

Fig. 4.2 (continued)

from unipolar depression (AUROC=0.86), and from ADHD (AUROC=0.82; Youngstrom, Frazier, et al., 2008). The authors suggest that these screeners are particularly useful in "ruling out" bipolar disorder through low scores; however, high scores indicate slightly higher likelihood ratios than family history. A recent study including almost 800 children and adolescents has demonstrated the utility of the *PGBI: SF10* across a variety of settings (Freeman et al., 2011), including clinical and community-based.

The Parent General Behavior Inventory: Short Form 10 (P-GBI: SF10)

Subject ID#: ☐☐☐☐☐☐ Write numbers like these: |1|2|3|4|5|6|7|8|9|10|	Date: ☐☐/ ☐☐/ ☐☐☐☐ M M D D Y Y Y Y
Relationship to Child: ┌──────────────────────┐ └──────────────────────┘	

GENERAL BEHAVIOR INVENTORY
Parent Version (P-GBI) Short Form – H/B

Here are some questions about behaviors that occur in the general population. Think about how often they occur for your child. Using the scale below, select the number that best describes how often your child experienced these behaviors **over the past year**:

0	1	2	3
Never	Sometimes	Often	Very Often
Hardly Ever			Almost Constantly

Keep the following points in mind:

Frequency: you may have noticed a behavior as far back as childhood or early teens, or you may have noticed it more recently. In either case, estimate how frequently the behavior has occurred **over the past year.**

> For example: if you noticed a behavior when your child was 5, and you have noticed it over the past year, mark your answer **"often"** or **"very often almost - constantly"**. However, if your child has experienced a behavior during only one isolated period in his/her life, but not outside that period, mark your answer **"never - hardly ever"** or **"sometimes."**

Duration: many questions require that a behavior occur for an approximate duration of time (for example, "several days or more"). The duration given is a **minimum** duration. If your child usually experiences a behavior for shorter durations, mark the question **"never - hardly ever"** or **"sometimes."**

Changeability: what matters is not whether your child can get rid of certain behaviors if he/she has them, but whether these behaviors have occurred at all. So even if your child can get rid of these behaviors, you should mark your answer according to how frequently he/she experiences them.

Your job, then, is to rate how frequently your child has experienced a behavior, over the past year, for the duration described in the question. Please read each question carefully, and record your answer next to each question.

Fig. 4.3 The Parent General Behavior Inventory: Short Form 10. *Note*: Reprinted with permission from "Developing a ten-item mania scale from the Parent General Behavior Inventory for children and adolescents" by E. A Youngstrom, T. W. Frazier, C. Demeter, J. R. Calabrese, & R. L. Findling (2008), *Journal of Clinical Psychiatry, 69*, 831–839

Mood Disorders Questionnaire

The mood disorders questionnaire (*MDQ*) (Hirschfeld et al., 2000) is a self-report of manic symptoms for adults and is available online (http://www.dbsalliance.org/pdfs/MDQ.pdf). A cut score of 7 (out of 13) on the *MDQ* has demonstrated fair sensitivity (0.73) and excellent specificity (0.90) for differentiating bipolar disorder from healthy controls (Hirschfeld, Holzer, et al., 2003). Wagner et al. (2006) adapted

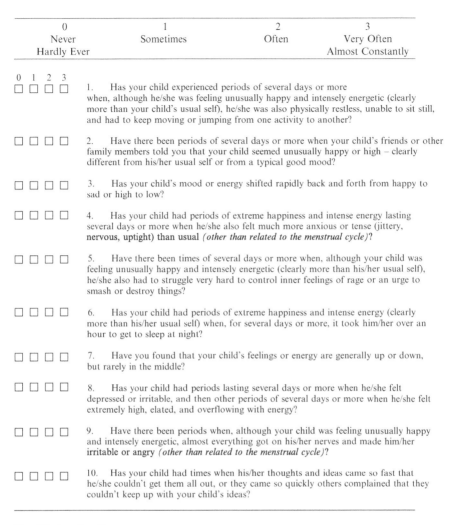

0	1	2	3
Never	Sometimes	Often	Very Often
Hardly Ever			Almost Constantly

0 1 2 3

☐ ☐ ☐ ☐ 1. Has your child experienced periods of several days or more when, although he/she was feeling unusually happy and intensely energetic (clearly more than your child's usual self), he/she was also physically restless, unable to sit still, and had to keep moving or jumping from one activity to another?

☐ ☐ ☐ ☐ 2. Have there been periods of several days or more when your child's friends or other family members told you that your child seemed unusually happy or high – clearly different from his/her usual self or from a typical good mood?

☐ ☐ ☐ ☐ 3. Has your child's mood or energy shifted rapidly back and forth from happy to sad or high to low?

☐ ☐ ☐ ☐ 4. Has your child had periods of extreme happiness and intense energy lasting several days or more when he/she also felt much more anxious or tense (jittery, nervous, uptight) than usual *(other than related to the menstrual cycle)*?

☐ ☐ ☐ ☐ 5. Have there been times of several days or more when, although your child was feeling unusually happy and intensely energetic (clearly more than his/her usual self), he/she also had to struggle very hard to control inner feelings of rage or an urge to smash or destroy things?

☐ ☐ ☐ ☐ 6. Has your child had periods of extreme happiness and intense energy (clearly more than his/her usual self) when, for several days or more, it took him/her over an hour to get to sleep at night?

☐ ☐ ☐ ☐ 7. Have you found that your child's feelings or energy are generally up or down, but rarely in the middle?

☐ ☐ ☐ ☐ 8. Has your child had periods lasting several days or more when he/she felt depressed or irritable, and then other periods of several days or more when he/she felt extremely high, elated, and overflowing with energy?

☐ ☐ ☐ ☐ 9. Have there been periods when, although your child was feeling unusually happy and intensely energetic, almost everything got on his/her nerves and made him/her irritable or angry *(other than related to the menstrual cycle)*?

☐ ☐ ☐ ☐ 10. Has your child had times when his/her thoughts and ideas came so fast that he/she couldn't get them all out, or they came so quickly others complained that they couldn't keep up with your child's ideas?

Fig. 4.3 (continued)

the *MDQ* into an adolescent version with self- and parent-report (*MDQ-Adolescent version*, MDQ-A). The *MDQ-A* (Fig. 4.4) completed by parents about their adolescent's symptoms demonstrated good sensitivity and specificity (0.72 and 0.81, respectively) at a cut-score of 5. Self-report was found to be not as useful as parent-report.

A similar version of the *MDQ* (*MDQ-Parent version*) was utilized in Youngstrom, Meyers, and colleagues (2005) screening tool comparison study and was found to discriminate children with bipolar disorder from non-bipolar children. This tool did

Mood Disorder Questionnaire - Adolescent Version
(MDQ-A)

Has there ever been a time for a week or more when your adolescent was not his/her usual self and...

	Yes	No
... felt too good or excited?	❑	❑
... was so irritable that he/she started fights or arguments with people?	❑	❑
...felt he/she could do anything?	❑	❑
... needed much less sleep?	❑	❑
... couldn't slow his/her mind down or thoughts raced through his/her head?	❑	❑
... was so easily distracted by things?	❑	❑
... had much more energy than usual?	❑	❑
... was much more active or did more things than usual?	❑	❑
... had many boyfriends or girlfriends at the same time?	❑	❑
... was more interested in sex than usual?	❑	❑
... did many things that were foolish or risky?	❑	❑
... spent too much money?	❑	❑
... used more alcohol or drugs?	❑	❑

If you checked YES to more than one of the above, have several of these ever ❑   ❑
happened to your adolescent during the same period of time?

How much of a problem did any of these cause your adolescent - like school problems, failing grades, problems with family and friends, legal troubles?
Please circle one response only.

     No problem   Minor problem   Moderate problem   Serious problem

Fig. 4.4 The Mood Disorder Questionnaire—Adolescent Version (MDQ-A). *Note*: Reprinted with permission from "Validation of the Mood Disorder Questionnaire for bipolar disorders in adolescents" by K. D. Wagner, R. M. A. Hirschfeld, G. J. Emslie, R. L. Findling, B. L. Gracious, & M. L. Reed, 2006, *Journal of Clinical Psychiatry, 67*, 827–830

not demonstrate statistical significance in favor of parent- over self-report (although there was a strong trend). The authors suggested using both the *P-GBI: SF10* and the *MDQ-P* as a multiple gating strategy, as both tools are different in format and content; however, if only one tool was to be used, the *P-GBI: SF10* was recommended.

Referral

While some children at risk of developing bipolar disorder will come to the attention of the school psychologist through direct observation or interaction, it is likely that the majority will be referred by other school-based professionals and paraprofessionals. In addition, parents may request to speak with the school psychologist or bring concerns to the attention of a Student Study Team (SST) or problem solving pre-referral team (of which the psychologist may be a member) about their child's social–emotional functioning. It is recommended that the referral process be continually evaluated to ensure those individuals with concerns regarding students have the ability to have their concerns heard and for the process to be efficient and effective.

The psychologist will also likely be involved in the referral process by referring parents and children evincing red flags (e.g., high score on a screening instrument and family history of bipolar disorder) to community resources. These might include referrals to county mental health, community groups and/or therapists, low-income health insurance agencies, and Social Security offices. To fill this role, school-based mental health professionals need to identify those local clinical resources that have expertise when it comes to the identification and treatment of youth with known or suspected bipolar disorder. Parents may also benefit from referrals to online resources, such as those listed in the Appendix.

Concluding Comments

The rate of bipolar disorder in children has increased substantially over the past decade. It is speculated that there are still large numbers of children that are mis- or un-identified. Misdiagnosis and under-diagnosis are problems that have significant implications for a child's life. Legislation places mandates on school districts through Child Find statutes for early identification of children with social–emotional challenges. School psychologists and other school-based mental health profession-als can expect to be involved in the case finding, screening, and referral process to identify children at risk for bipolar disorder.

Chapter 5
Diagnostic Assessment

In the USA a diagnosis of bipolar disorder is made utilizing criteria from the recently updated *Diagnostic and Statistical Manual of Mental Disorders*, now in its fifth edition (*DSM-5*; American Psychiatric Association [APA], 2013). While the diagnosis of bipolar disorder in adults is complex, it has been further complicated in children and adolescents by the demonstration of severely impaired individuals with a less classic presentation (e.g., less euphoria, less episodicity, more irritability), which the criteria, originally written for adults, was argued to not adequately capture. There was much speculation as to whether the revised *DSM-5* would alter the diagnostic criteria to account for this group of children and adolescents.

This chapter briefly outlines the changes to bipolar disorder diagnostic criteria from the *DSM-IV-TR* to *DSM-5* and provides information regarding diagnosis (e.g., episodes, subtypes, specifiers) according to *DSM-5* criteria, followed by discussions regarding the presentation of the disorder and the best practices regarding diagnosis in youth. As the *DSM-5* has been so recently published, much of the discussion regarding presentation will refer to research conducted under the guidelines of the *DSM-IV-TR*. While it is not expected that the responsibility of diagnosing bipolar disorder lies within the purview of school professionals, given its impact on school functioning and that school professionals may be the first contact with an impaired student, it is essential that these individuals are familiar with the criteria required to make the diagnosis and the issues surrounding this diagnosis for youth.

Diagnostic Criteria

Major Changes to Bipolar Disorder Diagnoses from DSM-IV-TR to DSM-5

As illustrated in Chapter 1 (see Fig. 1.1), several structural changes have been made to the diagnosis of bipolar disorders. "Rather than being subsumed under the Mood

S.R. Hart et al., *Identifying, Assessing, and Treating Bipolar Disorder at School*,
Developmental Psychopathology at School, DOI 10.1007/978-1-4614-7585-9_5,
© Springer Science+Business Media New York 2014

Disorders" umbrella, *DSM-5* includes Bipolar I Disorder, Bipolar II Disorder, Cyclothymic Disorder, Substance/Medication-Induced Bipolar and Related Disorder, Bipolar and Related Disorder Due to Another Medical Condition, Other Specified Bipolar and Related Disorder, and Unspecified Bipolar and Related Disorder under the umbrella: Bipolar and Related Disorders. These disorders continue to be characterized by the combination of episodes and level of severity of symptoms and/or impairment.

In addition to the restructuring and addition of several new bipolar diagnoses, several changes have been made within the diagnoses. These changes will be high-lighted in the appropriate sections of this chapter; however, two are important to briefly discuss here. First, what was a Mixed Episode in *DSM-IV-TR* is now a speci-fier for a manic, hypomanic or depressive episode in *DSM-5*. The purpose of the specifiers is to increase diagnostic specificity and create more homogeneous sub-groups to improve treatment selection and prognosis. Changing the mixed episode, where full criteria of both a (hypo)manic and depressive episode were required (except the duration criteria), to a course specifier, allows for subthreshold manic or depressive symptoms to be indicated within each episode. These subthreshold symp-toms are particularly important with regard to mania within unipolar depression, and evidence is accumulating that the presence of subthreshold manic symptoms within a depressive episode indeed represents a bipolar diathesis (see www.dsm5.org).

Second, much debate has occurred in the literature regarding whether the diag-nostic criteria of the *DSM-IV-TR* were appropriate for children, who might present with more chronic, primarily irritable symptoms. As indicated in Chapter 1, several different phenotypes were proposed to promote research in this area—the two of most interest being the Narrow (i.e., classic) and the Severe Mood and Behavioral Dysregulation (or Severe Mood Dysregulation [SMD]) phenotypes.

It appears that with the major revisions from *DSM-IV-TR* to the *DSM-5*, the less classically presenting individuals (i.e., those characterized more adequately by the SMD phenotype) will not be captured under a bipolar disorder diagnosis, but rather with a new disorder: Disruptive Mood Dysregulation Disorder (DMDD; originally proposed as Temper Dysregulation Disorder with Dysphoria; *DSM-5* Childhood and Adolescent Work Group, 2010). This disorder is located within the Depressive Disorders; however, as it is likely to characterize many children with a current *DSM-IV-TR* diagnosis of bipolar disorder (presumably the previous diagnosis of BP-NOS), a brief discussion follows.

In a consensus paper, the *DSM-5* Mood Disorders and Childhood and Adolescent Work Groups (2010) outlined the changes and rationale for the changes to the bipo-lar diagnosis. Within this document is a discussion regarding the introduction of DMDD and the relatively minor changes within the bipolar diagnoses. The work groups highlighted research into the SMD bipolar disorder phenotype originally proposed and researched by Leibenluft and colleagues (e.g., Leibenluft, 2011). As demonstrated by this body of research, those with the SMD phenotype are qualita-tively and quantitatively distinct from those with a classic presentation of bipolar disorder in youth. The classic and SMD phenotypes differed on important factors, such as outcomes, gender distribution, and family history. Importantly, those with SMD were more likely to develop anxiety or unipolar depression in adulthood, rather than episodic bipolar disorder (interested readers are referred to the consensus paper or Liebenluft, 2011, for a discussion of this research). Therefore, to further research and promote the understanding of these different presentations, the work group proposed the new depressive disorder, the addition of several disorders within the bipolar diagnoses that will provide opportunities for research among more homogeneous groups (e.g., adding time-specified subthreshold hypomania subcategories within the Other Specified Bipolar and Related Disorders; see "Subtypes" section for more discussion), and provided consistent wording within episodes emphasizing the episodic nature of bipolar disorder.

One final note regarding DMDD: while it is based primarily on research of the SMD phenotype, an important distinction exists. SMD included hyperarousal symptoms, which the work group determined would result in too much overlap with ADHD. Additionally, the work group was concerned regarding overlap with ODD; however, they determined that ODD or ADHD did not capture the significant impairment in mood for these youth. At the present, there is limited research specific to DMDD. One, relatively small study of inpatient children indicated it may reduce the rate of early-onset bipolar disorder (depending on rater and method; Marguiles, Weintraub, Basil, Grover, & Carlson, 2012). However, more questions regarding the stability and clinical utility of the disorder have been raised by the two other studies in this area (Axelson, et al., 2013; Copeland, Angold, Costello, & Egger, 2013). These two studies (larger and using community samples), demonstrated a disturbing overlap with ODD. Additionally, Axelson et al. (2013) reported only approximately ½ of the youth met criteria at both time points and did not differ from those without DMDD on mood symptoms (perplexing as DMDD is defined as a disorder of mood). *DSM-5* criteria for DMDD appear in Table 5.1. As evidenced by the criteria, this disorder exists in a hierarchy, in that if criteria are met for bipolar disorder, a bipolar diagnosis is made; however, if criteria are met for both ODD and DMDD, only a DMDD diagnosis is made. It is hoped that this new disorder will capture children and youth with significant impairment who experience chronic irritability and that future research into this group of youth will drive appropriate interventions and treatment options.

Episodes

Three mood episodes are described in the *DSM-5* in relation to a bipolar diagnosis. Two of these episodes are specific to a bipolar diagnosis (i.e., manic and hypomanic), and for a bipolar diagnosis to be made an individual must have experienced at least one manic or hypomanic episode in his or her lifetime. Evidence of a major depressive episode is typically found in the individual's past or present; however, it is not essential to a diagnosis of Bipolar I Disorder (although is required for a Bipolar II Disorder diagnosis).

Manic Episode

The *DSM-5* criteria for a manic episode are displayed in Table 5.2. A manic episode is characterized by a distinct period (at least 1 week, or less if hospitalization is required) of an abnormally and persistently elevated, expansive, or irritable mood

Table 5.1 *DSM-5* criteria for disruptive mood dysregulation disorder

A.	Severe recurrent temper outbursts manifested verbally (e.g., verbal rages) and/or behaviorally (e.g., physical aggression towards people or property) that are grossly out of proportion in intensity or duration to the situation or provocation.
B.	The temper outbursts are inconsistent with developmental level.
C.	The temper outbursts occur, on average, three or more times per week.
D.	The mood between temper outbursts is persistently irritable or angry most of the day, nearly every day, and is observable by others (e.g., parents, teachers, peers).
E.	Criteria A–D have been present for 12 or more months. Throughout that time, the person has not had 3 or more consecutive months when they were without all of the symptoms in Criteria A–D.
F.	Criteria A and D are present in at least two of three settings (i.e., at home, at school, with peers) and are severe in at least one of these.
G.	The diagnosis should not be made for the first time before age 6 years or after age 18 years.
H.	By history or observation, the age at onset of Criteria A–E is before 10 years.
I.	There has never been a distinct period lasting more than 1 day during which the full symptom criteria, except duration, for a manic or hypomanic episode have been met.
Note	Developmentally appropriate mood elevation, such as occurs in the context of a highly positive event or its anticipation, should not be considered as a symptom of mania or hypomania.
J.	The behaviors do not occur exclusively during an episode of major depressive disorder and are not better explained by another mental disorder (e.g., autism spectrum disorder, posttraumatic stress disorder, separation anxiety disorder, persistent depressive disorder [dysthymia])
Note	This diagnosis cannot coexist with oppositional defiant disorder, intermittent explosive disorder, or bipolar disorder, though it can coexist with others, including major depressive disorder, attention-deficit/hyperactivity disorder, conduct disorder, and substance use disorders. Individuals whose symptoms meet criteria for both disruptive mood dysregulation and oppositional defiant disorder should only be given the diagnosis of disruptive mood dysregulation disorder. If an individual has ever experienced a manic or hypomanic episode, the diagnosis of disruptive mood dysregulation should not be assigned.
K.	The symptoms are not attributable to the physiological effects of a substance or to another medical or neurological condition.

Note. Reprinted with permission PENDING from the Diagnostic and Statistical Manual of Mental Disorders, Fifth Edition (Copyright © 2013), American Psychiatric Association

and persistently increased goal-directed activity or energy. Changes to the *DSM-5* criteria for mania include the inclusion of increased energy as a core symptom, providing consistent wording across episodes (i.e., adding, "…and present most of the day, nearly every day…" to hypo(manic) episodes consistent with major depressive episode), and emphasizing the episodicity of bipolar disorder through addition of "…and represents a noticeable change from usual behavior…" to the B criterion. It is hoped that these somewhat subtle changes will increase diagnostic precision. For example, it has been suggested that clients may be more likely to remember or recognize increases in energy, rather than changes in mood (see www.dsm5.org for the rationale regarding these changes).

Elevated mood is characterized by euphoria, with an individual feeling unusually good, cheerful, or "high." People who know the individual well will recognize this

Table 5.2 *DSM-5* criteria for manic episode

A.	A distinct period of abnormally and persistently elevated, expansive, or irritable mood and abnormally and persistently increased activity or energy, lasting at least 1 week and present most of the day, nearly every day (or any duration if hospitalization is necessary).
B.	During the period of mood disturbance and increased energy or activity, three (or more) of the following symptoms (four if the mood is only irritable) are present to a significant degree, and represent a noticeable change from usual behavior:

    1. Inflated self-esteem or grandiosity

    2. Decreased need for sleep (e.g., feels rested after only 3 hours of sleep)

    3. More talkative than usual or pressured to keep talking

    4. Flight of ideas or subjective experience that thoughts are racing

    5. Distractibility (i.e., attention too easily drawn to unimportant or irrelevant external stimuli) as reported or observed

    6. Increase in goal-directed activity (either socially, at work or school, or sexually) or psychomotor agitation (i.e., purposeless non-goal directed activity)

    7. Excessive involvement in pleasurable activities that have a high potential for painful consequences (e.g., engaging in unrestrained buying sprees, sexual indiscretions, or foolish business investments)

C.	The mood disturbance is sufficiently severe to cause marked impairment in social or occupational functioning or to necessitate hospitalization to prevent harm to self or others, or there are psychotic features.
D.	The episode is not attributable to the direct physiological effects of a substance (e.g., a drug of abuse, a medication, or other treatment) or to another medical condition.
Note	A full manic episode that emerges during antidepressant therapy (e.g., medication, electroconvulsive therapy) but persists at a fully syndromal level beyond the physiological effect of that treatment is suufficient evidence for a manic episode and, therefore, a bipolar I diagnosiss.

Note. Reprinted with permission PENDING from the Diagnostic and Statistical Manual of Mental Disorders, Fourth Edition, Text Revision (Copyright © 2000), American Psychiatric Association

mood as excessive in comparison with the typical state. Expansive mood is described as an unceasing and indiscriminate enthusiasm for interpersonal, sexual, or occupational interactions. Increased energy represents a nonspecific, overall change in energy levels and should not be confused with the Criterion B symptom of "increase in goal-directed activity," which a specific and detailed inquiry. The changes in overall energy level represent a hallmark characteristic of a (hypo)manic episode.

Irritability may also exemplify the individual's mood disturbance and is defined as "persistent anger, a tendency to respond to events with angry outbursts or blaming others, or an exaggerated sense of frustration over minor matters" (APA, 2000, p. 349). The irritability seen in youth with bipolar disorder is qualitatively different from irritability in typically developing individuals or individuals displaying other psychopathology by its intensity, frequency, and aggressive out-of-control behavioral qualities (Biederman et al., 2005). Early research coined the term "affective storms" to describe the aggressive temper outbursts, which can last for prolonged periods of time (e.g., several hours) as a result of the severe irritability characterizing early-onset bipolar disorder (Davis, 1979). More recent research indicates that approximately ⅓ to ¾ of youths may experience "rage attacks," described by researchers as "severe anger associated with psychomotor agitation and verbal and/or physical aggressivity, lasting a minimum of 20 minutes, occurring at least twice per week, most weeks, during the preceding year" (Staton, Volness, & Beatty, 2008, p. 207).

It will be interesting to see what happens with the introduction of DMDD in this area. Previous research has clearly indicated that euphoria or elation is a common symptom; however, irritability is also commonly reported in youth with a classic presentation of bipolar disorder. A recent meta-analysis documented that an average of approximately 80 % of cases report irritability as a symptom and approximately 70 % report euphoria or elation, obviously with a majority reporting *both* (Kowatch, Youngstrom, Danielyan, & Findling, 2005). Mood lability (e.g., alternation between euphoria and irritability) is often documented in both adults and youth (APA, 2000). Elation is highly specific to bipolar disorder; however, irritability is not. Therefore, evidence of elated mood helps to rule in a diagnosis of bipolar disorder, while irritability may be an indicator of a multitude of other diagnoses or problems, and is therefore not as helpful when making a diagnosis (Youngstrom, Birmaher, & Findling, 2008). While the presence of elated mood is useful for ruling *in* bipolar disorder, its absence should not rule *out* bipolar disorder. In the aforementioned meta-analysis, reported rates of elated mood varied from 45 to 87 %, indicating that in some studies less than ½ of cases reported this symptom (Kowatch et al., 2005). If a clinician required elated mood as a necessary marker, it is likely that a bipolar disorder would be missed.

In addition to the overall disturbance in mood, three (or four if the mood is irritable) additional symptoms must be present for a manic episode to be established. Table 5.3 describes these additional symptoms and presents examples of what these might look like in school-aged children.

Finally, impairment is an essential element in documenting a manic episode, which is defined as a marked impairment in an area of functioning, the presence of psychotic features, or symptom severity significant enough to cause hospitalization. A manic episode cannot be established if the symptoms are due to the physiological effects of a substance, unless the symptoms persist beyond the physiological effects of that treatment. Manic episodes may represent the most studied and identifiable characteristic of bipolar disorder. While the bipolar spectrum is extremely heterogenous (e.g., bipolar II disorder vs. bipolar I disorder) and developmentally it may look quite different, the large number of different combinations of symptoms (which may present differently) reveals heterogeneity within the identification of a manic episode. In other words, one individual may present with an elevated mood, sleeping only 2- or 3-hours per night, sexual promiscuity (e.g., sneaking out of the house to engage in sexual activities with indiscriminant partners), and increased distractibility (e.g., not being able to stay on-track for more than a minute but becoming distracted by things such as noises in the hallway or thoughts in her head), which results in significant impairment in her friendships/relationships while the other areas of her life remain relatively intact and unaffected. Another may evidence extreme irritability and aggression (e.g., being sent to the principal for throwing books in the library after a minor comment intended as a joke by a peer), racing

Table 5.3 Examples of mania in school-aged children and youth

Symptom	Comment	Example—young(er) child	Example—adolescent
Inflated self-esteem/grandiosity	May be challenging to differentiate from developmentally appropriate imaginary play, but seems to be youth has an estimation of abilities that are not based in reality, are inappropriate to context and cause impairing consequences. When confronted about these abilities, will rarely "give up" on them, despite tangible evidence to the contrary.	Child states that he is Superman and jumps off the balcony to prove it to his family.	In the middle of a basketball game, a first year freshman player (and benchwarmer) stands up and begins coaching the team, calling time-outs, and talking with the referee because his coach "doesn't know what he's doing."
Decreased need for sleep	Not simply a lack of sleep, but not being tired in spite of little sleep; is not merely a lack of desire to sleep but youth is physically challenged to sleep.	Child wanting mother to read story after story at night time without getting sleepy or falling asleep; parents wake in the middle of the night to find child up and playing in room—in spite of getting only 3 hours of sleep, child not able to take a nap the next day.	Teen up on computer when parents go to bed, parents wake around 3 a.m. to find teen still up, teen complains of not being tired, parents take laptop and ground teen, but still wake in the morning to find teen watching TV. Doesn't seem tired all day despite claiming did not sleep.
Talkativeness	Speech can be pressured, loud, rapid, and difficult to interrupt. Youth may continue to speak at length without recognizing consequences (e.g., getting in trouble in the class).	Family has to leave movie because child cannot stop talking; student constantly raises hand and talks before being called on.	Teacher observes student following peers around continuing to talk to them as they walk away from her, she would then turn and begin talking to someone else without engaging with them and without waiting to join the situation.
Flight of ideas/racing thoughts	Typically developing children have difficulty defining this. Children and youth might describe it as an "energizer bunny" in their brain.	Child becomes so agitated while trying to explain his thinking that he punches his teacher and throws his chair down.	Teacher reports not being able to follow student's train of thought as her thoughts jump from one thing to another without making logical connections.

(continued)

Table 5.3 (continued)

Symptom	Comment	Example—young(er) child	Example—adolescent
Distractibility	Can demonstrate extreme difficulties focusing; may become distracted by internal (e.g., racing thoughts) or external stimuli.	Teacher reports student cannot stay focused on one thing, but drifts from activity to activity, group to group.	Student becomes frustrated with other students in the class because they are making so much noise (teacher reports other students were appropriately working).
Goal-directed activity	May be defined as "mission mode," once child becomes engaged in one activity, may find it hard to transition to another activity.	Student is suspended because he destroyed school property (ripped up books) and threw scissors when demanded that he stop working on his project.	Teen decided he "must" construct a skate ramp in his backyard and won't talk to friends, finish homework, or come in to eat until he is finished.
Pleasurable activities	This might look like excessive risk-taking, novelty-seeking, and hypersexuality. Hypersexuality is important because it is very specific to bipolar disorder (once abuse is ruled out).	Nine-year-old is suspended from school for accessing pornography on the school computer; a 10-year-old girl is referred for drawing two figures having sex and naked pictures of boys.	Twelve-year-old becomes pregnant after having sexual relationships with indiscriminate partners; 16-year-old has his license revoked after two speeding tickets of excessive speed.

thoughts (e.g., teacher unable to follow his string of comments and questions as they seem not to be connected to each other), and delusions (e.g., convinced his parents and teachers are conspiring to kill him), resulting in impairment in all areas of functioning and hospitalizations. Both may meet criteria for a manic episode, but would be quite different from each other. Therefore, it is challenging to make any grand sweeping statements about what mania is, as it can look drastically different from individual to individual.

However, sufficient research has allowed for some generalizations and associations. For example, manic episodes typically begin suddenly and frequently following psychosocial stressors (although it has been shown that as the disorder progresses, particularly without treatment, manic episodes may onset spontaneously); in many cases (50–70 %), manic episodes immediately precede or follow a major depressive episode with no period of recovery separating; and manic episodes tend to be recurrent, with more than 90 % of individuals reporting one single manic episode experiencing future episodes (APA, 2013). Manic episodes have been negatively correlated with cognitive functioning, which in turn, strongly predicts future psychosocial functioning, leading again to the importance of early intervention and treatment in order to prevent future episodes (Jaeger, Berns, Loftus, Gonzalez,

& Czobor, 2007; Martínez-Arán et al., 2004). Manic symptoms are also strongly associated with rapid cycling, history of alcohol dependence, and number of hospitalizations (Bauer, Kirk, Gavin, & Williford, 2001; Levine, Chengappa, Brar, Gershon, & Kupfer, 2001).

Importantly, while mania tends to be the defining feature of bipolar disorder for many in both professional and mainstream settings, individuals diagnosed with *any* bipolar disorder tend to spend significantly more time experiencing depressive symptoms, and those depressive symptoms are associated with far greater impairment (e.g., less ability to live independently, more suicidality, more social impairment, more work impairment; Levine et al., 2001; Manning, 2005; Miller, Uebelacker, Keitner, Ryan, & Solomon, 2004; Morriss et al., 2007).

Hypomanic Episode

Hypomanic episode criteria can be found in Table 5.4. Hypomania literally means "beneath" or "mild" mania and is identical to mania with the exceptions being the time required for the presence of symptoms, the level of impairment experienced, and the exclusion of psychotic features. The mood change experienced by the individual must be clearly different from the usual nondepressed mood and must be observable by others; however, it cannot be so significant as to cause marked impairment. The changes to hypomania in *DSM-5* are the same as the changes to mania.

Hypomania appears to have a mixed impact on individuals. When in an acute episode of hypomania, symptoms tend to result in adverse effects on overall social adjustment and more reports of interpersonal friction; however, when in a subsyndromal state, symptoms appear to increase performance, social, and leisure activities (Morriss et al., 2007). In addition, as individuals move from asymptomatic (i.e., no symptoms of hypomania) to a subsyndromal state, there are reported to be little changes on measures of psychosocial functioning (i.e., overall subjective satisfaction, role functioning such as work or school, functioning in interpersonal relationships, and ability to participate in recreation or hobbies). However, when moving from a subsyndromal state to an acute episode of hypomania, significant levels of impairment in these areas of functioning are reported (Judd et al., 2005).

Unrecognized and unreported hypomanic episodes are believed to be an important factor in missed bipolar diagnoses (Ghaemi, Ko, & Goodwin, 2001; Raman et al., 2007). Perhaps the most compelling arguments involve the idea that symptoms of hypomania overlap with normal and highly valued traits, such as high energy, work productivity, gregariousness, friendliness, and outgoingness (Doran, 2008). Individuals experiencing hypomania may state that they are having a "great day" or are feeling confident, vigorous, and happy. These individuals may be infectious, energizing those around them and drawing more upbeat individuals toward them. It is not likely to be a state where an individual feels like something is wrong or a sign of illness, but typically the opposite, a sign of strength and good mental health. Even when the mood is predominantly irritable, these symptoms may be viewed as part of an individual's "moody," "grouchy," or "touchy" personality. For

Table 5.4 *DSM-5* criteria for hypomanic episode

A.	A distinct period of abnormally and persistently elevated, expansive, or irritable mood, and abnormally and persistently increased activity or energy, lasting at least 4 consecutive days and present most of the day, nearly every day (or any duration if hospitalization is necessary).
B.	During the period of mood disturbance and increased energy and activity, three (or more) of the following symptoms have persisted (four if the mood is only irritable), represent a noticeable change from usual behavior, and have been present to a significant degree: 1. Inflated self-esteem or grandiosity 2. Decreased need for sleep (e.g., feels rested after only 3 hours of sleep) 3. More talkative than usual or pressure to keep talking 4. Flight of ideas or subjective experience that thoughts are racing 5. Distractibility (i.e., attention too easily drawn to unimportant or irrelevant external stimuli) as reported or observed 6. Increase in goal-directed activity (either socially, at work or school, or sexually) or psychomotor agitation 7. Excessive involvement in pleasurable activities that have a high potential for painful consequences (e.g., the person engages in unrestrained buying sprees, sexual indiscretions, or foolish business investments)
C.	The episode is associated with an unequivocal change in functioning that is uncharacteristic of the person when not symptomatic.
D.	The disturbance in mood and the change in functioning are observable by others.
E.	The episode is not severe enough to cause marked impairment in social or occupational functioning, or to necessitate hospitalization. If there are psychotic features, the episode is, by definition, manic.
F.	The symptoms are not due to the direct physiological effects of a substance (e.g., a drug of abuse, a medication, or other treatment).
Note	A full hypomanic episode that emerges during antidepressant treatment (e.g., medication, electroconvulsive therapy) but persists at a fully syndromal level beyond the physiological effect of that treatment is sufficient evidence for a hypomanic episode diagnosis. However, caution is indicated so that one or two symptoms (particularly increased irritability, edginess or agitation following antidepressant use) are not taken as sufficient for diagnosis of a hypomanic episode, nor necessarily indicative of a bipolar diathesis.

Note. Reprinted with permission PENDING from the Diagnostic and Statistical Manual of Mental Disorders, Fourth Edition, Text Revision (Copyright © 2000), American Psychiatric Association

these reasons, it is believed that individuals experiencing this state would not be likely to seek treatment or to vividly remember these time periods, and it is possible that even if he or she did, the most astute clinician may miss these signs.

A second and equally compelling argument has involved the overly strict and somewhat arbitrary *DSM-IV-TR* criteria. In a sample of almost 600 individuals drawn from a larger ($n = 4,547$) study and followed for 20-years, Angst and colleagues (2003) demonstrated that individuals who met the hypomania stem criterion (e.g., elevated, expansive, or irritable mood) did not differ from those who reported overactivity only (i.e., a behavioral indicator vs. a mood change indicator), that those who met the duration criterion (i.e., symptoms for 4 days) did not differ from those who did not (i.e., symptoms between 1 and 3 days), and that those who reported consequences from their symptoms did not differ from those who reported no such consequences. These individuals demonstrated no significant differences on important clinical validators, such as positive family history of mania/hypomania or depression, age of onset for symptoms, total number of days spent in hypomania or depression, treatment of depression, suicide attempts, comorbidities, or criminal offenses. These groups did demonstrate important differences from individuals diagnosed with unipolar depression as well as healthy controls. These findings establish that hypomanic symptoms (regardless of mood change, duration or consequences) are important clinical indicators.

Adding to this literature is a recent study that indicated the most common symptoms of hypomania included overactivity (92 %), elevated mood (86 %), and racing thoughts (69 %; Benazzi, 2007). This study further demonstrated that it was not essential to give priority to mood changes (i.e., the stem criterion of elevated, expansive, or irritable mood), but that acceptable sensitivity (90 %) and specificity (84 %) was established with a cut point at five of the nine symptoms (listing elevated and irritable mood with the additional symptoms). In other words, it was possible to establish a hypomanic episode by identifying at least five symptoms in a non-hierarchical manner. While this research assisted the *DSM-5* workgroup in the inclusion of overactivity (or increased energy) to the core symptom, the duration criterion was not altered. However, specific wording has been included in the Other Specified Bipolar and Related Disorder for clinicians to specify subsyndromal states (see "Subtypes" section).

Due to the challenges and the importance associated with the identification of hypomania, researchers stress the importance of clinicians utilizing collateral sources (significant others may be more likely to recognize signs), evaluating family history, looking beyond the presenting problem, and assessing carefully for the important hallmark traits of hypomania, including a decreased need for sleep and lack of daytime fatigue (Doran, 2008; Preston & Johnson, 2008).

Major Depressive Episode

DSM-5 criteria for a major depressive episode are presented in Table 5.5. The essential feature of an episode of major depression is a period of at least 2-weeks of either depressed mood or marked anhedonia (i.e., diminished interest or ability to gain pleasure from normally pleasurable activities). Descriptions of depression might include feeling "down in the dumps," "feeling nothing," and being "discouraged" or "hopeless." Some degree of loss of pleasure is typically always present. These individuals may present with a flat or blunted affect, that is, they do not show typical emotional expressiveness (e.g., monotone quality of voice, lack of expected range of facial expressions; APA, 2000). The only changes to this episode in *DSM-5* include elimination of the bereavement exclusion criteria. The rationale provided by the Mood Disorders Work Group (2012) discusses research in this area, concluding that well-constructed studies demonstrate no differences between bereavement-related or other stress-related depressions.

In addition to depressed mood or anhedonia, four other symptoms must be present during this time period (for a total of at least five). The symptoms of a major

Table 5.5 *DSM-5* criteria for a major depressive episode

A.	Five (or more) of the following criteria have been present during the same 2-week period and represent a change from previous functioning; at least one of the symptoms is either (1) depressed mood or (2) loss of interest or pleasure. *Note*: Do not include symptoms that are clearly due to a medical condition. 1. Depressed mood most of the day, nearly every day, as indicated by either subjective report (e.g., feels sad or empty) or observation made by others (e.g., appears tearful). *Note*: In children and adolescents, can be irritable mood. 2. Markedly diminished interest or pleasure in all, or almost all, activities most of the day, nearly every day (as indicated by either subjective account or observation). 3. Significant weight loss when not dieting or weight gain (e.g., a change of more than 5 % of body weight in a month), or decrease or increase in appetite nearly every day. *Note*: In children, consider failure to make expected weight gains. 4. Insomnia or hypersomnia nearly every day. 5. Psychomotor agitation or retardation nearly every day (observable by others, not merely subjective feelings of restlessness or being slowed down). 6. Fatigue or loss of energy nearly every day. 7. Feelings of worthlessness or excessive or inappropriate guilt (which may be delusional) nearly every day (not merely self-reproach or guilt about being sick). 8. Diminished ability to think or concentrate, or indecisiveness, nearly every day (either by subjective account or as observed by others). 9. Recurrent thoughts of death (not just fear of dying), recurrent suicidal ideation without a specific plan, or a suicide attempt or a specific plan for committing suicide.
B.	The symptoms cause clinically significant distress or impairment in social, occupational, or other important areas of functioning.
C.	The episode is not attributable to the physiological effects of a substance or another medical condition.
D.	The Major Depressive Episode is not better accounted for by Schizoaffective Disorder and is not superimposed on Schizophrenia, Schizophreniform Disorder, Delusional Disorder, or Psychotic Disorder Not Elsewhere Classified.
Note	Responses to a significant loss (e.g., bereavement, financial rin, losses from a natural disaster, a serious medical illness or disability) may include the feelings of intense sadness, rumination about the loss, insomnia, poor appetite, and weight loss noted in Criterion A, which may resemble a depressive episode. Although such symptoms may be understandable or considered appropriate to the loss, the presence of a major depressive episode in addition to the normal response to a significant loss should also be carefully considered. This decision inevitably requires the exercise of clinical judgment based on the individual's history and the cultural norms for the expression of distress in the context of loss.

Note. Reprinted with permission PENDING from the Diagnostic and Statistical Manual of Mental Disorders, Fourth Edition, Text Revision (Copyright © 2000), American Psychiatric Association

depressive episode are perhaps more familiar than the symptoms of (hypo)mania, and include disruptions in weight, sleep, activity, energy, and concentration, feelings of guilt or worthlessness, and suicidal thoughts and behaviors. Individuals may report craving certain foods (e.g., carbohydrates), waking in the middle of the night and being unable to fall back asleep, a slowed ability to respond physically, feeling too tired to accomplish even the smallest tasks, having difficulty remembering things, continually thinking about past failings, or thinking that family would be better if he or she was dead. These must be newly experienced symptoms or to have markedly worsened since pre-episode, and must persist for most of the day, nearly

Table 5.6 Differentiating bipolar disorders from unipolar depression

Family history of mania/bipolar diagnoses
Early onset of depression
More episodes (i.e., recurrences, typically 5 or more) of major depression
Atypical triad of depressive symptoms
•   Overeating (weight gain/increased appetite)
•   Oversleeping (hypersomnia)
•   Excessive physical fatigue
Marked irritability within depressive episodes
Evidence of hypomanic symptoms (irrespective of duration), particularly
•   Psychomotor agitation
•   Racing/crowded thoughts
Additional symptoms of atypical depression
•   Leaden paralysis
•   Interpersonal rejection sensitivity
Treatment response (either lack of response or medication-associated manic/hypomanic episodes)

every day for the 2-week period. Significant impairment or distress in an area of functioning must result and the symptoms cannot be the result of a substance or a medical condition and is not better accounted for by Schizoaffective Disorder or superimposed on psychotic disorders (APA, 2013).

In many studies of bipolar disorder, the index, or initial, episode is typically a major depressive episode, which complicates the process of diagnosis and treatment. As indicated in earlier chapters, the switch rate from unipolar to bipolar disorder is high, with many, large, longitudinal studies indicating approximately a 50 % conversion rate (Angst, Sellaro, Stassen, & Gamma, 2005) and evidence of (hypo)mania in a large portion of those with unipolar depressive diagnoses (Angst et al., 2011). While bipolar disorder shares major depressive episode with its unipolar counterpart, there do seem to be some differences (e.g., atypical depressive symptoms) in presentation and history, which are outlined in Table 5.6.

Individuals diagnosed with bipolar disorder tend to spend significantly more time experiencing depressive rather than manic/hypomanic symptoms. In fact, individuals have been estimated to experience depressive symptoms approximately four times more than manic/hypomanic symptoms (Miller et al., 2004), and between 30 and 50 % of the time, individuals with a bipolar diagnosis report experiencing these symptoms of depression (Judd et al., 2003). While subsyndromal states are more frequent, almost 15 % of the time it is estimated that full criteria are met for a major depressive episode (Judd et al., 2003).

Importantly, depressive symptoms have consistently been shown to be the most robust predictors of functional outcomes, and even modest subsyndromal levels of depression are important determinants (Bauer et al., 2001; Goetz, Tohen, Reed, Lorenzo, & Vieta, 2007; Huxley, & Baldessarini, 2007; Judd et al., 2005; Pope, Dudley, & Scott, 2007). Depressive symptoms tend to be positively correlated with psychosocial impairment (i.e., poor overall satisfaction, functioning in work, school, household, recreation or hobbies, and interpersonal relationships). In other words, as depressive symptoms increase, there is an equal increase in psychosocial impairment (Judd et al., 2005; Pope et al., 2007). In comparison to manic symptoms, it has been shown that depressive symptoms are at least as disabling and sometimes significantly more so than manic/hypomanic episodes (Judd et al., 2005). In addition, when depressive symptoms are evident within a manic episode, impairment is significantly greater (Goetz et al., 2007). Finally, individuals who attempt suicide almost always do so during a depressive phase (Angst, Stassen, Clayton, & Angst, 2002; Levine et al., 2001).

Subtypes

Bipolar disorder is categorized into subtypes according to the presentation of episodes. The main difference between the different types is the level of mania/hypomania. There are seven subtypes of bipolar disorder, and within bipolar I and bipolar II there are several designations required to identify the current episode an individual is experiencing and whether any specifiers are indicated. With the exception of changes to the episode criteria, addition of several new diagnoses, and re-designation of the bipolar disorder not otherwise specified (BP-NOS) category, no major changes were made from *DSM-IV-TR* to *DSM-5*.

Bipolar I Disorder

Bipolar I disorder is thought of as the more classic presentation. For an individual to receive this diagnosis, he or she must have experienced at least one manic episode within his or her lifetime. Bipolar I disorder is believed to be the more severe form of the disorder, as evidenced by more hospitalizations, lower Global Assessment of Functioning (GAF) scores, higher rates of psychotic features, more rapid cycling, more mixed presentation, and more deaths due to cerebrovascular problems (Angst et al., 2002; Judd et al., 2003). However, individuals with this diagnosis have been shown to recover to their premorbid level of psychosocial functioning between episodes more so than their counterparts with a bipolar II diagnosis (Judd et al., 2003).

Bipolar II Disorder

Bipolar II disorder is thought of as the more depressive presentation of the disorder. A manic (or mixed episode from research with the *DSM-IV-TR* criteria) cannot have been present in the individual's history to receive this diagnosis. Bipolar II disorder is believed to be more chronic, as individuals with this diagnosis experience significantly more depressive episodes and have more episodes (in general) per year with shorter inter-episode intervals (i.e., less time asymptomatic) than individuals with a bipolar I diagnosis (Judd et al., 2003). In addition, more anxiety disorders, particularly social phobias, have been demonstrated to coexist in individuals with a bipolar II diagnosis (Judd et al., 2003). Angst, Sellaro, et al. (2005) noted that approximately 40 % of individuals with a bipolar II diagnosis converted to a bipolar I diagnosis in the 20 years of their study, with men more likely to switch than women.

Cyclothymic Disorder

Cyclothymia is characterized by chronic fluctuating moods involving periods of hypomania and depression, without meeting full criteria for a (hypo)manic or major depressive episode (or mixed episode with criteria from *DSM-IV-TR*). The symptoms of manic and major depressive episodes are used for this diagnosis. Cyclothymia is considered a less severe presentation, with shorter, less severe periods of symptoms and not occuring with the regularity of bipolar I or II disorders. Additionally, symptoms must have been present for at least 2-years (or 1-year if diagnosing youth; APA, 2013). The symptoms must not be better explained by schizophrenia, schizophreniform disorder, delusional disorder, or psychotic disorder NOS, and cannot be due to the effects of a substance or general medical condition. Significant distress or impairment must result from the symptoms in an area of functioning.

Cyclothymia is thought to be a relatively rare disorder, occurring in approximately less than 1–2 % of individuals (Angst et al., 2003; APA, 2013). It is suggested that it begins early in life and may reflect a predisposition to other mood disorders. In fact, there appears to be a 15–50 % risk that an individual with cyclothymic disorder will subsequently develop a bipolar I or II disorder (APA, 2013). There is much less research on cyclothymia than other bipolar subtypes; however, a recent study has indicated that cyclothymia tends to onset earlier than either bipolar I or II disorder, that individuals with this diagnosis tend to experience depressive symptoms prior to hypomanic symptoms, and that individuals with this disorder are more likely to have family members with mood disorders than are those with ADHD or Disruptive Behavior Disorders (Van Meter, Youngstrom, Youngstrom, Feeny, & Findling, 2011).

Substance/Medication-Induced Bipolar and Related Disorder

It has been proposed that the exclusion criteria in *DSM-IV-TR* (hypo)manic episode of a substance-caused switch to (hypo)mania may provide one reason why a bipolar disorder may be missed. For example, Ghaemi and colleagues (2001) discussed research that demonstrated that a large portion of individuals with a substance-caused (i.e., antidepressant) switch to (hypo)mania progress to spontaneous episodes of (hypo)mania months or years later, indicating that this phenomenon might represent a sign of susceptibility to bipolar disorder and should not be excluded from the diagnosis. In addition to changes in the exclusionary criteria of a (hypo)manic episode in *DSM-5*, is the introduction of a specific subtype related to substance-induced bipolar disorder. This disorder was previously a substance-induced mood disorder. In order to meet criteria for this disorder, a person must meet the criteria for a manic episode and the symptoms must be associated with the advent of a substance.

Bipolar and Related Disorder Due to Another Medical Condition

This diagnosis was altered from a more general mood disorder to the bipolar specific disorder in the new *DSM-5*. As such, the criteria for a manic episode must be met, impairment must be significant, and the onset must be due to the effects of a medical condition.

Other Specified and Unspecified Bipolar and Related Disorder

Previously termed bipolar disorder not otherwise specified (BP-NOS), these subtypes are used when coding a bipolar disorder that does not meet criteria for any of the specific bipolar disorders defined, or when there is inadequate or contradictory information about symptoms (APA, 2013). Due to the heterogeneity inherent in the NOS subtype, generalizations about individuals with this diagnosis were previously difficult to make. *DSM-5* has moved toward more specificity by dividing this category, with several additional subcategories: (a) Subsyndromal Hypomania—Short Duration: characterized by sufficient number and duration of depressive symptoms, and sufficient hypomania symptoms but insufficient duration; (b) Subsyndromal Hypomania—Insufficient Symptoms: characterized by sufficient number and duration of depressive symptoms, and sufficient duration but insufficient number of hypomania symptoms; (c) Other Bipolar CNEC: characterized by atypical presentations of symptoms; and (d) Bipolar CNEC with insufficient information to make a specific diagnosis: reserved for situations when an individual presents with bipolar symptoms but a clinician is unable to gather sufficient information to make a formal diagnosis resulting in or from an uncertainty about primary vs. secondary nature of bipolar disorder, a patient who is unwilling or unable to provide information about symptoms or history, or when a clinician does not have the necessary time or training to make a thorough assessment.

Specifiers

The purpose of the *DSM-IV-TR* course specifiers is to increase diagnostic specificity, create more homogeneous subgroups, assist in treatment selection, and improve prognosis (APA, 2000). The specifiers are divided into three subgroups, specifiers that describe: (a) the clinical status; (b) the features; and (c) the course of current, most recent, or recurrent episodes. Only the specifiers describing the clinical status are coded in the diagnosis.

Specifiers Describing the Clinical Status of the Current (or Most) Recent Mood Episode

If an individual is currently experiencing an episode, the diagnostic code would indicate a severity specifier; if not currently experiencing an episode, the diagnostic code specifier would address the status of remission. A hypomanic episode does not require a clinical status specifier. These specifiers are identified in the fifth digit of the code for the disorder.

Severity

The severity specifier is categorized by mild, moderate, and severe. Severity is judged by the intensity of the symptoms, the degree of impairment, and the need for supervision. A mild episode indicates few additional symptoms over the number required for a diagnosis with intensity distressing but manageable and minor impairment in functioning. A moderate episode is characterized by number and intensity of symptoms, and functional impairment greater than mild but less than severe. Severe episodes require substantially more symptoms than needed for the diagnosis, seriously distressing and unmanageable intensity of the symptoms, and markedly impaired functioning.

Remission

Full remission requires at least two-months without evidence of significant symptoms. Partial remission is coded if symptoms are still present without meeting criteria or if less than two-months of remission is documented.

Specifiers Describing Features of the Current Episode (or Most Recent Episode if Currently in Partial or Full Remission)

These specifiers describe the symptoms or course features of the current or most recent episode. They include with: (a) anxious distress (b) mixed features, (c) melancholic, or (d) atypical features, (e) psychotic features, (f) catatonic, or (g) peripartum onset.

With Anxious Distress

Anxious distress is new to *DSM-5* and is coded if at least two symptoms (i.e., feeling keyed up or tense, feeling unusually restless, difficulty concentrating due to worry, fear something awful will happen, feeling out of control; APA, 2013) present during the majority of days within a (hypo)manic or major depressive episode. Anxious distress is fairly common in both bipolar and unipolar depression, and has been associated with deleterious clinical course, including increased suicide risk, longer duration of illness, and greater treatment nonresponse (APA, 2013).

Table 5.7 Additional symptoms required for coding of atypical depression

Significant weight gain or increase in appetite

Hypersomnia

Leaden paralysis (i.e., heavy, leaden feelings in arms or legs)

Long-standing pattern of interpersonal rejection sensitivity (not limited to episodes of mood
  disturbance) that results in significant social or occupational impairment

Note. Adapted from the Diagnostic and Statistical Manual of Mental Disorders, Fourth Edition, Text Revision (APA, 2000)

With Mixed Features

Previously an episode in *DSM-IV-TR*, mixed features is now a specifier, which is coded along with either a (hypo)manic or major depressive episode. In that way, full criteria must be met for any of the episodes along with three symptoms of the other episode present during the majority of days (e.g., manic with mixed features would require full criteria met for a manic episode with three symptoms of a major depressive episode present). Importantly, this change allows for clinicians to note mixed features of a major depressive episode in a diagnosis of Major Depressive Disorder. This is important, as this is considered to be a significant risk factor for the switch to bipolar disorder (APA, 2013).

With Melancholic Features

This specifier is only indicated if a major depressive episode is the current (or most recent) episode. It is characterized by a loss of pleasure or interest in all (or almost all) activities, or a lack of reactivity to usually pleasurable stimuli (e.g., not becoming happy as the result of good news). The loss of pleasure is described as a "near-complete absence" not merely a "diminution" (APA, 2013, p. 151). In addition to these stem criteria, three of the following additional symptoms must be present: (a) distinct quality of depressed mood, (b) feeling worse in the morning, (c) wakening earlier than typical (at least two hours before the usual time), (d) marked psychomotor agitation or retardation, (e) significant anorexia or weight loss, or (f) feelings of excessive guilt.

With Atypical Features

This specifier only applies if the current (or most recent) episode is major depression. Current *DSM-5* criteria require mood reactivity (i.e., mood brightening in response to an actual or potentially positive event) as a stem criterion, with at least two of the following additional features as listed in Table 5.7. The symptoms must be present for a 2-week period and criteria cannot be met for melancholic or catatonic features during the same episode (APA, 2013).

There is special interest in this specifier in regards to bipolar disorder. In a study of almost 600 individuals drawn from a larger, population-based sample, and followed for over 20-years, atypical depression was found to be significantly more common in females and associated with an early-onset of the disorder, bipolar diagnoses (specifically bipolar II disorder), and a family history of mania (Angst et al., 2006). This study demonstrated that mood reactivity was a non-specific symptom of depression and supported a non-hierarchically defined syndrome (i.e., requiring a number of symptoms with mood reactivity as one symptom, not a stem criterion).

This study further demonstrated that an atypical triad (i.e., overeating, oversleeping, and excessive physical fatigue) was the most useful combination of symptoms for differentiating bipolar from unipolar depression; in fact, the combination of two of these three symptoms is almost three times more likely to appear in a bipolar than a unipolar depression (Angst et al., 2006). Although more individuals with bipolar disorder (40%) exhibited this type of depression, individuals with unipolar depression (28%) also displayed this atypical triad. In general, the group of individuals demonstrating this combination of overeating, oversleeping, and excessive fatigue was significantly more likely to have experienced more severe depression (both in terms of number of symptoms and length of time spent experiencing symptoms), more cognitive impairment (i.e., reduced memory, concentration, and decision-making), higher rates of treatment and work impairment, and more comorbidities (particularly with social phobia, binge eating, and migraine headaches). Individuals with a bipolar II diagnosis who presented with this atypical triad demonstrated the highest rates of treatment, hospitalizations, and suicide attempts, with the longest duration of illness (Angst et al., 2006).

With Psychotic Features

Psychotic features in bipolar disorder are typically mood-congruent (i.e., consistent with the nature of the episode). When these features are mood-incongruent (i.e., the content has no relation to the nature of the episode) it may predict a poorer prognosis. In addition, psychotic features tend to ebb and flow with the episodes (e.g., as an individual moves from an active manic episode to euthymia, or recovery, the psychotic features tend to disappear), which helps to differentiate bipolar disorder from schizophrenia, where the psychotic features tend to remain stable throughout the course of the disorder (Pavuluri, Herbener et al., 2004).

With Catatonic Features

This specifier refers to a major depressive, manic, or mixed episode. Catatonia is characterized by marked psychomotor disturbance through motoric immobility (e.g., waxy flexibility), excessive motor activity (i.e., purposeless movement without being the result of external stimuli), extreme negativism (e.g., motiveless resistance), mutism, peculiar movements (e.g., posturing), echolalia (i.e., senseless repetition of word or phrase just heard) or echopraxia (i.e., repetitive imitation of movements of another person). Two of these features must be present to indicate catatonic features. This phenomenon is fairly rare, with estimates up to 35% of inpatients; however, it is believed that the majority of those cases occur in conjunction with a mood disorder diagnosis (APA, 2013).

With Peripartum Onset

This specifier can be applied to either current or most recent major depressive or (hypo)manic episode if the onset is within four-weeks after childbirth. Previously called "postpartum onset", this was changed as a majority of these episodes begin prior to delivery (APA, 2013). This type of onset of symptoms is particularly worrisome when psychotic features are present (especially when these include delusional thoughts about the infant). Psychotic features are believed to be more common in mothers giving birth to their first child, and the risk for this type of onset is increased if there is a prior history of postpartum onset (particularly if psychotic features were evident), presence of a mood diagnosis (particularly bipolar I disorder), or family history of bipolar disorder (APA, 2013).

Specifiers Describing Course of Recurrent Episodes

These specifiers describe an individual's course of the disorder and include with seasonal pattern or with rapid cycling. It is believed that an individual's course will remain fairly consistent (e.g., if a seasonal component was present in the past, it is likely there will continue to be a seasonal pattern to the course).

Seasonal Pattern

This specifier applies to the onset and offset of the symptoms of a major depressive episode. It is relevant if there is a regular temporal relationship between onset and remittance of depressive symptoms and particular times of the year. The typical pattern involves onset of symptoms in the fall or winter with remittance in the spring. Depressive episodes that occur in a seasonal pattern are often characterized by lack of energy, hypersomnia, overeating, weight gain, and carbohydrate craving. The *DSM-IV-TR* indicates that younger individuals, females, and those living in higher latitudes demonstrate more seasonal patterns. While this specifier is currently only applicable to a major depressive episode, it is indicated that manic or hypomanic episodes may also be linked to a particular season (APA, 2000). In addition, a recent, large, survey study indicated that sleep problems in individuals with an early-onset might be intensified at particular times of the year (e.g., after daylight savings time ends; Lofthouse et al., 2007).

Rapid Cycling

Rapid cycling refers to the number of mood episodes within the last 12-months. According to the *DSM-5*, rapid cycling applies if an individual experiences four or more episodes within the past year (APA, 2013). The episodes must meet episode criteria in both number of symptoms and duration. There was confusion related to this phenomenon, as the terms "cycling" and "episode" had been used somewhat interchangeably with the *DSM-IV-TR* criteria (particularly with a mixed episode), and as the term "rapid cycling" has been used in different studies to describe different amounts of time, (e.g., from four episodes per year to more than 365 changes per year). Researchers have attempted to clarify this by defining cycling more specifically. Geller, Tillman, and Bolhofner (2007) suggested that the term cycling should only be used to describe daily phenomena (i.e., pronounced shifts in mood and energy from one extreme to the other); therefore, ultra-rapid cycling would refer to mood switches every few days during an episode and ultradian cycling would refer to mood changes multiple times daily during an episode. Therefore, Geller and colleagues recommend that the term "rapid cycling" (in the *DSM-IV-TR* sense) should be replaced with "multiple episodes per year" to avoid confusion and to allow comparisons of early-onset individuals, who tend to exhibit multiple mood switches per day.

In general, longitudinal research demonstrates that rapid cycling carries with it a significantly poorer prognosis and greater impairment (e.g., Goetz et al., 2007). Coryell and colleagues (2003) followed almost 350 individuals with a bipolar diagnosis for almost 15-years. Within this sample approximately 25% displayed a rapid cycling course and over 50% of those individuals had no periods of remission (i.e., two months symptom-free) within a one-year period. This group was more likely to be female and to have an early-onset of the disorder (i.e., prior to 17-years-old). These individuals were shown to experience significantly more depressive symptoms, and were three times more likely to attempt suicide, significantly more likely to make an attempt with high intent for death, to make an attempt of high lethality (i.e., requiring medical care), and to have multiple attempts.

A second, one-year longitudinal study (*n* = 539) also indicated that individuals with a rapid cycling course were more likely to be female and to have an early age of onset (Kupka et al., 2005). In addition, these individuals demonstrated a longer time from onset of symptoms to first medication treatment. Rapid cycling was associated with a prior history of dysphoric mania/hypomania, treatment with antidepressants, substance-induced episodes, anxiety disorder, drug abuse or dependence, childhood physical or sexual abuse, and a parental history of substance abuse and mood disorder. Individuals with rapid cycling were seven times more likely to experience (hypo) manic episodes and twice as likely to experience depressive episodes as individuals without rapid cycling; however, almost 40% of the time was spent experiencing a depressive mood state. Interestingly, the duration of a major depressive episode was not related to the number of previous episodes, but the duration of a manic/hypomanic episode was (individuals with rapid cycling spent 27% of the time manic/hypomanic vs. 8% of the time for non-rapid cyclers) and the duration increased progressively as a function of the episode frequency, lending credence to the kindling theory.

Presentation in Children and Adolescents

The diagnosis of early-onset bipolar disorder has been a controversial topic in practice, research, and public arenas. The number of publications regarding this topic has increased exponentially over the last decade, with discrepancies evident in findings making generalizations difficult. However, many of these discrepancies have been evaluated in terms of research methodology and it now appears that much more consensus has arisen to describe this diagnosis.

Most Common Symptoms of Mania

Mania has, by far, been the most controversial aspect of the diagnosis in early-onset of the disorder. It has been demonstrated that youth experience many problematic symptoms. One study of 130 youth (3-years to 17-years) found that over 95 % of these children exhibited *at least* five of the eight symptoms of mania (Staton et al., 2008). Kowatch and colleagues (2005) determined that the most prominent symptom reported in the literature reviewed for their meta-analysis was increased energy. However, most of the symptoms were reported by over 70 % of cases, indicating that the majority of individuals experienced a multitude of symptoms. Table 5.8 displays the symptoms, weighted rates, and confidence intervals reported in this meta-analysis. Again, it is important to note the confidence interval, as in some cases (e.g., poor judgment) it is rather large.

It has been argued that mania can be validly recognized in children as young as 3-years-old (Luby & Belden, 2006). Faedda, Baldessarini, Glovinsky, and Austin (2004) reported that symptomatic onset occurred before age 3-years in 74 % of the children included in their study. Danielyan, Pathak, Kowatch, Arszman, and Johns (2007) indicated an average age of onset of bipolar disorder as 5-years of age. The

Table 5.8 Most common early-onset bipolar disorder symptoms

Symptom	Weighted rate % (95 % confidence interval)
Increased energy	89 (76–96)
Distractibility	84 (71–92)
Pressured speech	82 (69–90)
Irritability	81 (55–94)
Grandiosity	78 (67–85)
Racing thoughts	74 (51–88)
Decreased need for sleep	72 (53–86)
Euphoria/elation	70 (45–87)
Poor judgment	69 (38–89)
Flight of ideas	56 (46–66)
Hypersexuality	38 (31–45)

Note. Adapted from Kowatch et al. (2005)

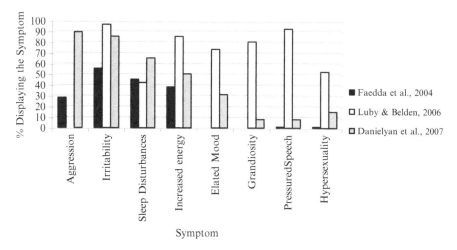

Fig. 5.1 Most common presenting symptoms in three large studies of young children

most common presenting or initial symptoms from these studies are presented in Fig. 5.1. Some differences arise due to methodological issues (e.g., operational definitions of elated mood, instruments used to assess symptoms). However, early-onset bipolar mania appears to be characterized by a predominantly irritable mood with a multitude of additional symptoms (including elation). It will be interesting to see what happens with the introduction of the DMDD diagnosis, which is characterized by irritable mood.

It is important to note that in addition to decreases in sleep—a current symptom for diagnosis—sleep disturbances are commonly reported to accompany the disorder. Chapter 3 provided a discussion related to this topic. As these challenges with sleep are commonly associated with impairment a more thorough assessment—that is, beyond assessing for simple decreases in sleep—is warranted.

Developmental Aspects

Early-onset bipolar disorder tends not to look like its counterpart (i.e., adult- or late-onset), although how much like the classic bipolar disorder an early-onset form is still remains open for debate. Interestingly, retrospective studies with adults typically indicate that symptom onset was younger than 19-years-old for approximately 60 % of adults (Hauser et al., 2007). Therefore, logical questions follow regarding the developmental progression of the disorder, i.e., whether early-onset bipolar disorders evolve into the more classic presentation as a function of age. Longitudinal research is just now emerging to help address these questions. However, there are some limitations with the current status of this research (e.g., small sample sizes, lack of consensus on terms such as rapid cycling, short or inconsistent follow-up periods), and it may still be some time before conclusions can be definitively drawn.

Early vs. Late Onset

When comparing cross-sectional studies of early- with late-onset (i.e., onset after 18-years-old) samples there are some important differences. In general, an early-onset tends not to look like the more classic version of the disorder and is associated with a more chronic, severe, and complicated course (Carter, Mundo, Parikh, & Kennedy, 2003). In particular, individuals with an early-onset have demonstrated more than a twofold increase in the risk of developing rapid cycling, and were significantly more likely to report suicidal ideation, to experience mixed episodes, to demonstrate comorbid Axis I diagnoses, and to abuse substances (Birmaher et al., 2006; Carter et al., 2003; Geller et al., 2002). These individuals are significantly less likely to recover from an episode; demonstrate less mood reactivity (i.e., being unable to console when angry or depressed), and significantly more likely to experience irritability (vs.elation) as a predominant mood; to be highly sensitive to rejection; to evidence fewer, but longer episodes; to exhibit treatment resistance to medications; to experience more symptoms in between episodes; and to relapse after a shorter period of time, than their late-onset counterparts (Birmaher et al., 2006; Chang, Steiner, & Ketter, 2000; Geller et al., 2002).

There is debate regarding the course of early-onset bipolar disorder. Some researchers argue that chronic mood dysregulation with a gradual onset of symptoms and underlying irritability for months or even years, is evidence of an early-onset of the disorder, while others argue that this diagnosis should not be conferred without a more episodic presentation (e.g., clear fluctuations in mood and energy with a distinct onset). Youngstrom, Birmaher and colleagues (2008) suggest that mood disturbance may fall along a continuum of episodicity, with the bipolar I (i.e., the more "classic" version of longer and more discrete episodes) on one extreme, moving into briefer and more frequent mood episodes describing the rapid cycling type, and finally on the other extreme, chronic mood dysregulation (labeled borderline personality in adults). Alternatively, it may be that there are two distinct types of bipolar disorder, with associated patterns and outcomes (e.g., episodic version that is more responsive to lithium; Youngstrom, Birmaher, et al., 2008). It is likely this debate will continue for some time and it will be important for consumers to be cognizant of the diagnostic criteria (e.g., the clinical phenotypes discussed in Chapter 1) utilized in the research. Again, it will be interesting to see how the DMDD diagnosis influences this conversation.

Prepubertal- vs. Adolescent-Onset

The few studies specifically addressing these two groups provide evidence of differences in symptoms and outcomes as a result of whether symptom onset occurs before or after puberty (i.e., 12-years-old), although authors contend that similarities outweigh differences between these groups. In general, an earlier onset of the disorder is associated with worse outcomes (Birmaher et al., 2006). It appears that an adolescent-onset of the disorder is more like the adult-onset (or classic) form of the disorder and to report "depressed mood" with a "suddenness" of symptom onset

(Jerrell & Shugart, 2004; Masi, Perugi, Millepiedi, et al., 2006). Adolescents are more likely to meet strict *DSM* criteria (e.g., the "narrow" phenotype), while the "broad" phenotype (i.e., nonepisodic symptoms of severe irritability and hyper-arousal without the hallmark symptoms of elated mood or grandiosity; Leibenluft, Charney, Towbin, Bhangoo, & Pine, 2003) is more typical of the prepubertal- or childhood-onset bipolar disorder (Masi, Perugi, Millepiedi, et al., 2006). Individuals with a prepubertal-onset are significantly more likely to be male, to exhibit a chronic course (little recovery from episodes), to have high comorbidity with ADHD and ODD/CD, to be prescribed a stimulant medication, to report feelings of detachment from others, and to demonstrate hypervigilance, than their adolescent-onset counterparts (Jerrell & Shugart, 2004; Masi, Perugi, Millepiedi, et al., 2006).

Evidence-Based Practice: The Gold Standard of Diagnosis

Obviously, as research continues to proliferate in this area and knowledge increases, best practices will incorporate that new information into the assessment of bipolar disorder. In a thorough review of the current literature, Youngstrom, Findling, Youngstrom, and Calabrese (2005) presented 12 recommendations for an evidence-based assessment approach of early-onset bipolar disorder (Table 5.9). They stress that diagnosis is a complicated process, with three of the most vital pieces of information being base rates (or the probability of a disorder occurring in a particular setting), family history, and screening information. Utilizing these three elements in the diagnostic process greatly increases the likelihood of an accurate diagnosis and the reader is referred to this article for a more in-depth discussion. Other researchers recommend that, in addition to assessing those individuals presenting with possible symptoms of mania, an assessment of bipolar disorder should be considered for individuals referred for depressive symptoms (including a diagnosis of unipolar depression), anxiety, and suicidal ideation, or following criminal offenses (Culver, Arnow, & Ketter, 2007), and the Food and Drug Administration (FDA, 2007a) has suggested routine screening for bipolar disorder in individuals for whom antide-pressant medications are being considered.

In addition to the screening measures recommended in Chapter 4, there are several structured and semi-structured interview tools utilized in the diagnosis of mental health disorders in youth. Renou, Hergueta, Flament, Mouren-Simeoni, and Lecrubier (2004) conducted a review of tools available for use with children and adolescents, and determined that the *Schedule for Affective Disorders and Schizophrenia for School-Age Children—Present and Lifetime Version* (K-SADS-PL; Kaufman et al., 1997) provided the best test-retest reliability for affective disorders. However, the authors noted substantial limitations for all of the tools, including the length of time required to administer (i.e., most of the tools took over 4-hours and multiple sittings to administer), the amount of clinician/researcher training required, and the complicated nature of the systems (not only during initial phases of assessment, but also in the need to continually check for the presence of each diagnostic criterion throughout treatment).

Table 5.9 Twelve recommendations for an evidence-based approach to the assessment of early-onset bipolar disorder

1.	*Be open to the possibility of a bipolar diagnosis in children and youth.*
2.	*Establish a reasonable base rate estimate for the context in which the child is seen.* A base rate is the probability or likelihood of seeing a particular disorder in a particular setting; a 5 % base rate is a good place to start for school professionals.
3.	*Gather a detailed family history.* Again, presence of bipolar disorder in relatives increases the likelihood of bipolar disorder. A diagnosis in a first-degree relative confers the most risk (odds ratios—OR of 5), while second degree relatives confer approximately half that risk (OR of 2.5). Ask about mental health treatment history (without relying on respondents to have received a diagnosis).
4.	*Use screening instruments.* Chapter 4 described several excellent screening instruments. These screeners can actually offer more important information than family history. Low scores on screeners can reduce the OR by a factor of 10, while high scores on parent screeners can increase the OR by a factor of 8.
5.	*Use an actuarial approach to estimating risk of bipolar disorder.* This is a complicated process combining OR of base rates, family history, and screening test scores.
6.	*Involve collateral informants.*
7.	*Be alert for spontaneous changes in mood compared to baseline functioning.* This is especially important if a child or youth meet criteria for another disorder, and clinicians are encouraged to gather detailed information regarding the longitudinal course of past functioning and mood states.
8.	*If concerned about the possibility of bipolar disorder, gather information about "handle" symptoms of bipolar disorder.* The "handle" symptoms include elevated mood, grandiosity, pressured speech, racing thoughts, and hypersexuality. It is recommended that clinicians are familiar with differential diagnoses associated with these symptoms.
9.	*Extend the "window" of assessment.* It is recommended that assessment not only be retrospective but an ongoing process during treatment.
10.	*Assess key constructs during treatment.* Once a diagnosis is made, it is important to continue to assess the symptoms of the disorder through screeners and clinician-rated instruments.
11.	*Be a critical consumer of the literature.*
12.	*Continue personal education on the topic of early-onset bipolar disorder.*

Note. Adapted from Youngstrom, Findling, et al. (2005)

Interestingly, one study utilizing the *K-SADS-PL* found that the psychiatrist's time was reduced by half when a trained diagnostic interviewer initially assessed the child prior to the psychiatrist appointment (Hughes et al., 2005). Particularly in relation to bipolar disorder, researchers at Washington University in St. Louis have adapted the *K-SADS-PL* mania and rapid cycling sections demonstrating excellent inter-rater reliability, high 6-month stability for mania diagnosis, and validity for parent and teacher reports (Geller et al., 2001). Unfortunately, this tool is currently only utilized in research settings.

Finally, several mnemonics have been offered to assist in the diagnosis of bipolar disorder. The first is used to remember the constellation of possible symptoms or mania (Table 5.10) and the second to remember the constellation of possible symptoms of depression (Table 5.11).

Table 5.10 Mnemonic to remember the symptoms of mania

D	Distractibility
I	Insomnia (or indiscretion—excessive involvement in pleasurable activities)
G	Grandiosity
F	Flight of ideas/racing thoughts
A	Activity increase
S	Speech (or sleep deficit)
T	Thoughtlessness

Note. Carlat (1998)

Table 5.11 Mnemonic to remember the symptoms of depression

S	Sleep disorder (either increase or decrease)
I	Interest deficit (anhedonia)
G	Guilt (worthlessness, hopelessness, regret)
E	Energy deficit
C	Concentration deficit
A	Appetite disorder (either increase or decrease)
P	Psychomotor retardation or agitation
S	Suicidality

Note. Carlat (1998)

Concluding Comments

Diagnosis of early-onset bipolar disorder is complex. At present, early-onset bipolar disorder is characterized by severe irritability with many additional symptoms of mania, a chronic course, multiple mood switches per day, very high rates of comorbidity (particularly with the disruptive behavior and anxiety disorders), and suicidal thoughts and behaviors. While it is not expected that school professionals will be making this diagnosis, it is essential that they are aware of the symptoms required for episode criteria, are aware of the differences between an early-onset and a late-onset of the disorder, and recognize the best practices for diagnosis.

Chapter 6
Psycho-educational Assessment

While diagnosis of bipolar disorder is not expected to fall within the duties of school professionals, psycho-educational assessment may be required for a child or adolescent with this diagnosis (or suspected of having this disorder) the opportunity for successful participation in his/her educational experiences. School personnel must be capable of and prepared to engage in those activities. While a level of expertise is expected for psychologists in general assessment practices, specific knowledge is needed to engage in the psycho-educational assessment of students with a bipolar disorder.

In complete contrast to research regarding diagnosis, very little has focused to date on the arena of education. However, several studies have demonstrated the potential impact of this disorder on the educational experience. For example, despite comparable college entrance levels and intelligence, adults with bipolar disorder complete fewer years of education (i.e., 16 % earned a degree compared to 47 % of controls; Glahn, Bearden, Bowden, & Soares, 2006). Specifically in relation to children and youth, again despite an average level of intelligence, approximately 58 % with an early-onset of the disorder received tutoring, 41 % were educated in a special class, and 22 % repeated a grade (Biederman et al., 2005). Unfortunately, at a 4-year follow-up, these numbers were not much improved (Wozniak et al., 2011). One study reported that the most pronounced difficulties were in relation to math and that only 58 % of individuals with an early-onset of the disorder graduated high school on schedule (in comparison to 85 % with a unipolar depression diagnosis and 92 % of healthy controls; Lagace & Kutcher, 2005). In addition, many of the deficit areas noted in this heterogeneous population (e.g., executive functions) will likely compromise the student's ability to successfully participate in the classroom.

That being said, a diagnosis of bipolar disorder does not automatically translate into qualification for special education, nor does it unequivocally mean that an assessment is warranted. This chapter focuses on the issues regarding psycho-educational assessment of a child or adolescent diagnosed with, or suspected of having, bipolar disorder.

S.R. Hart et al., *Identifying, Assessing, and Treating Bipolar Disorder at School*,
Developmental Psychopathology at School, DOI 10.1007/978-1-4614-7585-9_6,
© Springer Science+Business Media New York 2014

Why, When, and How to Assess

To "…ensure that all children with disabilities have available to them a free appropriate public education … designed to meet their unique needs and prepare them for further education, employment and independent living… and to ensure that the rights of children with disabilities and parents of such children are protected" [20 U. S. C. § 1400 (d)(1)], a full and individual initial evaluation (i.e., a psycho-educational evaluation) shall be conducted in accordance with Sections 1414 (a) and (b) of the Individuals with Disabilities Education Improvement Act (IDEA) of 2004 (Pub. L. 108–446) to establish eligibility for special education. There are two requirements for eligibility, (a) a disability according to education code, and (b) the need for special education as a result of that disability [20 U. S. C. § 1401 (3)(A)]. Therefore, suspicion of an *educational* disability that is *adversely affecting* the child's education is reason for assessment. However, while it cannot delay provision of appropriate services to a child, general education interventions must have been considered, and where appropriate, utilized [20 U. S. C. § 1412 (a)(5)].

Best practices in the assessment of emotional and behavioral disorders calls for school teams to be guided by a three-tiered service delivery model (McConaughy & Ritter, 2008). Tier 1 includes interventions that are provided to the entire population (e.g., universal prevention programs, school-wide rules and expectations for behavior). If conditions were appropriate and the student was still struggling, then more specific data should be acquired and the team should work together to develop appropriate Tier 2 interventions. These interventions are more targeted and individualized while still implemented within the general educational setting (e.g., preferential seating, positive behavioral support system). If Tier 1 and 2 interventions are determined to have been effectively developed, delivered, and monitored, yet the child is still struggling significantly, it is suggested that the team move to Tier 3. It is at this point that assessment of the child, the context, and the potential reasons for the lack of success with prior interventions, would be considered. Tier 3 would also include more intensive interventions, more frequent outcome progress monitoring, and potentially special education services.

Assessment is an investigation, with the assessor accumulating evidence to either support or refute qualification and to describe the child's educational needs (regardless of qualification issues). This, and similar, approaches offers the opportunity to accumulate evidence to assist in the determination of eligibility and the description of the child's educational needs, while providing the student support and interventions of increasing intensity as warranted, prior to the initiation of an official assessment. The child is not left to fail until *enough* failure in the general education environment warrants an assessment for special education, but provided with ever-increasingly intense interventions as a means of determining the least restrictive environment for the child's education.

Section 504 of the Rehabilitation Act of 1973 (29 U. S. C. § 701 *et seq.*) was enacted to prevent discrimination against individuals of all ages with disabilities and along with IDEA (2004) dictates the educational rights of children or youth with disabilities. To qualify for the accommodations, modifications, and rights available under Section 504, an individual must demonstrate a "physical or mental impairment" that "substantially limits one or more … major life activities" [29 U. S. C. § 705 (20)(B)(i)]. Section 504 is a function of general education and is not considered special education. With a diagnosis of bipolar disorder, it is probable that Section 504 will provide protection for the student and the authors strongly recommended that a 504 Accommodation and Modification Plan (heretofore referred to as a 504 Plan) be created and implemented based on the student's needs.

As emphasized throughout this book, students with an early-onset of bipolar disorder are a heterogeneous group, with differing levels of impairment in many different arenas. Depending on the youth, it may be that special education is not currently required, but that a 504 Plan with appropriate accommodations and modifications along with Tier 1 and 2 interventions will allow the student to benefit from his/her education. The IDEA (2004) mandate of least restrictive environment is essential when determining the need for assessment and services [20 U. S. C. § 1412 (a)(5)]. Again, if the student's educational needs can be met in the general education environment with the supports available in that setting, this is preferable to the more restrictive special education. By definition, bipolar is an episodic disorder, with frequent mood changes and energy levels waxing and waning throughout the individual's life. It is quite likely that the youth's needs will change substantially over the course and changing demands of his or her education, attempts to establish and maintain a stable medication regimen, and the natural course or progression of the disorder. It is therefore important for the youth's program to remain flexible and to monitor the student to evaluate if the needs have changed and an assessment is subsequently warranted. In other words, regardless of special education status, this student should be on the radar of school professionals (especially school mental health professionals).

Once the decision is made to move forward and permission is obtained from the individual holding educational rights for the child, it is proposed that the assessment will proceed in the following five steps: (a) clarification of specific referral questions(s), (b) development of an assessment strategy, (c) data collection, (d) data analysis and triangulation, and (e) development of conclusions and an intervention plan. The remainder of this chapter will focus on these steps in regard to a student diagnosed with (or suspected of having) bipolar disorder.

Step 1: Clarification of Specific Referral Question(s)

The first step in the assessment process is to become clear on the reason(s) for referral, i.e., the referral question(s). It is likely that throughout the activities associated with the general education interventions, concerns have been continually refined, with data supporting a deeper understanding of the child's needs. With that in mind, IDEA (2004) requires that the child be assessed in all areas of suspected disability [20 U. S. C. § 1414 (b)]; therefore, it is important to have a *comprehensive* understanding of what the concerns are. In general, areas to consider might include behavioral, emotional, social, cognitive, academic, motor/physical, or speech and language. One important element necessary to clarify the referral question(s) and determine the course of the assessment is determining the suspected educational disability or eligibility category. While behavioral concerns may be at the forefront for referring parties, it is important for assessors to remember there are many aspects to a thorough psycho-educational assessment.

Eligibility Category

Individuals with an early-onset of bipolar disorder may present with a multitude of challenges. As bipolar is viewed primarily as a disorder of mood, the default assumption may be an assessment to determine eligibility for special education as a student with an Emotional Disturbance (ED). However, as indicated in the earlier chapters of this book, bipolar is a neurological disorder that results in fluctuations (sometimes hourly and at times drastic) causing deficits in energy and alertness, impairment in executive functioning (e.g., attention, memory), and multiple medications (with side effects potentially resulting in drowsiness and cognitive "dulling"). In addition, the disturbances in sleep pervasive *throughout* the disorder (e.g., in phases of recovery as well as active episodes) may result in challenges for the student during the academic demands placed upon him/her in the classroom (e.g., difficulties maintaining alertness during the day). As such, it may be equally appropriate to assess the child or adolescent for eligibility as a student with an Other Health Impairment (OHI). Educational criteria for both ED and OHI are listed in Table 6.1.

In the "Analysis of Comments and Changes" section published in the Code of Federal Regulations (34 C. F. R. § 300, pp. 46547–46743; US Department of Education, 2006), a discussion occurred regarding adding bipolar disorder (among others) to the list of examples provided (e.g., asthma, ADHD, diabetes). Changes were not made to the definition, however, the reason for this was that the list had not been intended to be exhaustive and the disorders requested to have added were "… commonly understood to be health impairments" and as such, unnecessary to include (US Department of Education, 2006, p. 46550). This further supports that, as recognized by federal entities, bipolar disorder is equally appropriate to evaluate as an OHI designation.

While a student with a bipolar diagnosis may qualify in either category, many parent groups are advocating for an OHI versus an ED categorization. There are potential benefits and costs associated with each category (see Table 6.2). While it is clear from IDEA (2004) that a *child's unique needs* drive services (and not eligibility classification; 20 U. S. C. § 1401 [29]), the unfortunate reality in some districts is that it might be challenging for a student classified as OHI to access

Table 6.1 ED [300.8(c)(4)] and OHI [300.8(c)(9)] Eligibility Criteria

(i) *Emotional disturbance* means a condition exhibiting one or more of the following characteristics over a long period of time and to a marked degree that adversely affects a child's
educational performance:

   (A) An inability to learn that cannot be explained by intellectual, sensory, or health factors.

   (B) An inability to build or maintain satisfactory interpersonal relationships with peers and
teachers.

   (C) Inappropriate types of behavior or feelings under normal circumstances.

   (D) A general pervasive mood of unhappiness or depression.

   (E) A tendency to develop physical symptoms or fears associated with personal or school
problems.

(ii) Emotional disturbance includes schizophrenia. The term does not apply to children who are
socially maladjusted, unless it is determined that they have an emotional disturbance under
paragraph (c)(4)(i) of this section.

Other health impairment means having limited strength, vitality, or alertness, including a
heightened alertness to environmental stimuli, that results in limited alertness with respect to
the educational environment, that

(i) Is due to chronic or acute health problems such as asthma, attention deficit disorder or
attention deficit hyperactivity disorder, diabetes, epilepsy, a heart condition, hemophilia, lead
poisoning, leukemia, nephritis, rheumatic fever, sickle cell anemia, and Tourette syndrome.

(ii) Adversely affects a child's educational performance.

Table 6.2 Comparison of special education categories

ED	OHI
Likely easier to access special programs/classes	Label less stigmatizing
Can be an accurate representation (i.e., significant challenges with mood and emotion)	Can be an accurate representation (i.e., a chronic neurobiological disorder that results in significant fluctuations in strength, vitality, and alertness)
Draws attention to mood issues (and might imply the student should be able to control behaviors)	Implies a medical condition that is outside of the student's control (and might encourage more sympathy for the student and the challenges experienced as a result)
Represents the presentation (the symptoms) of the disorder	Represents the origin (the brain) of the disorder

specialized programs and classes. It is then up to school personnel to advocate for
the student's needs and to demonstrate the appropriateness of the OHI category.
As in any assessment, the eligibility category should be decided on by an IEP team
in a case-by-case manner. Recognizing the potentially stigmatizing effect of an ED
label, it is recommended that an assessor thoughtfully reflect on this issue. Readers
interested in a further discussion of this topic are encouraged to access Gilcher,
Field, and Hellander (2004).

Table 6.3 Example of a detailed referral statement for a student with a bipolar disorder

[Student] is an 8-year-old, second grade, Filipino student, referred for a psycho-education
    evaluation by SST due to behavioral and emotional concerns. [Student] is reported to have a
    low frustration tolerance with intense emotional reactions to events, resulting in frequent
    displays of aggressive (e.g., pushing others, threatening classmates with violence, fighting)
    and disruptive (e.g., crying, yelling, leaving class) behaviors. [Student] also demonstrates
    hyperactive behaviors (e.g., interrupts teacher, talks "constantly" to classmates while they
    are trying to work, walks around class during independent work, kicks his chair, "fiddles"
    with things in his desk). This testing is designed to help determine (a) if [Student]
    demonstrates a disability according to state and federal criteria, particularly as a student
    with an Emotional Disturbance, (b) if he needs special education as a result of an identified
    disability, and (c) to document his present levels of functioning and educational needs so as
    to develop an appropriate educational program.

Referral Statement

In general, the referral statement included in a report guides the reader through the
body of the report and summarizes the reasons for the assessment. It should include
pertinent identifying information (e.g., name, age, and grade of the child), the referral source, the specific concerns guiding the assessment, and the proposed outcomes
of the assessment. Table 6.3 provides an example of a detailed referral statement
from the psycho-educational report of a student with a bipolar disorder.

Step 2: Develop Assessment Strategy

The second step in the process is to develop a comprehensive, detailed, and appropriate
assessment plan. Steps 2 and 3 are driven by the question, "What information do I need
and how will I get it?" As such, the assessor needs to gather information related to bipolar disorder as well as general information regarding the student's abilities. From whom
the information will be acquired (e.g., parent, child, teacher, psychiatrist) is important to
factor into the planning phase and if necessary releases of information will need to be
signed prior to data collection. If there are several individuals involved in the assessment
process, coordinating these efforts will be an important activity at this time.

Become Familiar with the Disorder

As with any psycho-educational assessment, the assessor should have knowledge
regarding the individual's suspected disability [20 U. S. C. § 1414 (b)(3)(iv)]. Along
with educational criteria, become familiar with the signs and symptoms of early-
onset bipolar disorder, the red flags that might indicate onset or recurrence, and how
this disorder might impact the student. Learn about the medications currently used

Table 6.4 Questions to ask before conducting the psycho-educational assessment

Is the student currently symptomatic?

How will the student's mood episode and symptoms impact the testing situation or the validity of the results?

What is the length of time the student can be expected to engage in highly demanding cognitive tasks?

Is the student in the process of stabilizing medications, creating variability in levels of mood, energy, and alertness?

What side effects are commonly associated with the current medications?

How will these side effects affect the testing situation and the student's ability to complete the tasks?

Does the student have substantial levels of anxiety that will make coming into a new room with a new person for a new experience incapacitating?

Is the student's sleep/wake cycle such that he/she is very drowsy in the morning and doesn't fully wake until mid-afternoon?

Will suspected deficits in processing areas affect the testing (e.g., if processing speed deficits are evident, choose general cognitive ability tests not heavy on processing speed demands)?

to treat this disorder and the side effects associated with them. In addition, identify resources in the area that may prove helpful for professionals and families (e.g., therapists in the area with experience working with this unique population). In conjunction with this text, the Appendix provides some useful Websites and books to further advance this endeavor.

Testing Considerations

While the diagnostic assessment would find the presentation of bipolar symptoms to be important to the assessment process, the psycho-educational assessment may find such symptoms a challenge to obtaining valid test results. Thus, to collect valid results, it is important to consider certain things prior to direct testing. In addition to the general considerations (e.g., "…is this particular test valid for this particular student at this particular point in time?"), a student with bipolar disorder may present with further issues needing consideration. A list of some of the questions that may need to be asked as a part of such consideration is provided in Table 6.4. Asking questions such as these prior to psycho-educational testing should promote a valid and meaningful assessment in compliance with IDEA [20 U. S. C. § 1414 (b)].

Domains of Assessment

While assessment is a fluid process, with the assessor continually evaluating the information obtained *throughout* the assessment in order to guarantee a comprehensive and thorough evaluation, it is important before beginning to have a general guideline for the domains that will be assessed. Assessment should be guided by "… strategies that provide relevant information that directly assists persons in determining the educational needs of the child" [20 U. S. C. § 1414 (b)(3)(C)]. As such, information should be obtained regarding the student's past and present functioning, including any evidence of the red flags of bipolar disorder discussed in the previous chapters, as well as functioning in general domains and in areas of potential impairment. Due to the high rate of suicidality in this population, the assessor must not shy away from inquiring about these thoughts, feelings, and actions. In addition, the assessor should be cognizant of and incorporate strengths of the student into the assessment plan. Table 6.5 offers some ideas for areas and questions to consider.

Table 6.5 Domains to consider for psycho-educational assessment

General area	Specific area	Questions
Background	Family History	What is the family's mental health history?
		Have any first-degree relatives received a diagnosis of bipolar disorder (or other mood disorder, anxiety disorder, and/or a substance abuse disorder?
		Have any family members been hospitalized due to mental health difficulties?)
		Are any first-degree relatives prescribed medications for mental health reasons? If so, what is their response to these medications?
	Psychosocial Functioning & Health Histories	Any prior diagnoses for the student?
		Any evidence of the red flags of bipolar disorder in history?
		Any prior behavioral/emotional concerns?
		Have there been any hospitalizations?
		Prior medications (and response)?
		Any physical health concerns?
		Were developmental milestones met within age-appropriate timeframes?
	Past Academic Functioning	What are the student's previous levels of academic functioning?
		Any history of academic concerns?
		Any prior evaluations or assessments?
		Any history with special education?
		What are the student's academic strengths?
		What areas does the student enjoy?
		What do teacher comments indicate?
Psychosocial	Interpersonal	How does the student relate and interact with peers and teachers?
		What are family interactions like?
		What level of stressors does the student have in his or her life?
		How does the student cope with conflict?
		Is the student active in any activities in the community that require interactions with others (e.g., sports teams)?
		Who does the student enjoy spending time with?
		What interpersonal strengths does the student have (e.g., class comedian)?

(continued)

Table 6.5 (continued)

General area	Specific area	Questions
	Intrapersonal	Is the student currently symptomatic (is there evidence of mania or depression)?
		What is the student's dominant mood?
		What is the *quality* of the mood state (e.g., intensity and severity)?
		What is the *quantity* of mood states (e.g., how often is the student's mood cycling)?
		How does the student feel about him or herself?
		What level of insight does the individual have about his or her challenges or symptoms?
		Any evidence of psychotic features?
		Any evidence of suicidality?
Cognitive	General Abilities	What is the student's overall level of cognitive functioning?
		How stable are the student's abilities?
		What are the student's strengths?
		What type of cognitive tasks does the student seem or report to enjoy?
	Executive Functions	Planning, regulation (e.g., inhibition/initiation), attention and memory abilities?
		Does the student struggle with transitions?
		What should be expected from the student according to his or her developmental level (e.g., inconsistencies associated with typically developing adolescent)?
	Processing Abilities	Sensory-motor, processing speed, and visual processing abilities?
		What are the student's processing strengths (e.g., is the student an artist with excellent fine-motor abilities)?
Health	Current health status	Does the student have any current diagnoses?
		Current medications?
		Current health (physical or mental) issues?
		What are the student's sleep patterns?
		How are the student's vision and hearing abilities?
Academic	Current achievement levels	What is the student's current functioning in academic arenas?
		Is the student struggling academically? If so, is the student struggling in general, or more so in particular areas?
		Is it possible there is a Learning Disability?
		What are the student's academic strengths?
		What does the student enjoy about school?
		What are the student's favorite subjects?
Comorbidities	ADHD	Has the student received a diagnosis?
		Are the attention deficits and/or hyperactivity associated with mania?
		Is the student prescribed stimulant medications (without a bipolar diagnosis) and has there been a manic-like reaction to these?
		What interventions have been attempted to work with these issues?

(continued)

Table 6.5 (continued)

General area	Specific area	Questions
	Anxiety	Has the student received a diagnosis?
		Does the student display significant anxiety or phobias?
		Are fears primarily related to harm coming to self or to others?
		Does the student display ritualistic obsessions and compulsions?
		Does the student display perfectionistic tendencies?
		Has the student received counseling related to these challenges?
		Is the student prescribed medications to deal with these symptoms?
	ODD/CD	Has the student received a diagnosis?
		Does oppositional behavior tend to ebb and flow with symptoms of mania?
		Does the student display remorse after problematic behaviors?
		Have medication choices reflected this diagnosis, or are there additional medications prescribed to deal with these symptoms?
	Substance Abuse	Has the student received a diagnosis?
		What substances is the student using?
		How often does the student use these substances?
		What is the context of use (e.g., with friends, by self)?
		Are individuals concerned with student's experimentation and risk-taking behaviors?
		Does the student also display suicidal thoughts and behaviors?
	Others?	Does the student have any further diagnoses?
		How do these diagnoses impact the student's functioning?
		Are there medications associated?
		Is the student receiving counseling or services related to these diagnoses?

Step 3: Data Collection

During this step the assessor should be mindful of the importance of obtaining information from multiple sources (e.g., teacher and parent) through multiple methods (e.g., observations and rating scales; 20 U. S. C. § 1414 [b]). This multidimensional approach allows for the fact that children's behavior often varies in different contexts. Best practices in the assessment of emotional and behavioral difficulties calls for information to be collected from parent reports, teacher reports, and direct assessment of the child (McConaughy & Ritter, 2008).

In relation to bipolar disorder, certain information may be more valuable when collected from certain informants. For example, information about internalizing issues (e.g., depressive symptoms) or sleep difficulties may be best obtained directly from the student, as parents might miss these "secret" symptoms (Lofthouse,

Fristad, Splaingard, & Kelleher, 2007; Merrell, 2008), while rating scales assessing manic symptoms may be more valuable to obtain from parents versus teachers or students, as parent ratings are significantly more accurate than teacher ratings and self-ratings are no better than chance at predicting bipolar disorder (Youngstrom et al., 2004; Youngstrom, Meyers et al., 2005).

During the assessment, information will be obtained through both indirect and direct methods. In addition, a functional behavioral assessment (FBA) may be necessary in order to adequately understand the student and prepare for interventions. The goal of the assessment is not simply to establish eligibility for special education, but more importantly to develop a plan that will support the student's success in the educational setting [20 U. S. C. § 1414 (b)(4)(A)].

Indirect Assessment

Methods of obtaining information that are removed from direct observation of behaviors are designated as indirect (Gresham, 2007). Record review, interviews, questionnaires, and rating scales are all examples of indirect methods used in the assessment of a student with bipolar disorder.

Record Review

Conducting a thorough review of all available records is an important first step in collection of the "… relevant functional, developmental, and academic" data necessary for the assessment [20 U. S. C. § 1414 (b)(2)(A)]. The cumulative folder can provide invaluable data regarding the student's past functioning in the classroom, with peers, and in response to interventions attempted. The cumulative folder will contain accessible sources, such as report cards, teacher comments, disciplinary records, and prior SST meeting notes, among others. Depending on the student, a variety of additional records may be available, such as clinician reports, hospitalization records, and previous psycho-educational evaluations.

Interviews and Questionnaires

It is likely that a substantial amount of information will be obtained through a mixture of interviews and questionnaires with a variety of individuals. Questionnaires have the advantage of inquiring about a wide variety of topics (i.e., they have breadth) and of allowing the informant to complete at their leisure. However, the technique is somewhat limited (e.g., the informant may answer the outlined questions without elaboration, or the questionnaire may not elicit information about additional issues unique to the specific student). Therefore, following up with an interview is likely to improve the quality (i.e., depth) of information obtained. For example, a developmental and health history questionnaire might be sent home eliciting general information regarding milestones and background information, and the assessor may choose to follow up with specific questions related to bipolar disorder and more in depth mental health information in an interview. In addition, it is preferable to follow-up with an interview regarding sensitive information that a respondent may hesitate to put, or elaborate on, in writing (e.g., hospitalizations).

There are several different techniques of interviewing, such as structured (e.g., the *ChIPS*), semi-structured (e.g., the *K-SADS-PL,* both discussed in the previous chapter) and traditional or unstructured. These exist on a continuum allowing increasing flexibility in the interview process (e.g., a traditional interview is much more open-ended and adaptable to the situation and less rigid than a structured interview; Merrell, 2008). Regardless of the technique, the assessor should have a general idea of the information being sought and to be organized and prepared for the interview. In addition, the assessor must keep in mind the informant, careful to establish rapport and cognizant of any issues specific to that interview (e.g., developmental age of the child).

Rating Scales

Rating scales, both broad- and narrow-band, are integral tools in an assessment of a student suspected of, or diagnosed with, bipolar disorder. Broad-band (also referred to as "omnibus") measures assess a wide range of problems, while narrow-band measures focus on a particular challenge, such as anxiety or attention (McConaughy & Ritter, 2008).

One broad-band measure that has received attention regarding early-onset bipolar disorder is the *Child Behavior Checklist* (CBCL; Achenbach, 1991). A relatively homogeneous *CBCL-Dysregulation Profile* (CBCL-DP) has been associated with early-onset bipolar disorder (Holtmann et al., 2007; Mick, Beiderman, Pandina, & Faraone, 2003). This profile included significantly elevated scores (t scores of 70 or higher) on the (a) Anxious/Depressed, (b) Attention Problems, and (c) Aggression subscales. The *CBCL* was also found to demonstrate differences between children diagnosed with ADHD, CD, and bipolar disorder. Children with bipolar disorder were found to score significantly higher than children with ADHD alone on the Aggression and Attention Problems subscale, and significantly higher than children with CD alone on the Aggression subscale, but significantly lower on the Delinquency subscale (Mick et al., 2003).

Unfortunately, in studies conducted after this meta-analysis, a consensus has not been reached as to the utility of this profile. For example, in one study with over 800 children, Faraone, Althoff, Hudziak, Monuteaux, and Biederman (2005) demonstrated that the profile could be used to accurately predict bipolar disorder in children (AUC of .97). However, in another large sample of over 3,000 children from a community mental health clinic, while a similar profile was demonstrated (i.e., elevated Aggression, Attention Problems, Delinquent Behavior, and Social Problems subscales), researchers indicated that using the *CBCL* profile to identify bipolar disorder was challenging, as many of the children seen in the clinic (without a bipolar disorder) had similarly elevated profiles (Youngstrom, Youngstrom, & Starr, 2005). In a recent evaluation of this profile, Althoff, Ayer, Rettew, and Hudziak (2010) recommended that the *CBCL-DP* not be tied to specific diagnoses, but used to identify children with profound problems in emotion regulation, also important for the identification of DMDD (see Chapter 5).

As with any assessment, it is important not to rely on any one measure (e.g., the *CBCL*) to make a determination. If the *CBCL* is administered, the assessor should use the information in conjunction with the additional information obtained during the assessment. As diagnosis is not the primary objective of the psycho-educational assessment, this information should be used to assist the Individualized Education Program (IEP) team determine whether or not the child qualifies for special education and to develop the student's plan (regardless of eligibility) to help him or her succeed in school. It is important to include these scores in a report, in case the student is referred to a clinician this professional may use them to corroborate information collected during that assessment.

Narrow-band measures of particular interest would include those mania-specific screening tools discussed in Chapter 4, as well as those assessing other specific symptoms or issues of concern (e.g., depression, anxiety, ADHD, executive functions). Regarding comorbidity or related symptoms, it may be wise to start with a broad-band measure and then follow-up with a narrow-band measure in elevated areas of concern.

Another scale developed and validated for use specifically in early-onset bipolar disorder, is the *Child Bipolar Questionnaire* (CBQ; Papolos, Hennen, Cockerham, Thode, & Youngstrom, 2006). The *CBQ* is longer than the screeners mentioned in Chapter 4, with 65 items (although authors purport that it requires approximately 10 minutes to complete). The *CBQ* has demonstrated good reliability and validity, with excellent specificity and good sensitivity. It has been translated into Spanish, French, Polish, and Portuguese, was normed on over 5,000 individuals aged 5–17, and is available online through the Juvenile Bipolar Research Foundation Website (see Resources Appendix; Papolos et al., 2006). Unfortunately, while there are scales measuring hypomania in adults, the authors are aware of no scales for use with youth at the time of this printing.

Direct Assessment

Direct methods assess behaviors at the time and place of actual occurrence (Gresham, 2007). Obtaining information through these methods will include observations of the student and testing of the student's abilities. Observations will be the focus of this discussion as testing (e.g., domains, considerations) has been discussed in prior sections.

Observations

Observations of a student's behaviors can take many forms, (e.g., anecdotal, systematic), have the advantage of being able to directly link to interventions, and are an essential element of any behavioral, social, or emotional assessment. Per Merrell (2008), "direct behavioral observation is a procedure in which observers develop operational definitions of the targeted behaviors of interest, observe the subjects, and systematically record their behaviors" (p. 64).

Best practices of emotional and behavioral assessment calls for observations of relatively short duration (e.g., 10–20 minutes) on different days, utilizing one or two randomly selected "control" students, and conducted in such a way that the target student is not aware of the observer or the observer is as unobtrusive in the situation as possible (McConaughy & Ritter, 2008). It is advised that behaviors are observed in relevant settings where problems are occurring as well as situations less problematic to allow for comparison. Observations might take the form of narrative recordings (i.e., the observer writes a description of events occurring within a given timeframe, such as descriptive time sampling, antecedent–behavior–consequence analysis, or daily logs) or systematic methods (i.e., operationally defining behaviors that can be recorded or rated, through continuous recording methods or time sampling; McConaughy & Ritter, 2008).

To make general statements regarding a typically developing student's functioning, multiple observations are required. Due to the variability in mood and behavior inherent in the nature of a bipolar disorder, it will be more challenging to make overall statements and the observation process will require substantially more time. If there is a pattern evident in the student's arousal state (e.g., drowsy in the morning from medications and manic in the afternoon), it is essential the student be observed in those different states. As some parents report that the child is able to "hold it together" during the school day, but "falls apart" at home (Papolos & Papolos, 2006), it may be enlightening to observe the student in the home as well.

In addition to planned, naturalistic observations of the student, the assessor also has the opportunity to observe the student during testing. This situation provides the assessor information on how the student problem-solves, his or her frustration-tolerance, energy level, attentional capacity, and informal interactions with unfamiliar individuals, among others. Braaten (2007) describes the clinical Mental Status Exam (MSE) with children and adolescents. The MSE includes observations regarding areas such as appearance and behavior, alertness/cognition, demeanor/attitude, thought processes, speech, mood, affect, insight/judgment, and ideation (homicidal or suicidal), and can be a helpful guide when evaluating how a student presents during testing. The author cautions that consideration of development is necessary when conducting an MSE with youth.

Functional Behavioral Assessment

An FBA is a set of procedures for gathering information that can be used to inform and maximize the effectiveness and efficiency of interventions. The proposed outcomes of an FBA include (a) providing a clear description of problematic (i.e., target) behaviors; (b) identifying the times, events, and situations that predict when target behaviors will and will not occur; (c) identifying the consequences that are serving to maintain target behaviors (i.e., the function of the behaviors); (d) developing hypotheses; and (e) collecting data to support the hypotheses (O'Neill et al., 1997).

According to O'Neill and colleagues, the goal of an FBA is to "…bring clarity and understanding to otherwise chaotic and confusing situations" (p. 3), with the hope that this understanding will promote effective interventions. The common strategies for collecting information for an FBA incorporate several methods already discussed, including informant methods (e.g., interviews, rating scales) and direct observations. The third strategy is to conduct a functional analysis, which consists of the systematic manipulation of specific variables that are or are not associated with the target behaviors.

Andersen, Kubisak, Field, and Vogelstein (2003) discuss conducting an FBA with a student diagnosed with bipolar disorder. The major challenge with this process is the development of appropriate hypotheses. The foundation of traditional analysis methods is the notion that all behavior is purposeful and that the consequences following a behavior are perceived as desired results. However, in the case of a student with bipolar disorder, the behavior may be the result of symptoms (i.e., either symptoms being displayed or the child attempting to deal with symptoms). In other words, the behavior is driven by the medical condition of the child and does not necessarily have the intent inherent in behaviors demonstrated by more typically developing children. The authors suggested that making matters even more complicated is that behaviors can be a matter of choice (or learning), a result of symptoms, or a combination of both choice and symptoms. As the goal of an FBA is to inform interventions, it is important to keep this in mind. For behaviors that involve choice, reductive and natural consequences may be appropriate, however, if the behaviors are actually a result of symptoms, it is likely that these types of interventions may drastically escalate the behaviors.

Step 4: Analysis and Triangulation

An efficient and effective assessor is engaging in data analysis throughout the assessment. However, once all data is acquired, the next logical step is to sit down and triangulate the information from all sources. The focus at this point in the assessment is to make sense of all the findings in conjunction, i.e., to create a comprehensive picture of this particular student at this particular point in time from all of the information obtained. It is important for the assessor to begin drawing conclusions from the available data while challenging the conclusions with, and remaining open to, alternative possibilities or explanations. Figure 6.1 is a psycho-educational summary worksheet that might be used to assist the evaluator with analyzing and triangulating the substantial amount of information collected throughout the assessment of a youth with bipolar disorder.

PSYCHO-EDUCATIONAL EVALUATION

Bipolar Disorder Summary Sheet

Name of student: _____ Birthdate: _____ Teacher & Grade: _____

Name of informant: _____ Date: _____ Method of collection: _____
Release? Y N ❑
Name of informant: _____ Date: _____ Method of collection: _____
Release? Y N ❑
Name of indormant: _____ Date: _____ Method of collection: _____
Release? Y N ❑
Name of informant: _____ Date: _____ Method of collection: _____
Release? Y N ❑

BACKGROUND INFORMATION

1. Family History:
    a. Any history of mood disorders in the student's immediate or extended family? If so, what is relation to the student? At what age was this diagnosed?

    b. Any other psychopathology in the student's family? If so, describe and specify relation.

    c. Any reports of other "odd" or "red flag" behaviors in family members (e.g., explosive behaviors, excessive spending)? If so, describe and specify relation.

    d. Are any relatives prescribed any medications for mental health reasons? If so, describe and specify relation.

    e. Any cultural or environmental issues to consider?

    f. Any history of substance abuse in the student's family? Relation? Substance? Frequency of use? Is the family member currently using?

2. Developmental History:
    a. Any "red flags" in student's developmental history?
        ❑ Significantly more periods of colic as an infant?
        ❑ Intense & prolonged temper tantrums
        ❑ Decreased need for sleep & lack of daytime fatigue
        ❑ Extreme irritability
        ❑ Periods of giddiness/extreme silliness
        ❑ Increased need for sleep & difficulty getting going in the morning
        ❑ Increased mood reactivity (responds intensely)
        ❑ Mood lability
        ❑ Intense emotional response
        ❑ Increased rejection sensitivity
        ❑ Separation anxiety
        ❑ Inflexibility
        ❑ Hyperactivity (high activity level)

Fig. 6.1 Psycho-educational summary worksheet

      ❏ Novelty seeking
      ❏ Aggression
      ❏ Atypical sexual behaviors
      ❏ Others? Specify: _____

      _____

b.   Any additional information that may offer clarification regarding student's difficulties (e.g., abuse or witness to trauma; intense family conflict; frequent ear infections)?

c.   General information gathered during developmental and health history (e.g., information regarding pregnancy, birth, and developmental milestones). Were there any concerns regarding development/early childhood?

3.   Family Stability (it is likely this information will NOT be used in report. However, it will be invaluable when developing an appropriate plan):

    a.   How well is the family functioning?

    b.   How capable are they of accessing resources?

    c.   How do the parents view the child's difficulties?

    d.   What is parents' view of mental health disorders?

    e.   Are there siblings? If so, how are they functioning?

4.   Educational Background:

    a.   How stable has the child's educational environment been (e.g., many different schools, many different teachers, etc.)?

    b.   How have teacher's described the student's behavior in the past?

    c.   How have teachers describe student's peer relationships?

    d.   Is there any evidence of "red flags"?

    e.   How have teachers described student's academic performance? Any history of special education?

5.   Medical & Mental Health History

    a.   Has the student ever been evaluated by an outside mental health professional? Was the student assigned a mental health diagnosis? Has the student ever been prescribed a mental health medication? If so describe.

    b.   Has the student ever been hospitalized (medical or psychiatric)? Have medical records been obtained (if psychiatric)? If so describe.

    c.   Has the student had a recent physical, including hearing & vision assessments? If so describe.

Fig. 6.1 (contiuned)

CURRENT ASSESSMELT

6. Is there any reason to believe that these results are not valid or reliable?

7. Socio-Emotional Functioning:
    a. Is there any evidence of manic/hypomanic symptoms (e.g., acts silly/goofy/giddy or angry/irritable)?

    b. Is there any evidence of depression (e.g., anhedonia that may result in provoking behaviors)? If so, is there any evidence of the atypical triad (i.e., overeating, oversleeping, excessive physical fatigue)?

    c. Is there any evidence of other "red flags" such as intense affective storms, sleep/wake cycle disturbances, aggression/poor frustration tolerance, emotional inflexibility, poor self-esteem regulation (either over-exaggeration of abilities or overly pessimistic of abilities), fear of harm, hypersexuality, sensory sensitivities, carbohydrate cravings, low threshold for anxiety?

    d. What have you noticed about the student from your observations? How does the student interact with peers? With teachers & other staff members?

    e. What did your observations say about student during testing?

    f. What have interviews with the student indicated about his/her emotional status? What does he/she say is difficult/challenging about school? What suggestions might he/she have for encouraging success?

    g. What have interviews with parents indicated about the student's emotional status? What are seen as primary concerns for the parents?

    h. What have interviews with teacher(s) & other staff indicated about the student's emotional status? What are the primary concerns for the teacher(s)/staff?

    i. Any evidence of suicidality?

    j. What have rating scales indicated about socio-emotional functioning in comparison to others the student's age? Is there a particular area of concern regarding behaviors? Is there a difference between ratings of parents, teacher(s) and student?
        i. Externalizing behaviors:

        ii. Internalizing behaviors:

        iii. Psychosomatic concerns:

        iv. Bizarre behaviors:

        v. Relationships:

8. Cognitive Abilities:
    a. Tests administered & results:
        i. Strengths:

        ii. Weaknesses & Needs:

        iii. Recommendations:

Fig. 6.1 (contiuned)

Executive Functions:

        b.   Tests administered & results:

              i.   Strengths:

              ii.   Weaknesses & Needs:

              iii.   Recommendations:

9.   Processing Areas:

        a.   Tests administered & results:

              i.   Strengths:

              ii.   Weaknesses & Needs:

Recommendations:

Other Results:

Fig. 6.1 (contiued)

Step 5: Conclusions and Next Steps

After all the information is analyzed and triangulated, the final step is to draw conclusions and plan next steps. It will include a determination of eligibility and need [20 U. S. C. § 1414 (b)(4)(A)], and a report must be completed that conveys that information to the IEP team [20 U. S. C. § 1414 (b)(4)(B)]. As indicated earlier in the chapter, two requirements must be satisfied in order for a student to qualify for special education, a disability and the need for special education [20 U. S. C. § 1401 (3)(A)]. While the IEP team makes the decision regarding special education, it is important for the assessor to address this point in the report to assist the team. A sample structure for a psycho-educational assessment report is included in Fig. 6.2. Planning appropriate next steps (e.g., goals for the IEP, interventions for target behaviors, ongoing monitoring of interventions) will be addressed in Chapter 7.

PSYCHO-EDUCATIONAL EVALUATION
Confidential Report

NAME:	DATE OF REPORT:
BIRTH DATE:	ASSESSMENT DATES:
AGE:	DISTRICT:
GRADE:	PARENT:
PRIMARY LANGUAGE:	ADDRESS:
TEACHER	EXAMINER:
PRIMARY LANGUAGE:	POSITION:

REASONS FOR REFERRAL

List important demographic information regarding the student, the referral source, and the particular concerns that resulted in, and the proposed outcomes of, the assessment. See Figure 6.2 for an example of a referral statement.

METHODS OF DATA COLLECTION & ASSESSMENT VALIDITY

Discuss the appropriateness of the assessment methods with the current student. List all the methods utilized in the assessment, including full titles of all tests used. If the test was administered by another source, include that person's name and title in a footnote attached to the test name.

—Parent, Student and Teacher Interviews
—Review of Records
—Behavioral Observations
—*Lists of tests administered*[1]

BACKGROUND INFORMATION

Developmental, Health, and Family History

Discuss information regarding the student's developmental milestones, any red flags in the student's history, health history (i.e., mental health, any hospitalizations, medications, vision, hearing, etc.) and family history (including family mental health).

   Language. Discuss primary language and method for determining this (e.g., indicated by parents on Home Language Survey). Discuss level of competence student has with primary language (e.g., through district or state-wide assessments).

Educational History

Discuss student's educational history (per cumulative folder, and prior teachers, parents, and student reports). Include any information regarding prior evaluations and/or experience with special education.

CURRENT ASSESSMENT RESULTS

Include brief description of the methods utilized (e.g., combination of direct and indirect methods) and explanation regarding standardization in order to make scores understandable. If including scores in an appendix, refer the reader to that portion of the report for this information.

---

[1] Additional tests administered by other members of the multi-disciplinary team with attached footnote such as: "The [test] was administered by [name], the Resource Specialist Program (RSP) teacher".

Fig. 6.2 Sample structure of a psycho-educational evaluation report

TEST TAKING BEHAVIOR

Discuss student's behavior while testing, including cooperation, rapport-building, energy, mood, concentration, atypical behaviors, etc. The informal "mental status exam" conducted would be appropriate to discuss here.

ADDITIONAL OBSERVATIONS

Discuss any additional observations made, including data summaries (e.g., percentage of time on task in particular settings), if possible.

PSYCHOSOCIAL FUNCTIONING

Areas should be listed in order of importance. It is likely with an evaluation of a student with bipolar disorder that psychosocial functioning will be of the most concern. Discuss student's functioning in interpersonal and intrapersonal areas.

PROBLEM SOLVING & REASONING ABILITIES

Discuss cognitive abilities. Include executive functions in this section.

PROCESSING ABILITIES

Discuss assessment in all processing areas that were assessed.

ACADEMIC FUNCTIONING

Discuss academic functioning, including grades and any academic testing.

SUMMARY AND RECOMMENDATIONS

Briefly summarize results from assessment. Triangulate and synthesize information regarding different areas of functioning and different information sources to make statements about the student's current levels of functioning. Connect past with present behavior or functioning. Address any conflicting information.

Discussion of Eligibility & Educational Need: Discuss in detail eligibility issues. Summarize the information utilized to make conclusions regarding eligibilityand include statement regarding final determination of eligibility will be made by the IEP team at the IEP meeting.

From this assessment the following recommendations are made:

Include 3-5 recommendations addressing the main concerns raised in the assessment.

_____   _____
(Name)   Date
(Title)

Fig. 6.2 (contiuned)

Concluding Comments

While diagnosis of a bipolar disorder does not automatically translate into eligibility for special education services, the impact of this disorder on the student's ability to access educational opportunities should heighten school personnel's awareness of the student and result in monitoring the student's progress to continually evaluate the need for assessment. A five-step assessment model has been described to help guide the assessor through the psycho-educational evaluation of a student suspected of, or diagnosed with an early-onset bipolar disorder.

Chapter 7
Treatment of Bipolar Disorder in Children and Adolescents

The growing interest in the diagnosis of bipolar disorder in youth has sparked subsequent interest and controversy related to the appropriate treatment of the disorder in this population. As such, authoritative bodies like the American Academy of Child and Adolescent Psychiatry (AACAP) have recently published practice parameters regarding the treatment of early-onset bipolar disorder. These guidelines advocate for first-line, primary psychopharmacological treatment with adjunct psychosocial therapy (McClellan et al., 2007).

While these interventions are primarily based in community settings, it is important for school-based professionals to be aware of the research related to the current medications and the adverse effects of those medications, as well as the psychosocial interventions utilized in the treatment of early-onset bipolar disorder in community settings. Unfortunately, the current body of literature related to this topic demonstrates significant limitations. This chapter will discuss the current literature related to these interventions and will extrapolate from it to discuss potential educational interventions (regrettably absent from the current body of research) to conclude.

Psychopharmacological Interventions

As previously mentioned, bipolar disorder is a lifelong and recurrent illness requiring lifelong treatment. Medications are an important factor in the course of this disorder for both youth and adults. Delay of psychopharmacological interventions is associated with more time depressed, greater severity of depression, more episodes, more rapid cycling, and fewer days euthymic (Post et al., 2010). Termination of medications is associated with significantly more relapse, often within 1 year of termination (Angst et al., 2002; Jairam, Srinath, Girimaji, & Seshadri, 2004). Therefore, it is assumed that medication, (the primary and initial focus of treatment) will receive ongoing attention from individuals with this diagnosis as well as their family members.

S.R. Hart et al., *Identifying, Assessing, and Treating Bipolar Disorder at School*,
Developmental Psychopathology at School, DOI 10.1007/978-1-4614-7585-9_7,
© Springer Science+Business Media New York 2014

Concerns Regarding Medication

At present, many of the medications prescribed to children and adolescents are done so "off-label", that is, these medications are not approved by the Food and Drug Administration (FDA) for the specific treatment of bipolar disorder and/or for use with children and adolescents. At this time, only *five* medications are approved for use in children and adolescents with bipolar disorder. For children 10-years and older, three atypical antipsychotics have received FDA approval: *risperidone* (treatment of acute mania), *aripiprazole* (acute mania and maintenance therapy), and *quetiapine* (acute mania and depression). For individuals 12 years and older, *lithium* is approved for treatment in all phases of bipolar disorder. Finally, the atypical antipsychotic, *olanzapine* (acute mania) has received FDA approval for use with children aged ≥13 years (Pfeifer, Kowatch, & DelBello, 2010; Zito et al., 2008).

However, common practice for the treatment of bipolar disorder includes many other medications (see Table 7.1 for a listing of frequently used medications), and many times includes a combination of both approved and "off-label" medications (i.e., polypharmacy; Pfeifer et al., 2010; Smarty & Findling, 2007). In fact, among youth treated in psychiatric practice, children and adolescents with bipolar disorder are the group most frequently prescribed two or more medications (87 % vs. 40 %; Duffy et al., 2005). While data with youth is limited, polypharmacy does seem to have benefits. The only randomized, double-blind, placebo-controlled

Table 7.1 Common mood stabilizing medications: generic and brand names

Generic name	Brand name(s)
Lithium[a]	Eskalith®, Lithobid®, Lithonate®, Lithotab®
Anticonvulsants/Antiepileptics	
Divalproex Sodium	Depakote®, Epival®
Valproic Acid/Valproate	Depakene®
Tiagabine	Gabitril®
Lamotrigine	Lamictal®
Gabapentin	Neurontin®
Carbamazepine	Tegretol®, Epitol®, Carbatrol®
Topiramate	Topamax®
Oxcarbazepine	Trileptal®
Zonisamide	Zonegram®
Atypical Antipsychotics	
Aripiprazole[b]	Abilify®, Abilify Discmelt®
Clozapine	Clozaril®
Ziprasidone	Geodon®
Risperidone[b]	Risperdal®
Quetiapine	Seroquel®
Olanzapine[c]	Zyprexa®, Zydis®

Note: [a]Approved for treatment of bipolar disorder in youth aged 12 and older
[b]Approved for treatment of acute and mixed mania in children and youth aged 10 and older
[c]Approved for treatment of bipolar disorder in yuth aged 13 and older

polypharmacy study in adolescents indicated that while 53 % of individuals in the monotherapy group (treatment with one medication—in this case divalproex sodium) responded favorably, 87 % of individuals in the polypharmacy group did (adjunct quetiapine; DelBello, Schwiers, Rosenberg, & Strawkoski, 2002).

In spite of a growing interest in pediatric pharmacology and increasing numbers of randomized controlled studies in children and adolescents, the effectiveness and safety of these various "off-label" medications have yet to be adequately established and close clinical monitoring is vital for children prescribed medications to treat bipolar disorder (McClellan et al., 2007; Smarty & Findling, 2007; Zito et al., 2008). There are several specific concerns discussed next: adverse effects and suicidal thoughts and behaviors.

Adverse Effects

Adverse[1], or side effects (e.g., weight gain, sedation) from medications prescribed to treat bipolar disorder can be significant. While these adverse effects are concerning, they may be particularly so for the developing brain and body of children and adolescents (Correll, 2008). Several recent reviews have occurred particularly evaluating the effect of antipsychotics on children and adolescents (Jensen, Buitelaar, Pandina, Binder, & Haas, 2007; Maayan & Correll, 2011). In these reviews, the most frequently reported adverse effects included weight gain, sedation, and somnolence (i.e., sleepiness). The weight gain ranged from an average of approximately 2 pounds over a 16-week period to over 20 pounds after a 12-month period. Most weight gain seemed to occur during the first 2–3 months of treatment, and then plateau. Follow-up with individuals who terminated the medications demonstrated that the weight gain did reverse (Jensen et al., 2007). Maayan and Correll (2011) highlight the need to specifically address age in this research, as weight gain may differentially impact individuals depending on the developmental periods. They also note that several antipsychotics (i.e., clozapine and olanzapine) seem to have weight independent, direct adverse effects on metabolic problems in youth.

Prospective studies have indicated that age-inappropriate weight gain early in life seems to have particularly deleterious effects in that obesity, metabolic abnormalities, and weight gain during childhood strongly predict obesity, metabolic syndrome, hypertension, cardiovascular morbidity, sleep apnea, osteoarthritis, and malignancy later in life (Correll, 2008). In addition, this weight gain may be particularly disheartening to the developing adolescent (psychosocially) and potentially a reason for noncompliance throughout life.

---

[1] A comprehensive discussion regarding the multitude of potential adverse effects of each of the medications used to treat bipolar disorder is beyond the scope of this text. However, it is crucial for school psychologists and other educational professionals to be aware of these effects. It is recommended that these professionals educate themselves through available individuals (e.g., psychiatrist, nurse) and resources (e.g., medication websites) on a case-by-case basis, and to ensure that a child's educational team is consistently reminded of these effects.

Additional potential adverse effects related to the endocrine system (e.g., hyperp-rolactinaemia—elevated levels in the blood of the peptide hormone prolactin, which is responsible for lactation), metabolism (e.g., diabetes, metabolic syndrome—a constellation of physical and laboratory features that predisposes individuals to ath-erosclerotic cardiovascular disease) and hematology (e.g., neutropenia—abnormally low levels of the white blood cell, neutrophil) deserve attention in the use of antipsy-chotics in children and adolescents (Correll, 2008; Jensen et al., 2007). Particularly for females, the use of valproate has been associated with Polycystic Ovary Syndrome (PCOS; Joshi & Robb, 2008). This association is by no means clearly understood (e.g., is PCOS a result of the bipolar disorder, the valproate, or the combination of both), and more research in this area is called for.

The impact of these medications on physical and sexual development is also of concern. While further study is recommended to determine the long-term safety of antipsychotics during puberty, Jensen and colleagues' (2007) review of the avail-able literature indicated no apparent inhibition of growth or sexual maturation with the use of risperidone after 1-year of treatment.

Stevens-Johnson Syndrome/Toxic Epidermal Necrolysis Spectrum

One particularly detrimental adverse reaction to several of the medications pre-scribed for bipolar disorder is Stevens–Johnson syndrome (SJS) or toxic epidermal necrolysis spectrum (TEN). SJS/TEN are severe adverse skin reactions involving extensive detachment of skin and erosion of the mucous membranes (Mockenhaupt et al., 2008). SJS and TEN are believed to be a single disease with the difference in the amount of skin detachment/lesions and the extent of surface area involved (TEN is more severe affecting at least 30 % of the body surface area). Although SJS/TEN are rare (approximately one to seven cases per million people per year), mortality rates are approximately 30 % for TEN and 1–3 % for SJS in adults. Mortality rates in children have been estimated at 7.5 % (Knowles & Shear, 2009). Additionally, individuals suffering from this reaction frequently endure lasting disability and are reluctant to use medications in the future (Mockenhaupt et al., 2008).

Medications of interest to the discussion of bipolar disorder that are known to be of high relative risk include the following: (a) anticonvulsants—lamotrigine, carba-mazepine, and phenytoin (Dilantin® or Phenytek®); (b) an antidepressant—sertraline (Zoloft®); (c) nonsteroidal anti-inflammatories (NSAID's)—oxicam type (e.g., Feldene®, Mobic®); and (d) an antibiotic—cotrimoxazole (Septra® or Bactrim®; Mockenhaupt et al., 2008). Additionally, combination therapy of lamotrigine with divalproex sodium or with the discontinuance of oral contraceptives may increase the risk (Pfeifer et al., 2010). Most reactions occur after several weeks of exposure to the medications (although some reactions were noted as early as 4 days), and experts recommend monitoring for at least a month for symptoms. Particularly with lamotrigine, slow dose escalation is recommended. SJS/TEN can begin with non-specific symptoms such as fever, cough, headaches, and a general feeling of malaise

Table 7.2 Signs and symptoms of Stevens–Johnson syndrome (SJS)

Several days prior to rash individual may experience:
- Fever
- Cough
- Sore throat
- Burning eyes

Signs and symptoms (seek immediate medical attention):
- Facial swelling
- Tongue swelling
- Hives
- Skin pain (particularly unexplained and widespread pain)
- Red or purple rash that spreads within hours to days
- Blisters on skin and mucous membranes (especially in your mouth, nose and eyes)
- Shedding (sloughing of skin)

Note. Adapted from "Stevens-Johnson syndrome: Symptoms" retrieved from the Mayo Clinic Website at: http://www.mayoclinic.com/health/stevens-johnson-syndrome/DS00940/DSECTION=symptoms

up to 2-weeks prior to the development of a rash, which typically appears first on the trunk and rapidly spreads to the face, neck, and extremities (see Table 7.2 for list of signs and symptoms; Knowles & Shear, 2009). The rash can form into blisters and blisters can appear on the eyes, mouth, and vaginal area. In the case of TEN, layers of the skin (in some cases hair and nails) can come away easily. It is imperative that individuals are carefully monitored at the first sign of a fever, and if a rash appears, the student should be immediately taken to the hospital.

Suicidal Thoughts and Behaviors

In 2003, the FDA issued a public health advisory regarding several reports of children and teenagers who were taking antidepressants attempting or completing suicide (Gibbons et al., 2007). More recently, as a result of a comprehensive review of almost 300 trials that consistently demonstrated a slight increase in suicidal thoughts and behaviors for individuals in early treatment, the FDA recommended makers of all antidepressant medications include a black box warning on their label (FDA, 2007a). This warning recommends that individuals of all ages started on antidepressant therapy be monitored closely for clinical worsening, suicidal thoughts and behaviors, or unusual changes in behavior (see Table 7.3; FDA, 2007b).

However, this warning also clearly states that the *reasons* for the prescription (e.g., depression) are alone associated with increases in the risk and remain *the most important causes* of suicidal thoughts and behaviors (FDA, 2007b). Gibbons et al. (2007) recently examined US and Dutch data on Selective Serotonin Reuptake Inhibitor (SSRI) prescription rates and suicide rates in children and adolescents. These researchers demonstrated that as prescription rates substantially increased from 1998 to 2003, rates of suicide substantially decreased (over 30 % in the USA).

Table 7.3 Symptoms to be vigilant for in relation to antidepressant treatment and suicidal thoughts and behaviors

Emergence of:	
Anxiety	Agitation
Panic attacks	Insomnia
Irritability	Hostility
Aggressiveness	Impulsivity
Akathisia (psychomotor restlessness)	(Hypo)mania
Worsening of depression	Increases in suicidal thoughts and behaviors
Other unusual changes in behavior	

Note. Adapted from "Revisions to product labeling" by the Food and Drug Administration, 2007b, available online from: http://www.fda.gov/cder/drug/antidepressants/antidepressants_label_change_2007.pdf

Unfortunately, following the warnings or health advisories issued by regulatory agencies in both countries, prescription rates have decreased while suicide rates have increased (almost 14 % in the USA; Gibbons et al., 2007). In the USA, this increase is the largest since the Centers for Disease Control and Prevention (CDC) began collecting this data in 1979 (Gibbons et al., 2007). An individual (or guardian) must carefully balance the risk with the need and benefit of these medications.

In addition to the black box warning, the FDA recommended changes to current language on product labeling (FDA, 2007b). These include adding a section on screening individuals for bipolar disorder, stressing that prior to initiating antidepressant treatment, it is essential for individuals with depressive symptoms to be adequately screened to determine if they are at risk.

Medications Used to Treat Bipolar Disorder

The treatment of bipolar disorder with medications has two goals: the reduction of current symptoms and the prevention of future symptoms (Preston & Johnson, 2008). As such, different medications may be called for in the treatment of the acute versus the maintenance phase and the different target symptoms of an episode (e.g., mania versus depression). In addition, rapid cycling, dysphoric mania, and comorbid conditions present further considerations for and complications to treatment.

The term "mood stabilizer" is often used in conjunction with the psychopharmacological treatment of bipolar disorder. Essentially, this applies to a medication that has both antimanic and antidepressant effects and is able to decrease the frequency and severity of episodes (Mondimore, 2006); therefore many different medications may be deemed mood stabilizers. Lithium remains the most researched mood-stabilizing agent in the treatment of bipolar disorder. Additional classes of medications include anticonvulsants, atypical antipsychotics, and antidepressants. Several recent publications have provided reviews of available medication studies; these reviews will be utilized in the following discussions.

Lithium

While a thorough discussion is beyond the scope of this chapter, briefly, lithium impacts several neurotransmitters (i.e., serotonin, dopamine, norepinephrine, and Gamma-Aminobutyric Acid) and demonstrates important neuroprotective effects (e.g., aids in the process of neurogenesis, prevents stress-induced loss of dendrites, increases volume of gray matter and amygdala; Findling & Pavuluri, 2008). While the status of research with lithium suffers from similar challenges as other medications (e.g., small samples, lack of randomized-controlled trials), current studies indicate that monotherapy with lithium may be effective in the treatment of acute mixed and manic states, with increasing evidence supporting its use in the treatment of bipolar depression with children and adolescents. In addition, in those individuals that do not experience a significant response to monotherapy, it appears to be an effective component of a combination regimen (Pfeifer et al., 2010; Smarty & Findling, 2007). Several innovative studies (The Collaborative Lithium Trials) are currently being conducted through contracts with the National Institute of Child Health and Human Development (NICHD) to further evaluate the efficacy of lithium in early-onset disorder (Findling et al., 2008).

Unfortunately, there are several downsides to the use of lithium. As it is an element, it is not metabolized, but absorbed in the gastrointestinal tract and excreted in the urine. Therefore, changes in hydration status or drugs that affect renal function may alter concentrations (e.g., restriction of water or sodium, caffeinated beverages, or NSAID's such as aspirin or ibuprofen). It has a narrow therapeutic index, meaning that the therapeutic and toxic levels are close, and blood-serum levels must be closely monitored to prevent toxicity (see Table 7.4 for symptoms; Findling & Pavuluri, 2008). The most common adverse effects reported in studies of children and adolescents include weight gain/increased appetite, nausea, headache, tremor, polyuria (increased production of urine), vomiting, and diarrhea; however, lithium is reported to be relatively well-tolerated (Smarty & Findling, 2007).

Anticonvulsants

Several medications originally prescribed as anticonvulsants (sometimes called antiepileptics) have demonstrated efficacy for the treatment of bipolar disorder in adults; however, existing data regarding early-onset bipolar disorder is typically restricted to case reports, retrospective chart reviews, open trials, and combination studies (Consoli, Deniau, Huynh, Purper, & Cohen, 2007; Smarty & Findling, 2007). The most common anticonvulsants currently being used with youth appear to be divalproex sodium or valproate, and carbamazepine.

At present, several open-label, prospective studies and randomized controlled trials indicate that divalproex sodium may be effective and well-tolerated in children and adolescents for the treatment of acute mixed and manic episodes while one, large, randomized, placebo-controlled, double-blind study indicated that treatment with divalproex sodium was not statistically superior to placebo (Consoli et al., 2007;

Table 7.4 Signs of lithium toxicity

Early signs of lithium toxicity:
• Ataxia
• Dysarthria
• Reduced motor coordination
Symptoms of mild toxicity:
• Listlessness
• Slurred speech
• Coarse tremors
Symptoms of moderate toxicity:
• More pronounced coarse tremors
• More pronounced ataxia
• Confusion
• Delirium
Symptoms of severe toxicity[a]:
• Seizures
• Coma

Note. Adapted from "Lithium" by R. L. Findling & P. M Pavuluri (2008), in B. Geller and M. P. DelBello (Eds), *Treatment of bipolar disorder in children and adolescents*, pp. 43–68

[a]Severe lithium toxicity can cause death

Kowatch, 2008; Pfeifer et al., 2010). Data regarding carbamazepine are also mixed, but may point to its place as an adjunct medication (McClellan et al., 2007; Smarty & Findling, 2007). Several open-label studies with adolescents support the benefits of lamotrigine monotherapy or combination therapy with additional mood stabilizers in bipolar depression and maintaining symptom control of both manic and depressive symptoms (Pavuluri, Henry et al., 2009; Smarty & Findling, 2007). Finally, data are sufficiently lacking in regards to topiramate, oxcarbazepine, and gabapentin (Pavuluri, Henry et al., 2009; Smarty & Findling, 2007).

Atypical Antipsychotics

Aside from lithium, only four antipsychotics are approved for use with children and adolescents (aripirazole, olanzapine, quetiapine, and risperidone). Atypical antipsychotic medications exert their effects (both therapeutic and adverse) through the binding of specific cellular receptors in the central nervous system (Frazier, Bregman, & Jackson, 2008). Similar to anticonvulsants, much further research is needed before making general statements regarding their efficacy with children and adolescents. Much of the current data for use with this population comes from case reports, retrospective chart reviews, combination studies, open-label studies, and acute (versus longitudinal) studies. Several brief, double-blind, placebo-controlled, mono- and co-therapy studies have demonstrated the potential effectiveness of aripiprazole, olanzapine, quetiapine, risperidone, and ziprasidone in treating the manic symptoms associated with bipolar disorder (Chang, 2008; Consoli et al., 2007; Frazier et al., 2008; Pfeifer et al., 2010; Smarty & Findling, 2007).

Antidepressants

At present, there are no prospective clinical trials of antidepressants in children and adolescents with bipolar disorder (Smarty & Findling, 2007). Recently, one, large, longitudinal study with adults has indicated that individuals prescribed an antide-pressant in conjunction with a mood stabilizer recover no faster than those pre-scribed a placebo and mood stabilizer. In addition, manic symptoms were more severe among individuals prescribed the antidepressant (Goldberg et al., 2007). This study seems to indicate that while there appears to be no added benefit to antide-pressant use, there remains the concern of destabilization of mood and potential "switching" from depression to mania.

Final Thoughts Regarding Psychopharmacological Treatment

Psychopharmacology is the primary and core element of treatment in early-onset bipolar disorder. While research is increasing in this area, at the present time, it is too early to make definitive statements about the efficacy and safety of these medi-cations for use with this population. Recognizing the adverse effects associated with current psychopharmacological treatments, professionals and families are seeking treatments with fewer deleterious effects; at times, despite a dearth of research indi-cating effectiveness and safety (Wozniak et al., 2007). Two of the more common and researched alternative approaches to treatment in bipolar disorder warrant a brief discussion.

Electroconvulsive Therapy

In adults electroconvulsive therapy (ECT) has been demonstrated to be an effective and safe treatment. Research is accumulating regarding its use for both manic and depressive symptoms, and AACAP includes a recommendation regarding ECT in its guidelines based on these studies with adults and several small studies with youth (McClellan et al., 2007). Interested readers are referred to Ghaziuddin et al., (2004) for further information regarding AACAP's guidelines on the use of this treatment with adolescents. In general, AACAP suggests that ECT should only be considered for adolescents diagnosed with bipolar I disorder who have severe episodes of mania or depression and are nonresponsive (or unable to take) standard medications

(McClellan et al., 2007). Adverse effects associated with this treatment can include headache, nausea, vomiting, muscle aches, short-term cognitive impairment (particularly memory), anxiety reactions, disinhibition, and altered seizure threshold (Ghaziuddin et al., 2004; McClellan et al., 2007).

Omega-3 Fatty Acids

Due to reported abnormalities in fatty acid composition of phospholipids in cell membranes of the brains of individuals with bipolar disorder, omega-3 fatty acid therapy has received some attention in the literature. Omega-3 fatty acids can be introduced in the form of a safe and well-tolerated nutritional supplement, and in studies of adults, have been associated with heart disease, cardiac mortality, and depression. One open-label, monotherapy study recently conducted with children and adolescents indicated that manic symptoms may be reduced in youth with bipolar disorder through the use of omega-3 fatty acids, with individuals reporting a modest decrease in manic symptoms during the course of the disorder (Wozniak et al., 2007). However, a randomized, controlled study indicated that there was no significant improvement in comparison to placebo (Gracious et al., 2010). Obviously, more research is required to fully understand the place of omega-3 fatty acids in the treatment of bipolar disorder, particularly as data from adult trials are not equivocal, and many questions remain regarding dosing, ratio of omega-3 to omega-6, and level of eicosapentaenoic (EPA) versus docosahexaenoic acid (DHA).

On a final note, noncompliance with psychopharmacological treatment is common in all age groups, and in recent studies of adolescents, has ranged widely from 16 to 76 % (Coletti, Leigh, Galleli, & Kafantaris, 2005; Patel, DelBello, Keck, & Strakowski, 2005; Drotar et al., 2007). In general, adherence rates tend to be higher in younger populations; however, studies of children with chronic illness indicate that less adequate family functioning is related to nonadherence (Riekert & Drotar, 2000). Recognizing the connection between termination of medications and relapse, as well as the indication that subsequent episodes tend to become progressively worse and possibly treatment refractory (Preston & Johnson, 2008), adherence to medication is, and family therapy is increasingly becoming, common elements of many psychosocial interventions. Youth prescribed these medications must be carefully monitored by physicians and school professionals need to be aware of potential adverse effects. It is critical for any comprehensive treatment plan to outline a process for all involved to communicate regarding medications.

Psychosocial Interventions

Important developmental growth occurs during childhood and adolescence; the onset of psychiatric disorders during these periods of time can disrupt these ongoing developmental processes. While medications focus on the core symptoms of bipolar

Table 7.5 Recommendations for areas to be considered in comprehensive psychosocial interventions

1.	Psychoeducational Therapy:	Information provided regarding heritability, symptoms, course, treatment options, and potential impact of disorder on functioning
2.	Relapse Prevention:	Focus on identifying factors that may precipitate (e.g., medication noncompliance, stressors) and reduce occurrence of (e.g., stress reduction, promotion of healthy sleep habits) relapse
3.	Individual Psychotherapy:	Support of psychological development, skill building, and monitoring of symptoms
4.	Social and Family Functioning:	Address the disruptions that occur in social, family, academic, and developmental functioning. Enhance relationships through communication and problem-solving skills
5.	Academic and Occupational Functioning:	Educational and occupational needs must not be forgotten. Consultation and communication with schools, participation in IEP's as needed to encourage healthy and appropriate environment
6.	Community Consultation:	Open communication and consultation between all necessary entities (e.g., juvenile justice, social welfare programs). Advocacy efforts important

Note. Adapted from "Practice parameter for the assessment and treatment of children and adolescents with bipolar disorder" by J. McClellan, R. Kowatch, R. L. Findling, W. Bernet, O. Bukstein, J. Beitchman, et al., 2007, *Journal of the American Academy of Child and Adolescent Psychiatry, 46,* pp. 107–125

disorder, this type of treatment does not necessarily address the associated functional and developmental impairments (McClellan et al., 2007). Controlled studies with children and adolescents are beginning to emerge and several programs demonstrating efficacy are briefly discussed. These programs share common elements (Miklowitz, Goodwin, Bauer, & Geddes, 2008) and extrapolating from the available literature with both youth and adults, AACAP has proposed several areas that psychosocial interventions should address (see Table 7.5; McClellan et al., 2007).

Family-Focused Treatment

Family-focused treatment (FFT) assumes that an episode of bipolar disorder creates a disruption in the entire family system (not just for the individual) and the purpose of treatment is to attain a new state of equilibrium within the system (Miklowitz, 2008). "Expressed emotion" (EE) is a measure of the emotional attitudes of caregivers toward a family member with a psychiatric disorder. Due to the link between high EE family environments and poorer outcomes, it is an important focus of the FFT approach (e.g., to improve communication between family members). A person is considered high

EE if he or she expresses a high number of critical comments, makes one or more statements of hostility, or shows emotional over-involvement (Morris, Miklowitz, & Waxmonsky, 2007).

The components of FFT consist of psychoeducation, communication enhancement training, and problem solving training, provided over 21 sessions (Morris et al., 2007). The goals of FFT for adolescents (modified from FFT with adults) include: (a) to increase adherence to medication and therefore decrease relapse, (b) to enhance knowledge of bipolar disorder, (c) to enhance communication and coping skills (e.g., lower EE), and (d) to minimize the psychosocial impairment associated with bipolar disorder (Young & Fristad, 2007). Readers interested in further reading are referred to Miklowitz, 2008.

FFT has been primarily studied in adult populations. Several large, randomized controlled trials (with samples between 100 and 300 subjects) have demonstrated efficacy in FFT as an adjunct to psychopharmacological interventions, with results (e.g., higher rates of medication compliance, lower symptoms, increased frequency of positive interactional behaviors, lower rates of hospitalization) evident upon completion through follow-up at 2-years (Morris et al., 2007). Several recent studies involving children and adolescents have demonstrated positive results (e.g., reduction in symptoms of mania), and one recent randomized trial indicated more recovery from depressive symptoms, fewer weeks experiencing depressive episodes, and a better overall trajectory for depressive symptoms of the FFT group in comparison to a three-session family-focused prevention relapse protocol (Miklowitz, Axeslon et al., 2008; Miklowitz et al. 2011; Morris et al., 2007; Young & Fristad, 2007).

Child- and Family-Focused Cognitive-Behavioral Therapy or RAINBOW

Child- and family-focused cognitive-behavioral therapy (CFF-CBT) is an adaptation of the FFT model to address the needs of younger children diagnosed with bipolar disorder and their families (ages 8 to 12; Pavuluri, Graczyk, Henry, & Carbray et al., 2004; Pavuluri, Graczyk, & Henry et al. 2004). CFF-CBT, also known as RAINBOW (an acronym with each letter introducing one component of the program; see Table 7.6), is conducted in 12 protocol-driven sessions consisting of family, child alone, parents alone, and parents with siblings. It is based on psychoeducational, cognitive-behavioral, and interpersonal psychotherapies (Young & Fristad, 2007).

Like FFT, CFF-CBT adheres to a vulnerability-stress model, proposing that stressful life events, EE, coping, and negative communication styles within families interact with a biological predisposition to elicit episodes. It is driven by three sets of factors: (a) an understanding of the affective circuitry of the brain and dysfunction associated with bipolar disorder, (b) the unique psychopathological characteristics of bipolar disorder, and (c) the environmental stressors in the family and educational environment (Pavuluri, Graczyk, Henry, & Carbray et al., 2004;

Table 7.6 CFF-CBT/RAINBOW program components

R	*R*outine: Encourage a predictable, simplified routine including sleep hygiene
A	*A*ffect Regulation: Emphasize consistent self-monitoring of moods and reducing EE
I	*I* Can Do It!: Assist with generating a list of positive self-statements to help child view self as positive and to increase more effective problem-solving
N	*N*o Negative Thoughts and Live in the *N*ow!: Teaches participants to differentiate and reframe unhelpful to helpful thoughts to facilitate effective problem-solving; also focuses on a "here and now" approach to reduce feelings of an overwhelming nature
B	*B*e a Good Friend: Teach and practice skills to establish and maintain friendships; also help parents develop a more balanced lifestyle involving "recharging batteries"
O	*O*h, How Can We Solve the Problem?: Problem-solving skills are explicitly taught and practiced; collaborative family problem-solving practices strongly encouraged, including finding solutions as well as developing a process for coming to solutions
W	*W*ays to Get Support: Assisting participants to identify appropriate individuals, times, and strategies to finding support

Note. Adapted from "Child- and family-focused cognitive-behavioral therapy for pediatric bipolar disorder: Development and preliminary results" by M. N. Pavuluri, P. A. Graczyk, D. B. Henry, J. A. Carbray, J. Heidenreich, D. J. Miklowitz, 2004, *Journal of the American Academy of Child and Adolescent Psychiatry, 45*, pp. 528–537

Pavuluri, Graczyk, & Henry et al. 2004). In several open trials, children and adolescents (ages 6–12) demonstrated significant improvements in symptoms of mania, depression, aggression, psychosis, sleep disturbances, and ADHD, as well as in overall psychosocial functioning (Pavuluri, Graczyk, Henry, & Carbray et al., 2004; West et al., 2009). A maintenance study indicated positive effects in symptoms and functioning over the 3-year period (West, Henry, & Pavuluri, 2007). Readers interested in further exploration of this program are referred to Pavuluri, 2008.

Multi-Family Psychoeducation Group and Individual Family Psychoeducation

Multi-Family Psychoeducation Group (MFPG) and Individual Family Psychoeducation (IFP) have a similar psychoeducational focus as FFT and CFF-CBT (i.e., education of the family about the child's disorder and necessary treatment, decreasing EE, improving symptom management, enhancing problem-solving, and improving communication; Young & Fristad, 2007). MFPG is organized to occur in eight, 90-min, concurrent sessions (i.e., parents with one therapist, children with another therapist). This format provides a unique opportunity to foster supportive relationships with other individuals struggling with similar issues (e.g., the challenge of parenting a child with bipolar disorder, other children with bipolar disorder). IFP was developed as a non-group format for families for whom MFPG was inappropriate (e.g., located in geographically remote areas). It is provided in 24 50-min sessions (20 manual-driven with 4 reserved for crises or to reinforce certain concepts; Young & Fristad, 2007).

One important technique for both forms of this therapy is "Thinking-Feeling-Doing" (Fristad, Davidson, & Leffler, 2007). This technique emphasizes the interactions between feelings, thoughts, and behaviors (i.e., "what I think/say about an event influences what I feel about the event and consequently what I do") in a concrete and developmentally appropriate way with scaffolding and reinforcing activities (see Fristad et al., 2007, for a detailed discussion of this technique). In addition to the basic components of MFPG, IFP contains a "Healthy Habits" component, which focuses on maintaining healthy sleep hygiene, improving nutrition, and increasing appropriate exercise activities (Young & Fristad, 2007).

A large, randomized trial of MFPG has recently been completed with children 8- to 12-years-old. Results indicated a decrease in mood (both depressive and manic) symptoms, with wait-listed clients also indicating similar response following treatment 1-year later (Fristad, Verducci, Walters, & Young, 2009). Additionally, pilot studies have demonstrated significant increases in knowledge about mood disorders, improved family interactions, improved ability to access appropriate services reported by parents, and for children, significant increases in perceived social support from parents, with a trend toward significant increases in perceived social support from peers compared to wait-listed families. In the IFP trial, mood symptoms improved significantly post-treatment and these improvements were maintained at 12-month follow-up (Young & Fristad, 2007).

Interpersonal and Social Rhythm Therapy for Adolescents (IPSRT-A)

Interpersonal and social rhythm therapy, a common treatment modality in adults with unipolar depression and bipolar disorder and in adolescents with unipolar depression has recently been adapted for use with adolescents with bipolar disorder (IPSRT-A; Hlastala, Kotler, McClellan, & McCauley, 2010). IPSRT is based on the theory that stressors in an individual's life stimulate new episodes of the illness, and the reduction of these stressors is the goal (Frank, 2005). Instability of circadian rhythms via psychosocial stressors (e.g., changes in social roles or routines, interpersonal stress, disruptions in sleep cycles) is a major focus of this therapy. IPSRT-A includes three essential components: (a) psychoeducation, (b) alleviating interpersonal stressors (e.g., fights with friends), and (c) development of structure, social routine, and sleep regularity (Hlastala et al., 2010). Treatment consisting of 16–18 sessions takes place over 20 weeks, with the primary participant being the adolescent and caregivers and other family members included for two to three family psychoeducation sessions. One pilot study has recently published results, indicating that adolescents demonstrated significant improvement on overall functioning, as well as depressive and manic symptoms (Hlastala et al., 2010).

Dialectical Behavior Therapy

Dialectical Behavior Therapy (DBT) is a relatively newly adapted treatment for bipolar disorder in youth. The main focus of DBT is emotional dysregulation (i.e., high sensitivity to emotional stimuli, extreme emotional intensity, and slow return to baseline state). Emotional dysregulation is a core feature of the disorder that is not expressly targeted by any other treatment program (Goldstein, Axelson, Birmaher & Brent, 2007). DBT, as proposed, is appropriate for adolescents and is delivered in an individual format over a 1-year period. The acute treatment period includes 24 weekly sessions over 6 months, with the continuation period consisting of 12 additional sessions tapering in frequency over the remainder of the year. Preliminary results of the pilot study are encouraging, with high treatment attendance, completion, and satisfaction ratings. Adolescents demonstrated significant improvement in suicidal thoughts and behaviors, self-injurious behaviors, emotional dysregulation, and depressive symptoms (Goldstein et al., 2007). Obviously further research is needed to demonstrate the efficacy of this treatment program.

Final Thoughts Regarding Psychosocial Interventions

The psychosocial interventions currently advocated for use with children and adolescents diagnosed with bipolar disorder share several important goals and features. These interventions seek to ensure medication compliance, to increase awareness about the disorder and associated issues, and to promote wellness through healthy habits (e.g., sleep integrity) and positive relationships. They are typically psychoeducational in nature, are based on cognitive-behavioral therapy, and incorporate both the child or adolescent and the parents. Skill building and problem-solving are often the focus of each (Young & Fristad, 2007). While incorporating a program like those described may be unfeasible for individuals based in the school setting, it is believed that components of these programs and techniques described therein can provide a useful foundation for school-based services. In addition, knowledge of these programs may be useful in advocating for students with their community mental health providers.

Educational Interventions

Unfortunately, there is a severe paucity of research related to the education of a child or adolescent with bipolar disorder. However, one can extrapolate from the available literature regarding impairments (see Chapter 3) that it is likely that a child or adolescent with bipolar disorder will benefit from support and interventions within the educational setting, regardless of qualification for special education. Chapter 6 outlined the components of a comprehensive psychoeducational assessment. The following discussion assumes the child assessed has qualified for special education services and the interventions appropriate for an educational setting would flow from this assessment.

As with all students (with an educationally defined disability) struggling to be successful in the educational environment, the development of an appropriate and comprehensive Individualized Education Program (IEP) treatment plan is essential. IDEA (2004) requires the consideration of: (a) strengths, (b) parents' concerns for enhancing the child's education, (c) results of the initial or most recent evaluation, and (d) academic, developmental, and functional needs [20 U. S. C. § 1414 (d)(3) (A)]. For children whose behaviors are impeding learning, special factors will necessarily be considered [20 U. S. C. § 1414 (d)(3)(B)]. While each individualized assessment provides direction in the development of this plan, several components can be briefly discussed.

IEP Teams and IEP Goals

According to IDEA (2004), the IEP team will consist of (1) parents, (2) at least one general education teacher (if the child participates in the general education environment), (3) at least one special education teacher/provider (i.e., a person responsible for implementing the IEP), (4) a local educational agency (LEA) representative, (5) an individual who can interpret the instructional implications of evaluation results, (6) additional individuals who have knowledge or special expertise regarding the child, and (7) the child, whenever appropriate [20 U. S. C. § 1414 (d)(1)(B)]. For a student with bipolar disorder, the additional members of the IEP team might include a psychiatrist, school-based nurse, community-based counselors, social workers, and/or any additional providers of community-based services.

If school-based mental health professionals are not particularly familiar with bipolar disorder, it is highly recommended that an expert (or individual with more specific knowledge and expertise) be available to help educate and prompt the educational team in order to provide the most effective IEP (this is often the case when working with individuals with an Autism Spectrum Disorder). As students with bipolar disorder may be connected with several agencies (e.g., "wrap-around" services) it will be crucial for all those actively involved to be present at IEP meetings and for communication between all team members to remain open throughout the year. Finally, it is stressed that an IEP team be sensitive and proactive, remaining open to meeting as frequently as needed, particularly when stabilizing a student on medications or an initial IEP plan is attempted. Bipolar disorder is characterized by varying symptomatology. The plan should be carefully monitored in order to evaluate the need for adjustment in order to best serve the child.

Annual, measurable goals are one element of an IEP plan. The objective of these goals is to assist the student in accessing the general education curriculum and to meet other educational needs resulting from the child's disability [20 U. S. C. § 1414 (d)(1)(A)(i)(II)]. These goals will naturally flow from the comprehensive assessment and discussion during the IEP meeting.[2] For a student with bipolar disorder, emotional and behavioral challenges may be the primary barriers to the general curriculum, and these issues may, at times, need to take precedence over academic goals. This is likely going to require a shift for the IEP team and, in this age of accountability, it may present a challenge for mental health professionals to suggest this shift. This is not to say that academics are not of concern, but simply that in order for learning to occur, the child must be reasonably emotionally stable.

Considerations for Programming

Potential considerations for programming, including accommodations and modifications, can be found in Table 7.7. An educational team will likely consider many of the areas presented when developing an appropriate IEP for a child or adolescent with bipolar disorder. This list is by no means comprehensive but is meant to stimulate thinking about students' needs. It is important to note that special education, related services and supplementary aids and services should be "… based on peer-reviewed research to the extent practicable" [20 U. S. C. § 1414 (d)(1)(A)(i)(IV)]. It will be important for research to provide evidence-based services and aids regarding students with bipolar disorder. Morris and Mather (2008) have recently published a volume including evidence-based interventions for students with behavioral (and learning) challenges. While bipolar disorder is not represented in this text, it does include chapters on related issues, such as depression, anxiety, and ADHD. Comorbidity and related symptoms are important to consider during treatment planning and this resource will be useful in that process.

Counseling

It is expected that individual and/or group counseling will be a part of the IEP for a student with bipolar disorder. School psychologists, counselors, and social workers will want to utilize components of the psychosocial interventions listed earlier.

---

[2]It seems to be common practice to develop a draft of the IEP, including goals, prior to an IEP meeting. The US Department of Education strongly recommends that if a draft is constructed, parents are provided a copy prior to the IEP meeting, so that they have an opportunity to review the recommendations and are better able to engage in full discussion of the proposals for the IEP (34 C. F. R. § 300, pp. 46678; Department of Education, August 14, 2006). In the case of a student with bipolar disorder, this is a particularly important consideration, as these IEP meetings may be fairly involved.

Table 7.7 Considerations for programming, including accommodations and/or modifications for the educational setting

Area		Possible Considerations for Programming
Mood	• Changes/Fluctuations • Mania • Depression • Irritability • Low self-esteem	• Provide psychoeducation regarding the disorder and the importance of medications to improve compliance • Designate a "go to" person for the student when he or she feels unable to cope. This should be a person the student trusts, feels safe with, and is involved in choosing • Give the student a "permanent pass" and a private signal that only he or she and the teacher know so that a private exit is possible in front of the rest of the class • Offer the student a private place to go to calm down when feelings are overwhelming • Schedule regular meetings (counseling) to work on calming and anger management techniques • Try to anticipate issues by reading a student's affect and questioning students. Allow student to "opt out" • Try to keep distractions to a minimum, tendency to become irritated by extraneous stimulation may increase when academic demands increase (e.g., noise from peers), if necessary, allow student a quiet place to work away from peers • One-on-one aid to prevent situations that may cause the student to lose control • Conduct an FBA/FAA to identify triggers that may cause the student to lose control and then develop a BSP/BIP to add to the IEP, which provides appropriate interventions for problematic behaviors. Include alternatives to punitive measures to punitive measures for problematic behaviors. Include alternatives to punitive measures for problematic behaviors • If part of student's treatment component involves light therapy, allow an area for student to receive treatment during the day • Allow student 5 min at end of period (or end of ½ hour) to talk to teacher or aide about any topic he or she wants, keep directing student in compassionate way back on track in the interim • Have a person the student "checks-in" with at the start of the day to see how the day is starting out. If the day is rough, the student is allowed an alternative activity in order to transition successfully into the classroom. This may also just be used to have student connect with another adult on campus • Allow choice in activities. For example, give list of possible tasks to complete and permit choice with which tasks to complete first, student will be given explicit time limit (e.g., 15 min of language arts activity, then switch to math worksheet) • Provide as much physical activity as possible. Allow student to run "important" errands to the office or move things around the room • Allow student to rejoin group after failure to control emotion. Provide opportunities for student to apologize, but "save face" • Be flexible and adaptable. Avoid confrontational interactions (e.g., keep emotion of voice, use short directives)

	• Mood charts to see how student's mood is fluctuating
	• Closely monitor medications
	• Develop a token economy system. Provide student with much reinforcement and encouragement
	• Have staffing separate from the IEP that involves brief discussion about bipolar disorder, and meet frequently with staff to provide support
	• Address depressive symptoms and internalizing behaviors (although externalizing challenges may be more salient to significant others)
	• Ensure open communication with all service care providers regarding mood, medications, and possible issues to address in counseling sessions
Relationship Concerns	• Poor peer relationships
	• Poor social skills
	• Misperception of intentions
	• Provide explicit teaching of skills, if possible in one-on-one situation
	• Teach student relaxation techniques
	• Assist student with identifying triggers in social situations and develop game plan for dealing with these situations
	• Assist student in recognizing the inflexibility regarding social situations and develop strategies for working through
	• Use visual imagery (have student imagine unsuccessful situation, then experiencing success in the same situation) and discuss what would need to happen to have success
	• Record student's interactions with peers and adults so that student evaluate and learn from his or her own experiences
	• Provide student with social skills groups where student may be able to role-play or practice skills taught
	• Provide as much supervision of peer interactions as possible (particularly during unstructured times of the day, such as lunch and recesses), and assist student as much as necessary
	• Provide private, but prompt feedback about interactions of peers
	• Help student navigate peer conflicts and help peers understand student's misunderstanding of his or her behaviors
	• Connect student with a peer "buddy" who can help keep student on-track
	• Education staff regarding student's diagnosis so that all staff that interact with student can assist student develop positive peer relationships

(continued)

Table 7.7 (continued)

Area	Possible Considerations for Programming
Medications	• Include medication education as part of meetings with school psychologist and personal therapist
• Side effects	• Provide written and oral information about side effects of medications to ALL staff members involved in student's day (including lunch staff)
• Frequent changes in doses and medications	• Allow student to keep a water bottle at his or her side (or desk) or have unlimited access to (non-caffeinated) fluids
• Noncompliance	• Allow unlimited access to the bathroom (with a private signal to the teacher as to where the student is going)
	• Provide place for student to take a nap so that he or she can continue with the school day (sleepiness typically subsides as the body adjusts to medication)
	• Schedule frequent breaks in cognitively taxing tasks
	• Provide extra time for work completion
	• Decrease workload and homework
	• Ensure good communication between home and school regarding medications and doses including changes in doses as this may result in changes in the student's behavior and the medications
	• Sign release of information so that student's physician/psychiatrist can communicate directly with school regarding the student's behavior and the medications
	• Monitor medication levels and mood fluctuations
	• Recognize the adverse effects and provide education for all staff in these effects (particularly rash)
Comorbid Diagnoses	• (Accommodations, modifications, and considerations appropriate for each comorbid diagnosis)
Sleep Cycle Disturbances	• Schedule academic classes later in the day when the student is more alert and emotionally available for learning
• Difficult to get going in the morning	• Allow student to take important tests later in the day when able to focus better
• Vivid and gory dreams	• Allow a later start time
• Shift in sleep cycle	• Check-in with student in the morning
	• Keep sleep log to understand the sleep cycle
	• Allow student to integrate into classroom demands after a "wake-up" period in a quiet space
	• Discuss with parents ideas for sleep routine (e.g., relaxation exercises, reading stories, soft music)

| Executive Function Issues/Cognitive Deficits | • Attention
• Organization
• Memory
• Time management
• Difficulty with transitions
• Problem-solving | • Seat student close to teacher where teacher can discretely get student's attention if needed
• Schedule frequent breaks
• Offer choices such as going to a study carrel in the library or to a quiet area outside the classroom
• Assign a "study buddy"
• Use a "travel folder" with one side marked for "to do" items and the other "completed" items
• Have student use a planner book and have teacher check that daily assignments are recorded properly. Parents can sign the planner as a way to increase home–school communication, and let parents know what homework is expected
• Have teacher or aide give student a prompt before leaving school (e.g., "what do I need to do tonight, and what materials would I need to accomplish it? I need: my coat, my lunch box, my math book, my planner, etc." The teacher could photocopy lists of typical items so that the student can check them off as they are put into his or her backpack. The same technique can be used at home
• Provide a second set of textbooks for home
• Teach student to number assignments in the order in which they should be done before beginning a homework session (prioritizing). Have student start with an assignment that is short and easy, but avoid saving the hardest or longest assignment for last. Have student estimate how much time it will take to complete each assignment and measure the estimates against the actual time (improving time management). Have him or her use a stopwatch to assign chunks of time to each step of a study plan to help him or her move on to the next step
• Teach student to preview questions at the end of each chapter to focus him or her on important concepts. The student should also preview photos, captions, and headings throughout the chapter before reading and when reviewing for a test
• Color-code subject folders and notebooks to match textbooks (e.g., if math book is orange, math folder should be orange)
• Explicitly teach student problem-solving strategies (e.g., first identify the problem, second think of alternative solutions, third attempt to solve, fourth recheck strategy to determine effectiveness, etc.) |

(continued)

Table 7.7 (continued)

Area	Possible Considerations for Programming
	• Have all teachers cue student as to transitions and the time they will occur
	• Allow student to finish tasks before moving on
	• Allow student to transitions ahead of the rest of the class (e.g., going to lunch room, library)
	• Use graphic organizers
	• Help student draw out and link important information
Difficulty with Transitions	• Have all teachers cue student as to transitions and the time they will occur
	• Allow student to finish tasks before moving on
	• Allow student to transition ahead of the rest of the class (e.g., going to lunch, library)
	Provide student with choices as to:
	• Which assignment is first (e.g., reading or math)
	• The amount of time spent working on each assignment
	• The number of problems the student will complete before moving on to another assignment
Hospitalizations	Set up a contingency plan, including:
	• How to discuss with class(es)
	• How to reintroduce to school (e.g., half-day for a week, how to discuss with the class where student has been, if student requires home/hospital)
	• What will be done regarding homework
	• How the school might support the family

Note. Adapted from S. R. Hart, "Bipolar disorder and the school psychologist", presentation for the CASP Summer Institute (2008), and J. Papolos, M. J. Hatton, S. Norelli, C. E. Garcia, & A. M. Smith, "The educational issues of students with bipolar disorder: Symptoms and accommodations" retrieved from http://www.jbrf.org/edu/forums/accommocations.html (2002)

In addition, Mennuti, Christner, and Freeman (2012) have recently edited a volume regarding CBT in educational settings. Encouragingly, bipolar disorder is represented in this second edition; additionally, many issues relevant to this group (e.g., anxiety) are present.

As indicated in Chapters 5 and 6, school-based professionals should be aware of potential psychosocial impairments. These students will likely benefit from basic skill building groups (e.g., anger management, coping skills, social skills) where they are explicitly taught skills with the opportunity to practice in a safe setting as well as to generalize to situations outside the group. Finally, topics such as suicidal ideation and substance abuse should not be avoided. These are significant issues in the life of an individual with bipolar disorder and the earlier and more directly (yet appropriately) they are addressed, the better.

Behavior Support Plan

As required by IDEA (2004), when behavior is impeding the learning (of the student or others), positive behavioral interventions and supports should be considered [20 U. S. C. § 1414 (d)(3)(B)]. A behavior support plan (BSP) should flow from a comprehensive functional behavioral assessment (FBA). That is, the summary statements from the FBA including the (a) situation (setting events and antecedents), (b) problematic behaviors, and (c) function of the behaviors or reinforcing outcomes, should form the foundation for the BSP. The objective of the BSP is to outline the changes in others' behaviors that will make the student's problematic behavior *irrelevant*, *inefficient*, and *ineffective*. Alternative or competing behaviors are identified to replace the problematic behaviors (O'Neill et al., 1997).

As indicated in Chapter 6, an FBA can be challenging with students with bipolar disorder (e.g., behavior as a result of symptomatology rather than volition). As such, the BSP should reflect accurate knowledge of the disorder and the nature of the student's challenges. This plan should also include a strategy to address potential crises (e.g., destabilization of mood, hospitalization). Finally, ongoing monitoring of the effectiveness of the plan is an important element with all BSP's, but particularly in the case of students with bipolar disorder. The variable nature of the disorder implies that flexibility is a necessity in working with these students.

Final Thoughts Regarding Educational Interventions

Interventions for the education of children and adolescents with bipolar disorder are severely lacking. However, extrapolating from the literature knowledge about the disorder and potential impairments, it is possible to begin to arrange a treatment plan. In addition to direct services provided to these students, indirect services are also crucial. Services provided to the families of these children and adolescents may, at times, be more important than the direct services provided to these students. These services might include referrals to outside agencies, provision of support resources (such as the Websites listed in the appendix), assistance with adjustment issues (e.g., stages of grief at the loss of a healthy child), and supporting the family in implementation of home-based interventions (e.g., consistent sleep routine). Additionally, providing support for those working closely with these students can go far in successful treatment. Educating all those involved in the student's daily life about bipolar disorder (e.g., teachers, administration, cafeteria workers, yard duties, bus drivers, office staff) will likely eliminate and prevent problematic behaviors. Finally, it will be helpful to create open communication between these individuals and allow a safe place to "vent" about frustrations and challenges while gently guiding this venting back to an education about the disorder and solutions to these challenges. These "behind the scenes" actions on the part of school mental health professionals can have a profound effect on the experience of a child or adolescent with bipolar disorder.

Concluding Comments

Bipolar disorder is a complex and challenging disorder, particularly in the event of an early-onset. Research in this area is quickly increasing; however, there still remain gaps in the literature. While there may be controversy about this disorder being over diagnosed, the reality is that these children and adolescents are being seen in the educational arena and research needs to provide educational professionals with evidence-based interventions. This final chapter has synthesized the current research available about medications (the first line of treatment) and psychosocial interventions. Finally, a discussion regarding the educational interventions was conducted by extrapolating from the available literature. It is hoped that in the future more direction, guidance, and treatment options will be available for these students, their families, and those professionals who work with them.

References

Achenbach, T. M. (1991). *Manual for the Child Behavior Checklist/4-18 and 1991 profile.* Burlington, VT: University of Vermont Department of Psychiatry.

Alloy, L. B., Abramson, L. Y., Urosevic, S., Walshaw, P. D., Nusslock, R., & Neeren, A. M. (2005). The psychosocial context of bipolar disorder: Environmental, cognitive, and developmental risk factors. *Clinical Psychology Review, 25,* 1043–1075. doi:10.1016/j.cpr.2005.06.006.

Althoff, R. R., Ayer, L. A., Rettew, D. C., & Hudziak, J. J. (2010). Assessment of dysregulated children using the Child Behavior Checklist: A receiver operating characteristic curve analysis. *Psychological Assessment, 22,* 609–617. doi:10.1037/a0019699.

Althoff, R. R., Faraone, S. V., Rettew, D. C., Morley, C. P., & Hudziak, J. J. (2005). Family, twin, adoption, and molecular genetic studies of juvenile bipolar disorder. *Bipolar Disorders, 7,* 598–609. doi:10.1111/j.1399-5618.2005.00268.x.

Alvarez, M.-J., Roura, P., Oses, A., Foguet, Q., Sola, J., & Arrufat, F.-X. (2011). Prevalence and clinical impact of childhood trauma in patients with severe mental disorders. *The Journal of Nervous and Mental Disease, 199,* 156–161. doi:10.1097/NMD.0b013e31820c751c.

American Psychiatric Association. (2002). *Practice guideline for the treatment of patients with bipolar disorder* (2nd ed.). Retrieved from http://www.psych.org/psych_pract/treatg/pg/Bipolar2ePG_05-15-06.pdf

American Psychiatric Association. (2013). *Diagnostic and statistical manual of mental disorders* (5th ed.). Washington, DC: Author.

American Psychiatric Association. (2000). *Diagnostic and statistical manual of mental disorders: Fourth edition-text revision (DSM-IV-TR).* Washington, DC: Author.

Andersen, M., Kubisak, J. B., Field, R., & Vogelstein, S. (2003). *Understanding and educating children and adolescents with bipolar disorder: A guide for educators.* Northfield, IL: Josselyn Center.

Anglada, T. (2006). *Intense minds: Through the eyes of young people with bipolar disorder.* Victoria, BC: Trafford Publishing.

Angst, J., Azorin, J.-M., Bowden, C. L., Perugi, G., Vieta, E., Gamma, A., et al. (2011). Prevalence and characteristics of undiagnosed bipolar disorders in patients with a major depressive episode: The BRIDGE study. *Archives of General Psychiatry, 68,* 791–798. doi:10.1001/archgenpsychiatry.2011.87.

Angst, J., Gamma, A., Benazzi, F., Ajdacic, V., Eich, D., & Rössler, W. (2003). Toward a re-definition of subthreshold bipolarity: Epidemiology and proposed criteria for bipolar-II, minor bipolar disorders and hypomania. *Journal of Affective Disorders, 73,* 133–146. doi:10.1016/S0165-0327(02)00322-1.

S.R. Hart et al., *Identifying, Assessing, and Treating Bipolar Disorder at School,* Developmental Psychopathology at School, DOI 10.1007/978-1-4614-7585-9, © Springer Science+Business Media New York 2014

Angst, J., Gamma, A., Benazzi, F., Silverstein, B., Ajdacic-Gross, V., Eich, D., et al. (2006). Atypical depressive syndromes in varying definitions. *European Archives of Psychiatry and Clinical Neuroscience, 256*, 44–54. doi:10.1007/s00406-005-0600-z.

Angst, J., Sellaro, R., Stassen, H. H., & Gamma, A. (2005). Diagnostic conversion from depression to bipolar disorders: Results of a long-term prospective study of hospital admissions. *Journal of Affective Disorders, 84*, 149–157. doi:1016/S0165-0327(03)00195-2.

Angst, J., Stassen, H. H., Clayton, P. J., & Angst, J. (2002). Mortality of patients with mood disorders: Follow-up over 34–38 years. *Journal of Affective Disorders, 68*, 167–181. doi:10.1016/S0165-0327(01)00377-9.

Arnold, L. E., Demeter, C., Mount, K., Frazier, T. W., Youngstrom, E. A., Fristad, M., et al. (2011). Pediatric bipolar spectrum disorder and ADHD: Comparison and comorbidity in the LAMS clinical sample. *Bipolar Disorders, 13*, 509–521. doi:10.1111/j.1399-5618.2011.00948.x.

Assion, H.-J., Brune, N., Schmidt, N., Aubel, T., Edel, M.-A., Basilowski, M., et al. (2009). Trauma exposure and post-traumatic stress disorder in bipolar disorder. *Social Psychiatry and Psychiatric Epidemiology, 44*, 1041–1049. doi:10.1007/s00127-009-0029-1.

Axelson, D. A., Birmaher, B., Strober, M. A., Goldstein, B. I., Ha, W., Gill, M. K., et al. (2011). Course of subthreshold bipolar disorder in youth: Diagnostic progression from bipolar disorders not otherwise specified. *Journal of the American Academy of Child and Adolescent Psychiatry, 50*, 1001–1016. doi:10.1016/j.jaac.2011.07.005.

Axelson, D. A., Birmaher, B., Strober, M., Gill, M. K., Valeri, S., Chiapetta, L., et al. (2006). Phenomenology of children and adolescents with bipolar spectrum disorders. *Archives of General Psychiatry, 63*, 1139–1148. doi:10.1001/archpsych.63.10.1139.

Balázs, J., Benazzi, F., Rihmer, Z., Rihmer, A., Akiskal, K. K., & Akiskal, H. S. (2006). The close link between suicide attempts and mixed (bipolar) depression: Implications for suicide prevention. *Journal of Affective Disorders, 91*, 133–138. doi:10.1016/j.jad.2005.12.049.

Bauer, M. S., Kirk, G. F., Gavin, C., & Williford, W. O. (2001). Determinants of functional outcome and healthcare costs in bipolar disorder: A high-intensity follow-up study. *Journal of Affective Disorders, 65*, 231–245. doi:10.1016/S0165-0327(00)00247-0.

Bearden, C. E., Glahn, D. C., Caetano, S., Olvera, R. L., Fonseca, M., Najt, P., et al. (2007). Evidence for distruption in prefrontal cortical functions in juvenile bipolar disorder. *Bipolar Disorders, 9*, 145–159. doi:10.1111/j.1399-5618.2007.00453.x.

Bella, T., Goldstein, T., Axelson, D., Obreja, M., Monk, K., Hickey, M. B., et al. (2011). Psychosocial functioning in offspring of parents with bipolar disorder. *Journal of Affective Disorders, 133*, 204–211. doi:10.1016/j.jad.2011.03.022.

Benazzi, F. (2007). Challenging DSM-IV criteria for hypomania: Diagnosing based on number of no-priority symptoms. *European Psychiatry, 22*, 99–103. doi:10.1016/j.eurpsy.2006.06.003.

Benes, F. M., & Berretta, S. (2001). GABAergic interneurons: Implications for understanding schizophrenia and bipolar disorder. *Neuropsychopharmacology, 25*, 1–27. doi:10.1016/S0893-133X(01)00225-1.

Bentall, R. P., Myin-Germeys, I., Smith, A., Knowles, R., Jones, S. H., Smith, T., et al. (2011). Hypomanic personality, stability of self-esteem and response styles to negative mood. *Clinical Psychology & Psychotherapy, 18*, 397–410. doi:10.1002/cpp.780.

Bhangoo, R. K., Dell, M. L., Towbin, K. E., Myers, F. S., Lowe, C. H., Pine, D. S., et al. (2003). Clinical correlates of episodicity in juvenile mania. *Journal of Child and Adolescent Psychopharmacology, 13*, 507–514. doi:10.1089/104454603322724896.

Biederman, J., Faraone, S., Chu, M. P., & Wozniak, J. (1999). Further evidence of a bidirectional overlap between juvenile mania and conduct disorder in children. *Journal of the American Academy of Child and Adolescent Psychiatry, 38*, 468–476. doi:10.1097/00004583-199904000-00021.

Biederman, J., Faraone, S., Mick, E., Wozniak, J., Chen, L., Ouellette, C., et al. (1996). Attention-deficit hyperactivity disorder and juvenile mania: An overlooked comorbidity? *Journal of the American Academy of Child and Adolescent Psychiatry, 35*, 997–1008. doi:10.1097/00004583-199608000-00010.

Biederman, J., Faraone, S., Wozniak, J., Mick, E., Kwon, A., Cayton, G. A., et al. (2005). Clinical correlates of bipolar disorder in a large, referred sample of children and adolescents. *Journal of Psychiatric Research, 39*, 611–622. doi:10.1016/j.jpsychires.2004.08.003.

Biederman, J., Kwon, A., Wozniak, J., Mick, E., Markowitz, S., Fazio, V., et al. (2004). Absence of gender differences in pediatric bipolar disorder: Findings from a large sample of referred youth. *Journal of Affective Disorders, 83*, 207–214. doi:10.1016/j.jad.2004.08.005.

Biederman, J., Petty, C. R., Byrne, D., Wong, P., Wozniak, J., & Faraone, S. V. (2009). Risk for switch from unipolar to bipolar disorder in youth with ADHD: A long term prospective controlled study. *Journal of Affective Disorders, 119*, 16–21. doi:10.1016/j.jad.2009.02.024.

Birmaher, B., Arbelaez, C., & Brent, D. (2002). Course and outcome of child and adolescent major depressive disorder. *Child and Adolescent Psychiatric Clinics of North America, 11*, 619–638. doi:10.1016/S1056-4993(02)00011-1.

Birmaher, B., Axelson, D., Goldstein, B., Strober, M., Gill, M. K., Hunt, J., et al. (2009). Four-year longitudinal course of children and adolescents with bipolar spectrum disorders: The course and outcome of bipolar youth (COBY) study. *The American Journal of Psychiatry, 166*, 795–804. doi:10.1176/appi.ajp.2009.08101569.

Birmaher, B., Axelson, D., Strober, M., Gill, M. K., Valeri, S., Chiapetta, L., et al. (2006). Clinical course of children and adolescents with bipolar spectrum disorders. *Archives of General Psychiatry, 63*, 175–183. doi:10.1001/archpsyc.63.2.175.

Birmaher, B., Axelson, D., Strober, M., Gill, M. K., Yang, M., Ryan, N., et al. (2009). Comparison of manic and depressive symptoms between children and adolescents with bipolar spectrum disorders. *Bipolar Disorders, 11*, 52–62. doi:10.1111/j.1399-5618.2008.00659.x.

Blader, J. C. (2011). Acute inpatient care for psychiatric disorders in the United States, 1996 through 2007. *Archives of General Psychiatry, 68*, 1276–1283. doi:10.1001/archgenpsychiatry.2011.84.

Blader, J. C., & Carlson, G. A. (2007). Increased rate of bipolar diagnoses among U. S. child, adolescent, and adult inpatients, 1996–2004. *Biological Psychiatry, 62*, 107–114. doi:10.1016/j.biopsych.2006.11.006.

Boomsma, D. I., Rebollo, I., Derks, E. M., van Beijsterveldt, T. C. E. M., Althoff, R. R., Rettew, D. C., et al. (2006). Longitudinal stability of the CBCL-juvenile bipolar disorder phenotype: A study of Dutch twins. *Biological Psychiatry, 60*, 912–920. doi:10.1016/j.biopsych.2006.02.028.

Braaten, E. (2007). *The child clinician's report-writing handbook*. New York, NY: Guilford Press.

Brieger, P., Röttig, S., Röttig, D., Marneros, A., & Priebe, S. (2007). Dimensions underlying outcome criteria in bipolar I disorder. *Journal of Affective Disorders, 99*, 1–7. doi:10.1016/j.jad.2006.08.012.

Bressert, S. (2007, February 23). *The causes of bipolar disorder (manic depression)*. Retrieved April 11, 2009, from http://psychcentral.com/lib/2007/the-causes-of-bipolar-disorder-manic-depression/

Brock, S. E., Jimerson, S. R., & Hansen, R. (2009). *Identifying, assessing, and treating ADHD at school*. New York: Springer.

Brock, S. E., Jimerson, S. R., & Hansen, R. L. (2006). *Identifying, assessing, and treating autism at school*. New York: Springer.

Brock, S. E., Sandoval, J., & Hart, S. (2006). Suicidal ideation and behaviors. In G. Bear & K. Minke (Eds.), *Children's needs III: Understanding and addressing the developmental needs of children*. Bethesda, MD: National Association of School Psychologists.

Carlat, D. J. (1998). The psychiatric review of symptoms: A screening tool for family physicians. *American Family Physician, 58*, 1617–1624. Retrieved from http://www.aafp.org/.

Carlson, G. A., & Glovinsky, I. (2009). The concept of bipolar disorder in children: A history of the bipolar controversy. *Child and Adolescent Psychiatric Clinics of North America, 18*, 257–271. doi:10.1016/j.chc.2008.11.003.

Carlson, G., & Kelly, K. (1998). Manic symptoms in psychiatrically hospitalized children—What do they mean? *Journal of Affective Disorders, 51*, 123–135. doi:10.1016/S0165-0327(98)00211-0.

Carter, A. S., & Briggs-Gowan, M. J. (2000). *Manual of the Infant-Toddler Social-Emotional Assessment*. New Haven, CT: Yale University Press.

Carter, A. S., Briggs-Gowan, M. J., & Davis, N. O. (2004). Assessment of young children's social-emotional development and psychopathology: Recent advances and recommendations for practice. *Journal of Child Psychology and Psychiatry, 45*, 109–134. doi:10.1046/j.0021-9630.2003.00316.x.

Carter, T. D. C., Mundo, E., Parikh, S. V., & Kennedy, J. L. (2003). Early age at onset as a risk factor for poor outcome of bipolar disorder. *Journal of Psychiatric Research, 37*, 297–303. doi:10.1016/S0022-3956(03)00052-9.

Chan, J., Stringaris, A., & Ford, T. (2010). Bipolar disorder in children and adolescents recognised in the UK: A clinic-based study. *Child and Adolescent Mental Health, 16*, 71–78. doi:10.1111/j.1475-3588.2010.00566.x.

Chang, K. D. (2008). The use of atypical antipsychotics in pediatric bipolar disorder. *Journal of Clinical Psychiatry, 69*(Suppl. 4), 4–8. www.psychiatrist.com.

Chang, K., Adleman, N., Wagner, C., Barnea-Goraly, N., & Garrett, A. (2006). Will neuroimaging ever be used to diagnose pediatric bipolar disorder? *Development and Psychopathology, 18*, 1133–1146. doi:10.1017/S09545794060548.

Chang, K. D., Steiner, H., & Ketter, T. A. (2000). Psychiatric phenomenology of child and adolescent bipolar offspring. *Journal of the American Academy of Child and Adolescent Psychiatry, 39*(4), 453–460. doi:10.1097/00004583-200004000-00014.

Chou, J. C.-Y. (2004). Review and update of the American Psychiatric Association practice guideline for bipolar disorder. *Primary Psychiatry, 11*(9), 73–84. www.primarypsychiatry.com.

Coletti, D. J., Leigh, E., Galleli, K. A., & Kafantaris, V. (2005). Patterns of adherence to treatment in adolescents with bipolar disorder. *Journal of Child and Adolescent Psychopharmacology, 15*, 913–917. doi:10.1089/cap.2005.15.913.

Colom, F., Vieta, E., Martinez-Arán, A., Reinares, M., Goikolea, J. M., Benabarre, A., et al. (2003). A randomized trial on the efficacy of group psychoeducation in the prophylaxis of recurrences in bipolar patients whose disease is in remission. *Archives of General Psychiatry, 60*, 402–407. doi:10.1001/archpsyc.60.4.402.

Consoli, A., Deniau, E., Huynh, C., Purper, D., & Cohen, D. (2007). Treatments in child and adolescent bipolar disorder. *European Child & Adolescent Psychiatry, 16*, 187–198. doi:10.1007/s00787-006-0587-7.

Conus, P., Cotton, S., Schimmelmann, B. G., Berk, M., Daglas, R., McGorry, P. D., et al. (2010). Pretreatment and outcome correlates of past sexual and physical trauma in 118 bipolar I disorder patients with a first episode of psychotic mania. *Bipolar Disorders, 12*, 244–252. doi:10.1111/j.1399-5618.2010.00813.x.

Correll, C. U. (2008). Weight gain and metabolic abnormalities in pediatric bipolar disorder. In B. Geller & M. P. DelBello (Eds.), *Treatment of bipolar disorder in children and adolescents* (pp. 361–391). New York, NY: Guilford Press.

Coryell, W., Solomon, D., Turvey, C., Keller, M., Leon, A. C., Endicott, J., et al. (2003). The long-term course of rapid-cycling bipolar disorder. *Archives of General Psychiatry, 60*, 914–920. doi:10.1001/archpsyc.60.9.914.

Cotter, D., Landau, S., Beasley, C., Stevenson, R., Chana, G., & MacMillan, L. (2002). The density and spatial distribution of GABAergic neurons, labeled using calcium binding proteins, in the anterior cingulate cortex in major depressive disorder, bipolar disorder, and schizophrenia. *Biological Psychiatry, 51*, 377–386. doi:10.1016/S0006-3223(01)01243-4.

Craddock, N., O'Donovan, M. C., Owen, M. J. (2005). The genetics of schizophrenia and bipolar disorder: Dissecting psychosis. *Journal of Medical Genetics, 42*, 193–204. doi:10.1136/jmg.2005.030718.

Crick, N. R., & Dodge, K. A. (1994). A review and reformulation of social information-processing mechanisms in children's social adjustment. *Psychological Bulletin, 115*, 74–101. doi:10.1037/0033-2909.115.1.74.

Culver, J. L., Arnow, B. A., & Ketter, T. A. (2007). Bipolar disorder: Improving diagnosis and optimizing integrated care. *Journal of Clinical Psychology, 63*, 73–92. doi:10.1002/jclp.20333.

Danielyan, A., Pathak, S., Kowatch, R. A., Arszman, S. P., & Johns, E. S. (2007). Clinical characteristics of bipolar disorder in very young children. *Journal of Affective Disorders, 97*, 51–59. doi:10.1016/j.jad.2006.05.028.

Davis, R. E. (1979). Manic-depressive variant syndrome of childhood: A preliminary report. *American Journal of Psychiatry, 136*, 702–706. http://ajp.psychiatryonline.org/journal.aspx?journalid=13.

DelBello, M. P., Schwiers, M. L., Rosenberg, H. L., & Strakowski, S. M. (2002). A double-blind, placebo-controlled study of quetiapine as adjunctive treatment for adolescent mania. *Journal of the American Academy of Child and Adolescent Psychiatry, 41*, 1216–1223. doi:10.1097/00004583-200210000-00011.

DelBello, M., Soutullo, C., Hendricks, W., Niemeier, R., McElroy, S., & Strakowski, S. (2001). Prior stimulant treatment in adolescents with bipolar disorder: Association with age at onset. *Bipolar Disorders, 3*, 53–57. doi:10.1034/j.1399-5618.2001.030201.x.

Deveney, C. M., Brotman, M. A., Decker, A. M., Pine, D. S., & Leibenluft, E. (2012). Affective prosody labeling in youths with bipolar disorder or severe mood dysregulation. *Journal of Child Psychology and Psychiatry, 53*, 262–270. doi:10.1111/j.1469-7610.2011.02482.x.

Diflorio, A., & Jones, I. (2010). Is sex important? Gender differences in bipolar disorder. *International Review of Psychiatry, 22*, 437–452. doi:10.3109/09540261.2010.514601.

Diler, R. S., Uguz, S., Seydaoglu, G., Erol, N., & Avci, A. (2007). Differentiating bipolar disorder in Turkish prepubertal children with attention-deficit hyperactivity disorder. *Bipolar Disorders, 9*, 243–251. doi:10.1111/j.1399-5618.2007.00347.x.

Doran, C. M. (2008). *The hypomania handbook: The challenge of elevated mood*. Philadelphia, PA: Lippincott Williams & Wilkins.

Drotar, D., Greenley, R. N., Demeter, C. A., McNamara, N. K., Stansbrey, R. J., Calabrese, J. R., et al. (2007). Adherence to pharmacological treatment for juvenile bipolar disorder. *Journal of the American Academy of Child and Adolescent Psychiatry, 46*, 831–839. doi:10.1097/chi.0b013e31805c7421.

DSM-5 Childhood and Adolescent Disorders Work Group (2010). *Justification for Temper Dysregulation Disorder with Dysphoria*. Retrieved from www.dsm5.org

DSM-5 Mood Disorders and Childhood and Adolescent Disorders Work Groups (2010). *Issues pertinent to a developmental approach to bipolar disorder in DSM-5*. Retrieved from www.dsm5.org

DSM-5 Mood Disorders Work Group (2012). *Proposal to eliminate bereavement exclusion criteria from major depressive episode in DSM-5*. Retrieved from www.dsm5.org

Duax, J. M., Youngstrom, E. A., Calabrese, J. R., & Findling, R. L. (2007). Sex differences in pediatric bipolar disorder. *The Journal of Clinical Psychiatry, 68*, 1565–1573. doi:10.4088/JCP.v68n1016.

Duffy, A., Alda, M., Hajek, T., Sherry, S. B., & Grof, P. (2010). Early stages in the development of bipolar disorder. *Journal of Affective Disorders, 121*, 127–135. doi:10.1016/j.jad.2009.05.022.

Duffy, F. F., Narrow, W. E., Rae, D. S., West, J. C., Zarin, D. A., Rubio-Stipec, M., et al. (2005). Concomitant pharmacotherapy among youths treated in routine psychiatric practice. *Journal of Child and Adolescent Psychopharmacology, 15*, 12–25. doi:10.1089/cap.2005.15.12.

Eckblad, M., & Chapman, L. J. (1986). Development and validation of a scale for hypomanic personality. *Journal of Abnormal Psychology, 95*, 214–222. doi:10.1037/0021-843X.95.3.214.

Emilien, G., Septien, L., Brisard, C., Corruble, E., & Bourin, M. (2007). Bipolar disorder: How far are we from a rigorous definition and effective management? *Progress in Neuro-Psychopharmacology & Biological Psychiatry, 31*, 975–996. doi:10.1016/j.pnpbp.2007.03.005.

Esposito-Smythers, C., Birmaher, B., Valeri, S., Chiapetti, L., Hunt, J., Ryan, N., et al. (2006). Child co-morbidity, maternal mood disorder, and perceptions of family functioning among bipolar youth. *Journal of the American Academy of Child and Adolescent Psychiatry, 45*, 955–964. doi:10.1097/01.chi.0000222785.11359.04.

Evans-Lacko, S. E., Zeber, J. E., Gonzalez, J. M., & Olvera, R. L. (2009). Medical comorbidity among youth diagnosed with bipolar disorder in the United States. *The Journal of Clinical Psychiatry, 70*, 1461–1466. doi:10.4088/JCP.08m04871.

Eyberg, S. M., & Ross, A. W. (1978). Assessment of child behavior problems: The validation of a new inventory. *Journal of Clinical Child Psychology, 7*, 113–116. doi:10.1080/15374417809532835.

Faedda, G. L., Baldessarini, R. J., Glovinsky, I. P., & Austin, N. B. (2004). Pediatric bipolar disorder: Phenomenology and course of illness. *Bipolar Disorders, 6*, 305–313. doi:10.1111/j.1399-5618.2004.00128.x.

Faraone, S. V., Althoff, R. R., Hudziak, J. J., Monuteaux, M., & Biederman, J. (2005). The CBCL predicts DSM bipolar disorder in children: A receiver operating characteristic curve analysis. *Bipolar Disorders, 7*, 518–524. doi:10.1111/j.1399-5618.2005.00271.x.

Faraone, S. V., Glatt, S. J., Su, J., & Tsuang, M. T. (2004). Three potential susceptibility loci shown by a genome-wide scan for regions influencing the age at onset of mania. *The American Journal of Psychiatry, 161*, 625–630. doi:10.1176/appi.ajp.161.4.625.

Fatemi, S. H., Stary, J. M., Earle, J. A., Araghi-Niknam, M., & Eagan, E. (2005). GABAergic dysfunction in schizophrenia and mood disorders as reflected by decreased levels of glutamic acid decarboxylase 65 and 67 kDa and Reelin proteins in cerebellum. *Schizophrenia Research, 72*, 109–122. doi:10.1016/j.schres.2004.02.017.

Faust, E. S., Walker, D., & Sands, M. (2006). Diagnosis and management of childhood bipolar disorder in the primary care setting. *Clinical Pediatrics, 45*, 801–808. doi:10.1177/0009922806295279.

Findling, R. L., Frazier, J. A., Kafantaris, V., Kowatch, R., McClellan, J., Pavuluri, M., et al. (2008). The collaborative lithium trials (CoLT): Specific aims, methods, and implementation. *Child and Adolescent Psychiatry and Mental Health, 2*, 21–34. doi:10.1186/1753-2000-2-21.

Findling, R. L., & Pavuluri, M. N. (2008). Lithium. In B. Geller & M. P. DelBello (Eds.), *Treatment of bipolar disorder in children and adolescents* (pp. 43–68). New York: Guilford.

Food and Drug Administration (2007a). FDA proposes new warnings about suicidal thinking, behavior in young adults who take antidepressant medications. *FDA News*. Retrieved from http://www.fda.gov/bbs/topics/NEWS/2007/NEW01624.html

Food and Drug Administration (2007b). *Revisions to product labeling*. Retrieved from http://www.fda.gov/cder/drug/antidepressants/antidepressants_label_change_2007.pdf

Frank, E. (2005). *Treating bipolar disorder: A clinician's guide to interpersonal and social rhythm therapy*. New York, NY: Guilford Press.

Frank, E., Kupfer, D. J., Thase, M. E., Mallinger, A. G., Swartz, H. A., Faiolini, A. M., et al. (2005). Two-year outcomes for interpersonal and social rhythm therapy in individuals with bipolar I disorder. *Archives of General Psychiatry, 62*, 996–1004. doi:10.1001/archpsyc.62.9.996.

Freeman, A. J., Youngstrom, E. A., Frazier, T. W., Youngstrom, J. K., Demeter, C., & Findling, R. L. (2011). Portability of a screener for pediatric bipolar disorder to a diverse setting. *Psychological Assessment, 24*, 341–351. doi:10.1037/s0025617.

Freeman, A. J., Youngstrom, E. A., Michalak, E., Siegel, R., Meyers, O. I., & Findling, R. L. (2009). Quality of life in pediatric bipolar disorder. *Pediatrics, 123*, e446–e452. doi:10.1542/peds.2008-0841.

Frazier, J. A., Bregman, H. R., & Jackson, J. A. (2008). Atypical antipsychotics in the treatment of early-onset bipolar disorder. In B. Geller & M. P. DelBello (Eds.), *Treatment of bipolar disorder in children and adolescents* (pp. 69–108). New York, NY: Guilford Press.

Fristad, M. A., Davidson, K. H., & Leffler, J. M. (2007). Thinking-feeling-doing: A therapeutic technique for children with bipolar disorder and their parents. *Journal of Family Psychotherapy, 18*, 81–103. doi:10.1300/J085v18n04_06.

Fristad, M. A., Verducci, J. S., Walters, K., & Young, M. E. (2009). Impact of multifamily psychoeducational psychotherapy in treating children aged 8 to 12 years with mood disorders. *Archives of General Psychiatry, 66*, 1013–1020. doi:10.1001/archgenpsychiatry.2009.112.

Galanter, C. A., & Leibenluft, E. (2008). Frontiers between attention deficit hyperactivity and bipolar disorder. *Child and Adolescent Psychiatric Clinics of North America, 17*, 325–346. doi:10.1016/j.chc.2007.11.001.

Geller, B., Bolhofner, K., Craney, J. L., Williams, M., DelBello, M. P., & Gundersen, K. (2000). Psychosocial functioning in a prepubertal and early adolescent bipolar disorder phenotype. *Journal of the American Academy of Child and Adolescent Psychiatry, 39*(12), 1543–1548. doi:10.1097/00004583-200012000-00018.

Geller, B., Craney, J. L., Bolhofner, K., Nickelsburg, M. J., Williams, M., & Zimerman, B. (2002). Two-year prospective follow-up children with a prepubertal and early adolescent bipolar disorder phenotype. *The American Journal of Psychiatry, 159*, 927–933. doi:10.1176/appi.ajp.159.6.927.

Geller, B., Tillman, R., & Bolhofner, K. (2007). Proposed definitions of bipolar I disorder episodes and daily rapid cycling phenomena in preschoolers, school-aged children, adolescents, and adults. *Journal of Child and Adolescent Psychopharmacology, 17*, 217–222. doi:10.1089/cap.2007.0017.

Geller, B., Williams, M., Zimerman, B., Frazier, J., Beringer, L., & Warner, K. L. (1998). Prepubertal and early adolescent bipolarity differentiate from ADHD by manic symptoms, grandiose delusions, ultra-rapid or ultradian cycling. *Journal of Affective Disorders, 51*, 81–91. doi:10.1016/S0165-0327(98)00175-X.

Geller, B., Zimerman, B., Williams, M., Bolhofner, K., Craney, J. L., DelBello, M., et al. (2001). Reliability of the Washington University in St Louis Kiddi Schedule for Affective Disorders and Schizophrenia (WASH-U-KSADS) mania and rapid cycling sections. *Journal of the American Academy of Child and Adolescent Psychiatry, 40*, 450–455. doi:10.1097/00004583-200104000-00014.

Ghaemi, S. N., Ko, J. Y., & Goodwin, F. K. (2001). The bipolar spectrum and the antidepressant view of the world. *Journal of Psychiatric Practice*, 287–297. doi:10.1097/00131746-200109000-00002

Ghaziuddin, N., Kutcher, S. P., Knapp, P., Bernet, W., Arnold, V., Beitchman, J., et al. (2004). Practice parameter for use of electroconvulsive therapy with adolescents. *Journal of the American Academy of Child and Adolescent Psychiatry, 43*, 1521–15399. doi:10.1097/01.chi.0000142280.87429.68.

Gibbons, R. D., Brown, C. H., Hur, K., Marcus, S. M., Bhaumik, D. K., Erkens, J. A., et al. (2007). Early evidence on the effects of regulators' suicidality warnings on SSRI prescriptions and suicide in children and adolescents. *The American Journal of Psychiatry, 164*, 1356–1363. doi:10.1176/appi.ajp.2007.07030454.

Gilcher, D., Field, R., & Hellander, M. (2004). The IDEA classification debate: ED or OHI? *CABF e Bulletin.* Retrieved from http://www.bpkids.org/site/DocServer/field_idea_classification.pdf?docID=169

Glahn, D. C., Bearden, C. E., Bowden, C. L., & Soares, J. C. (2006). Reduced educational attainment in bipolar disorder. *Journal of Affective Disorders, 92*, 309–312.

Goetz, I., Tohen, M., Reed, C., Lorenzo, M., & Vieta, E. (2007). Functional impairment in patients with mania: Baseline results of the EMBLEM study. *Bipolar Disorders, 9*, 45–52. doi:10.1111/j.1399-5618.2007.00325.x.

Gogtay, N., Ordonez, A., Herman, D. H., Hayashi, K. M., Greenstein, D., Vaituzis, C., et al. (2007). Dynamic mapping of cortical development before and after the onset of pediatric bipolar illness. *Journal of Child Psychology and Psychiatry, 48*, 852–862. doi:10.1111/j.1469-7610.2007.01747.x.

Goldberg, J. F., & Ernst, C. L. (2004). Clinical correlates of childhood and adolescent adjustment in adult patients with bipolar disorder. *The Journal of Nervous and Mental Disease, 192*, 187–192. doi:10.1097/01.nmd.0000116461.53411.ab.

Goldberg, J. F., Perlis, R. H., Ghaemi, S. N., Calabrese, J. R., Bowden, C. L., Wisniewski, S., et al. (2007). Adjunctive antipressant use and symptomatic recovery among bipolar depressed patients with concomitant manic symptoms: Findings from the STEP-BD. *The American Journal of Psychiatry, 164*, 1348–1355. doi:10.1176/appi.ajp.2007.05122032.

Goldstein, B. I. (2012). Recent progress in understanding pediatric bipolar disorder. *Archives of Pediatrics & Adolescent Medicine, 166*, 362–371. doi:10.1001/archpediatrics.2011.832.

Goldstein, B. I., & Bukstein, O. G. (2010). Comorbid substance use disorders among youth with bipolar disorder: Opportunities for early identification and prevention. *The Journal of Clinical Psychiatry, 71*, 348–358. doi:10.4088/JCP.09r05222gry.

Goldstein, B. I., Strober, M. A., Birmaher, B., Axelson, D. A., Esposito-Smythers, C., Goldstein, T. R., et al. (2008). Substance use disorders among adolescents with bipolar spectrum disorders. *Bipolar Disorders, 10*, 469–478. doi:10.1111/j.1399-5618.2008.00584.x.

Goldstein, T. R. (2009). Suicidality in pediatric bipolar disorder. *Child and Adolescent Psychiatric Clinics of North America, 18*, 339–352. doi:10.1016/j.chc.2008.11.005.

Goldstein, T. R., Axelson, D. A., Birmaher, B., & Brent, D. A. (2007). Dialectical behavior therapy for adolescents with bipolar disorder: A 1-year open trial. *Journal of the American Academy of Child and Adolescent Psychiatry, 46*, 820–830. 10.1097.chi.0b013e31805c1613.

Goldstein, T. R., Birmaher, B., Axelson, D., Goldstein, B. I., Gill, M. K., Esposito-Smythers, C., et al. (2009). Psychosocial functioning among bipolar youth. *Journal of Affective Disorders, 114*, 174–183. doi:10.1016/j.jad.2008.07.001.

Goldstein, T. R., Birmaher, B., Axelson, D., Ryan, N. D., Strober, M. A., Gill, M. K., et al. (2005). History of suicide attempts in pediatric bipolar disorder: Factors associated with increased risk. *Bipolar Disorders, 7*, 525–535. 1111/j.1399-5618.2005.00263.x.

Goldstein, T. R., Miklowitz, D. J., & Mullen, K. L. (2006). Social skills knowledge and performance among adolescents with bipolar disorders. *Bipolar Disorders, 8*, 350–361. doi:10.1111/j.1399-5618.2006.00321.x.

Gottesman, I. I., Laursen, T. M., Bertelsen, A., & Mortensen, P. B. (2010). Severe mental disorders in offspring with 2 psychiatrically ill parents. *Archives of General Psychiatry, 67*, 252–257. doi:10.1001/archgenpsychiatry.2010.1.

Gracious, B. L., Chirieac, M. C., Costescu, S., Finucane, T. L., Youngstrom, E. A., & Hibbeln, J. R. (2010). Randomized, placebo-controlled trial of flax oil in pediatric bipolar disorder. *Bipolar Disorders, 12*, 142–154. doi:10.1111/j.1399-5618.2010.00799.x.

Greene, R. W., & Doyle, A. E. (1999). Toward a transactional conceptualization of oppositional defiant disorder: Implications for assessment and treatment. *Clinical Child and Family Psychology Review, 2*, 129–148. doi:10.1023/A:1021850921476.

Greenwood, T. A., Alexander, M., Keck, P. E., McElroy, S., Sadovnick, A. D., Remick, R. A., & Kelsoe, J. R. (2001). Evidence for linkage disequilibrium between the dopamine transporter and bipolar disorder. *American Journal of Medical Genetics, 105*, 145–151. doi:10.1002/1096-8628.

Gresham, F. (2007). Response to intervention and emotional and behavioral disorders: Best practices in assessment for intervention. *Assessment for Effective Intervention, 32*, 214–222. doi:10.1177/15345084070320040301.

Grisso, T. (2008). Adolescent offenders with mental disorders. *The Future of Children, 18*, 143–162. 10.1353.foc.0.0016.

Guyer, A. E., McClure, E. B., Adler, A. D., Brotman, M. A., Rich, B. A., Kimes, A. S., et al. (2007). Specificity of facial expression labeling deficits in childhood psychopathology. *Journal of Child Psychology and Psychiatry, 48*, 863–871. doi:10.1111/j.1469-7610.2007.01758.x.

Hamrin, V., & Iennaco, J. D. (2010). Psychopharmacology of pediatric bipolar disorder. *Expert Reviews of Neurotherapy, 10*, 1053–1088. 10.1586.ERN.10.86.

Harpaz-Rotem, I., Leslie, D. L., Martin, A., & Rosenheck, R. A. (2005). Changes in child and adolescent inpatient psychiatric admission diagnoses between 1995 and 2000. *Social Psychiatry and Psychiatric Epidemiology, 40*, 642–647. doi:10.1007/s00127-005-0923-0.

Harpaz-Rotem, I., & Rosenheck, R. A. (2004). Changes in outpatient psychiatric diagnosis in privately insured children and adolescents from 1995 to 2000. *Child Psychiatry and Human Development, 34*(4), 329–340. doi:10.1023/B:CHUD.0000020683.08514.2d.

Hauser, M., Pfennig, A., Özgürdal, S., Heinz, A., Bauer, M., & Juckel, G. (2007). Early recognition of bipolar disorder. *European Psychiatry, 22*, 92–98. doi:10.1016/j.eurpsy.2006.08.003.

Hayden, E. P., & Nurnberger, J. I. (2006). Molecular genetics of bipolar disorder. *Genes, Brain, and Behavior, 5*, 85–95. doi:10.1111/j.1601-183X.2005.00138.x.

Henin, A., Beiderman, J., Mick, E., Hirshfeld-Becker, D. R., Sachs, G. S., Wu, Y., et al. (2007). Childhood antecedent disorders to bipolar disorder in adults: A controlled study. *Journal of Affective Disorders, 99*, 51–57. doi:10.1016/j.jad.2006.09.001.

Henin, A., Mick, E., Biederman, J., Faraone, S. V., Fried, R., Wozniak, J., et al. (2007). Can bipolar disorder-specific neuropsychological impairments in children be identified? *Journal of Consulting and Clinical Psychology, 75*, 210–220. doi:10.1037/0022-006X.75.2.210.

Henry, D. B., Pavuluri, M. N., Youngstrom, E., Birmaher, B. (2008). Accuracy of brief and full forms of the Child Mania Rating Scale. *Journal of Clinical Psychology, 64*, 368–381. doi:10.1002/jclp.20464.

Hirschfeld, R. M. A., Williams, J. B. W., Spitzer, R. L., Calabrese, J. R., Flynn, L., Keck, P. E., ... Zajecka, J. (2000). Development and validation of a screening instrument for bipolar spectrum disorder: The Mood Disorder Questionnaire. *American Journal of Psychiatry, 157*, 1873–1875. doi:10.1176/appi.ajp.157.11.1873.

Hirschfeld, R. M., Lewis, L., & Vornik, L. A. (2003). Perceptions and impact of bipolar disorder: How far have we really come? Results of the National Depressive and Manic-Depressive Association 2000 survey of individuals with bipolar disorder. *The Journal of Clinical Psychiatry, 64*, 161–174. doi:10.4088/JCP.v64n0209.

Hirschfeld, R. M. A., Holzer, C., Calabrese, J. R., Weissman, M., Reed, M., Davies, M., ... Hazard, E. (2003). Validity of the Mood Disorder Questionnaire: A general population study. *American Journal of Psychiatry, 160*, 178–180. doi:10.1176/appi.ajp.160.1.178.

Hlastala, S. A., Kotler, J. S., McClellan, J. M., & McCauley, E. A. (2010). Interpersonal and social rhythm therapy for adolescents with bipolar disorder: Treatment development and results from an open trial. *Depression and Anxiety, 27*, 457–464. doi:10.1002/da.20668.

Holtmann, M., Bölte, S., Goth, K., Döpfner, M., Plück, J., Huss, M., et al. (2007). Prevalence of the CBCL-pediatric bipolar disorder phenotype in a German general population sample. *Bipolar Disorders, 9*, 895–900. doi:10.1111/j.1399-5618.2007.00463.x.

Horn, K., Roessner, V., & Holtmann, M. (2011). Neurocognitive performance in children and adolescents with bipolar disorder: A review. *European Child & Adolescent Psychiatry, 20*, 433–450. doi:10.1007/s00787-011-0209-x.

Houston, J. E., Shevlin, M., Adamson, G., & Murphy, J. (2011). A person-centred approach to modelling population experiences of trauma and mental illness. *Social Psychiatry and Psychiatric Epidemiology, 46*, 149–157. doi:10.1007/s00127-009-0176-4.

Hua, L. L., Wilens, T. E., Martelon, M., Wong, P., Wozniak, J., & Biederman, J. (2010). Psychosocial functioning, familiarity, and psychiatric comorbidity in bipolar youth with and without psychotic features. *The Journal of Clinical Psychiatry, 72*, 397–405. doi:10.4088/JCP.10m06025yel.

Hughes, C. W., Emslie, G. J., Wohlfahrt, H., Winslow, R., Kashner, R. M., & Rush, A. J. (2005). Effect of structured interviews on evaluation time in pediatric community mental health settings. *Psychiatric Services, 56*, 1098–1103. doi:10.1176/appi.ps.56.9.1098.

Huxley, N., & Baldessarini, R. J. (2007). Disability and its treatment in bipolar disorder patients. *Bipolar Disorders, 9*, 183–196. doi:10.1111/j.1399-5618.2007.00430.x.

Individuals with Disabilities Education Improvement Act. (2004). Retrieved from www.ed.gov/about/offices/list/osers/osep/index.html

Jaeger, J., Berns, S., Loftus, S., Gonzalez, C., & Czobor, P. (2007). Neurocognitive test performance predicts functional recovery from acute exacerbation leading to hospitalization in bipolar disorder. *Bipolar Disorders, 9*, 93–102. doi:10.1111/j.1399-5618.2007.00427.x.

Jairam, R., Srinath, S., Girimaji, S. C., & Seshadri, S. P. (2004). A prospective 4–5 year follow-up of juvenile onset bipolar disorder. *Bipolar Disorders, 6*, 386–394. doi:10.1111/j.1399-5618.2004.00149.x.

Jensen, P. S., Buitelaar, J., Pandina, G. J., Binder, C., & Haas, M. (2007). Management of psychiatric disorders in children and adolescents with atypical antipsychotics: A systematic review of published clinical trials. *European Child & Adolescent Psychiatry, 16*, 104–120. doi:10.1007/s00787-006-0580-1.

Jerrell, J. M., McIntyre, R. S., & Tripathi, A. (2010). A cohort study of the prevalence and impact of comorbid medical conditions in pediatric bipolar disorder. *The Journal of Clinical Psychiatry, 71*, 1518–1525. doi:10.4088/JCP.09m05585ora.

Jerrell, J. M., McIntyre, R. S., & Tripathi, A. (2011). Childhood treatment with psychotropic medication and development of comorbid medical conditions in adolescent-onset bipolar disorder. *Human Psychopharmacology: Clinical and Experimental, 26*, 451–459. doi:10.1002/hup.1227.

Jerrell, J. M., & Prewette, E. D. (2008). Outcomes for youths with early- and very-early-onset bipolar I disorder. *The Journal of Behavioral Health Services and Research, 35*, 52–59. doi:10.1007/s11414-007-9081-3.

Jerrell, J. M., & Shugart, M. A. (2004). Community-based care for youths with early and very-early onset bipolar I disorder. *Bipolar Disorders, 6*, 299–304. doi:10.1111/j.1399-5618.2004.00129.x.

Jolin, E. M., Weller, E. B., & Weller, R. A. (2008a). Anxiety symptoms and syndromes in bipolar children and adolescents. *Current Psychiatry Reports, 10*, 123–129. doi:10.1007/s11920-008-0022-5.

Jones, S. H., & Bentall, R. P. (2008). A review of potential cognitive and environmental risk markers in children of bipolar parents. *Clinical Psychology Review, 28*, 1083–1095. doi:10.1016/j.cpr.2008.03.002.

Joseph, M. F., Frazier, T. W., Youngstrom, E. A., & Soares, J. C. (2008). A quantitative and qualitative review of neurocognitive performance in pediatric bipolar disorder. *Journal of Child and Adolescent Psychopharmacology, 18*, 595–605. doi:10.1089/cap.2008.064.

Joshi, G. G., & Wilens, T. (2009). Comorbidity in pediatric bipolar disorder. *Child and Adolescent Psychiatric Clinics of North America, 18*, 291–319. doi:10.1016/j.chc.2008.12.005.

Joshi, P. T., & Robb, A. S. (2008). Polycystic ovary syndrome. In B. Geller & M. P. DelBello (Eds.), *Treatment of bipolar disorder in children and adolescents* (pp. 333–360). New York, NY: Guilford Press.

Judd, L. L., & Akiskal, H. S. (2003). The prevalence and disability of bipolar spectrum disorders in the US population: Re-analysis of the ECA database taking into account subthreshold cases. *Journal of Affective Disorders, 73*, 123–131. doi:10.1016/S0165-0327(02)00332-4.

Judd, L. L., Akiskal, H. S., Schettler, P. J., Coryell, W., Maser, J., Rice, J. A., et al. (2003). The comparative clinical phenotype and long term longitudinal episode course of bipolar I and II: A clinical spectrum or distinct disorders? *Journal of Affective Disorders, 73*, 19–32. doi:10.1016/S0165-0327(02)00324-5.

Judd, L. L., Akiskal, H. S., Schettler, P. J., Endicott, J., Leon, A. C., Solomon, D. A., et al. (2005). Psychosocial disability in the course of bipolar I and II disorders. *Archives of General Psychiatry, 62*, 1322–1330. doi:10.1001/archpsyc.62.12.1322.

Kato, T. (2008). Molecular neurobiology of bipolar disorder: A disease of 'mood-stabilizing nuerons'? *Trends in Neurosciences, 31*, 495–503. doi:10.1016/j.tins.2008.07.007.

Kamphaus, R. W., & Reynolds, C. R. (2007). *The behavioral and emotional screening system.* Autsin, TX: Pearson Assessment.

Kamphaus, R. W., Thorpe, J., Winsor, A. P., Kroncke, A., Dowdy, E., & VanDeventer, M. (2007). Development and predictive validity of a teacher screener for child behavioral and emotional problems at school. *Educational and Psychological Measurement, 67*, 342–356. doi:10.1177/0 0131644070670021001.

Kaufman, J., Birmaher, B., Brent, D., Rao, U., Flynn, C., Moreci, P., et al. (1997). Schedule for Affective Disorders and Schizophrenia for School-Age Children—Present and Lifetime Version (KSADS-PL): Initial reliability and validity data. *Journal of the American Academy of Child and Adolescent Psychiatry, 36*, 980–988. doi:10.1097/00004583-199707000-00021.

Keenan-Miller, D., & Miklowitz, D. J. (2011). Interpersonal functioning in pediatric bipolar disorder. *Clinical Psychology: Science and Practice, 18*, 342–356. doi:10.1111/j.1468-2850.2011.01266.x.

Kempton, M. (2008). *Bipolar disorder neuroimaging database (BiND).* Retrieved June 4, 2008, from http://sites.google.com/site/bipolardatabase/

Kempton, M., Geddes, J. R., Ettinger, U., Williams, S. C. R., & Grasby, P. M. (2008). Meta-analysis, database, and meta-regression of 98 structural imaging studies in bipolar disorder. *Archives of General Psychiatry, 65*, 1017–1032. doi:10.1001/archpsyc.65.9.1017.

Kerner, B., Lambert, C. G., & Muthén, B. O. (2011). Genome-wide association study in bipolar patients stratified by co-morbidity. *PLoS One, 6*, 1–10. doi:10.1371/journal.pone.0028477.

Kessler, R. C., Adler, L., Barkley, R., Biederman, J., Conners, C. K., Demler, O., et al. (2006). The prevalence and correlates of adult ADHD in the United States: Results from the National Comorbidity Survey Replication. *The American Journal of Psychiatry, 163*, 716–723. doi:10.1176/appi.ajp.163.4.716.

Kilbourne, A. M., Cornelius, J. R., Han, X., Pincus, H. A., Shad, M., Salloum, I., et al. (2004). Burden of general medical conditions among individuals with bipolar disorder. *Bipolar Disorders, 6*, 368–373. doi:10.1111/j.1399-5618.2004.00138.x.

Kim, E. Y., & Miklowitz, D. J. (2002). Childhood mania, attention deficit hyperactivity disorder and conduct disorder: A critical review of diagnostic dilemmas. *Bipolar Disorders, 4*, 215–225. doi:10.1034/j.1399-5618.2002.01191.x.

Knowles, S., & Shear, N. H. (2009). Clinical risk management of Stevens-Johnson syndrome/toxic epidermal necrolysis spectrum. *Dermatologic Therapy, 22*, 441–451. doi:10.1111/j.1529-8019.2009.01260.x.

Kovacs, M., Kovacs, M., & Pollack, M. (1995). Bipolar disorder and comorbid conduct disorder in childhood and adolescence. *Journal of the American Academy of Children and Adolescent Psychiatry, 34,* 526–529. www.jaacap.com.

Kowatch, R. A. (2008). Mood stabilizers. In B. Geller & M. P. DelBello (Eds.), *Treatment of bipolar disorder in children and adolescents* (pp. 109–125). New York, NY: Guilford Press.

Kowatch, R. A., Youngstrom, E. A., Danielyan, A., & Findling, R. L. (2005). Review and meta-analysis of the phenomenology and clinical characteristics of mania in children and adolescents. *Bipolar Disorders, 7,* 483–496. doi:10.1111/j.1399-5618.2005.00261.x.

Krishnan, K. R. R. (2005). Psychiatric and medical comorbidities of bipolar disorder. *Psychosomatic Medicine, 67,* 1–8. doi:10.1097/01.psy.0000151489.36347.18.

Kupka, R. W., Luckenbaugh, D. A., Post, R. M., Suppes, T., Altshuler, L. L., Keck, P. E., et al. (2005). Comparison of rapid-cycling and non-rapid-cycling bipolar disorder based on prospective mood ratings in 539 outpatients. *The American Journal of Psychiatry, 162,* 1273–1280. doi:10.1176/appi.ajp.162.7.1273.

Kutcher, S., Robertson, H. A., & Bird, D. (1998). Premorbid functioning in adolescent onset bipolar I disorder: A preliminary report from an ongoing study. *Journal of Affective Disorders, 51,* 137–144. doi:10.1016/S0165-0327(98)00212-2.

Kwapil, T. R., Miller, M. B., Zinser, M. C., Chapman, L. J., Chapman, J., & Eckblad, M. (2000). A longitudinal study of high scorers on the hypomanic personality scale. *Journal of Abnormal Psychology, 109,* 222–226. doi:10.1037/0021-843X.109.2.222.

Labbe, C. (2007, September 1). *Studies refine understanding of treatments for bipolar disorder.* Retrieved from http://www.nimh.nih.gov/press/miklowitz_golbergstep.cfm

Labbe, C. (2007, September 6). *Global survey reveals significant gap in meeting world's mental health care needs.* Retrieved from http://www.nimh.nih.gov/press/wang_globalhealth.cfm

Lacerda, L. T., Keshavan, M. S., Hardan, A. Y., Yorbik, O., Brambilla, P., Sassi, R. B., et al. (2004). Anatomic evaluation of the orbitofrontal cortex in major depressive disorder. *Biological Psychiatry, 55,* 353–358. doi:10.1016/j.biopsych.2003.08.021.

Lachman, H. M., Papolos, D. F., Saito, T., Yu, Y. M., Szumlanski, C. L., & Weinshilboum, R. M. (1996). Human catechol-O-methyltransferase pharmacogenetics: description of a functional polymorphism and its potential application to neuropsychiatric disorders. *Pharmacogenetics, 6,* 243–250. Retrieved from http://journals.lww.com/jpharmacogenetics/pages/default.aspx.

Lagace, D. C., & Kutcher, S. P. (2005). Academic performance of adolescents with bipolar disorder. *Directions in Psychiatry, 25,* 111–117. doi.

Lam, D. H., Watkins, E. R., Hayward, P., Bright, J., Wright, K., Kerr, N., et al. (2003). A randomized controlled study of cognitive therapy for relapse prevention for bipolar affective disorder: Outcome of the first year. *Archives of General Psychiatry, 60,* 145–152. doi:10.1001/archpsyc.60.2.145.

Lasky, T., Krieger, A., Elixhauser, A., & Vitiello, B. (2011). Children's hospitalizations with a mood disorder diagnosis in general hospitals in the United States 2000–2006. *Child and Adolescent Psychiatry and Mental Health, 5,* 27–35. doi:10.1186/1753-2000-5-27.

Leahy, R. L. (2007). Bipolar disorder: Causes, contexts, and treatments. *Journal of Clinical Psychology: In Session, 83,* 417–424. doi:10.1002/jclp.20360.

LeBuffe, P.A., & Naglieri, J A. (2003). *The Devereux Early Childhood Assessment Clinical Form (DECA-C): A measure of behaviors related to risk and resilience in preschool children.* Lewisville, NC: Kaplan Press.

Leibenluft, E. (2011). Severe mood dysregulation, irritability, and the diagnostic boundaries of bipolar disorder in youths. *The American Journal of Psychiatry, 168,* 129–142. doi:10.1176/appi.ajp.2010.10050766.

Leibenluft, E., Charney, D. S., Towbin, K. E., Bhangoo, R. K., & Pine, D. S. (2003). Defining clinical phenotypes of juvenile mania. *The American Journal of Psychiatry, 160,* 430–437. doi:10.1176/appi.ajp.160.3.430.

Leibenluft, E., Rich, B. A., Vinton, D. T., Nelson, E. E., Fromm, S. J., Berghorst, L. H., et al. (2007). Neural circuitry engaged during unsuccessful motor inhibition in pediatric bipolar disorder. *The American Journal of Psychiatry, 164,* 52–60. doi:10.1176/appi.ajp.164.1.52.

Levine, J., Chengappa, K. N. R., Brar, J. S., Gershon, S., & Kupfer, D. J. (2001). Illness characteristics and their association with prescription patterns for bipolar I disorder. *Bipolar Disorders,*
3, 41–49. doi:10.1034/j.1399-5618.2001.030106.x.

Lewinsohn, P. M., Klein, D. N., & Seeley, J. R. (1995). Bipolar disorders in a community sample
of older adolescents: Prevalence, phenomenology, comorbidity and course. *Journal of the*
American Academy of Child and Adolescent Psychiatry, 34, 454–463.
doi:10.1097/00004583-199504000-00012.

Lewinsohn, P. M., Seeley, J. R., & Klein, D. N. (2003). Bipolar disorder in adolescents:
Epidemiology and suicidal behavior. In B. Geller & M. P. DelBello (Eds.), *Bipolar disorder in*
childhood and early adolescence (pp. 7–24). New York, NY: Guilford Press.

Lofthouse, N., Fristad, M., Splaingard, M., & Kelleher, K. (2007). Parent and child reports of sleep
problems associated with early-onset bipolar spectrum disorders. *Journal of Family Psychology,*
21, 114–123. doi:10.1037/0893-3200.21.1.114.

Lorberg, B., Wilens, T. E., Martelon, M., Wong, P., & Parcell, T. (2010). Reasons for substance use
among adolescents with bipolar disorder. *The American Journal on Addictions, 19*, 474–480.
doi:10.1111/j.1521-0391.2010.00077.x.

Luby, J., & Belden, A. (2006). Defining and validating bipolar disorder in the preschool period.
Development and Psychopathology, 18, 971–988. doi:10.1017/S0954579406060482.

Luckenbaugh, D. A., Findling, R. L., Leverich, G. S., Pizzarello, S. M., & Post, R. M. (2009).
Earliest symptoms discriminating juvenile-onset bipolar illness from ADHD. *Bipolar*
Disorders, 11, 441–451. doi:10.1111/j.1399-5618.2009.00684.x.

Maayan, L., & Correll, C. U. (2011). Weight gain and metabolic risks associated with antipsychotic medications in children and adolescents. *Journal of Child and Adolescent*
Psychopharmacology, 21, 517–535. doi:10.1089/cap.2011.0015.

Manning, J. S. (2005). Burden of illness in bipolar depression. *The Primary Care Companion to*
The Journal of Clinical Psychiatry, 7(6), 259–267. doi:10.4088/PCC.v07n0601.

Martínez-Arán, A., Vieta, E., Reinares, M., Colom, F., Torrent, C., Sánchez-Moreno, J., et al.
(2004). Cognitive function across manic or hypomanic, depressed, and euthymic states in bipolar disorder. *The American Journal of Psychiatry, 161*, 262–270. doi:10.1176/appi.ajp.161.2.262.

Masi, G., Perugi, G., Toni, C., Millepiedi, S., Mucci, M., Bertini, N., et al. (2006). Attention-deficit
hyperactivity disorder—bipolar comorbidity in children and adolescents. *Bipolar Disorders, 8*,
373–381. doi:10.1111/j.1399-5618.2006.00342.x.

Masi, G., Perugi, G., Millepiedi, S., Mucci, M., Toni, C., Bertini, N., et al. (2006). Developmental
differences according to age at onset in juvenile bipolar disorder. *Journal of Child and*
Adolescent Psychopharmacology, 16, 679–685. doi:10.1089/cap.2006.16.679.

McClellan, J., Kowatch, R., Findling, R. L., Bernet, W., Bukstein, O., Beithchman, J., et al. (2007).
Practice parameter for the assessment and treatment of children and adolescents with bipolar
disorder. *Journal of the American Academy of Child and Adolescent Psychiatry, 46*, 107–125.
doi:10.1016/j.jaac.2011.09.019.

McClure-Tone, E. B. (2010). Social cognition and cognitive flexibility in BD. In D. J. Miklowitz
& D. Cicchetti (Eds.), *Understanding bipolar disorder: A developmental psychopathology*
perspective (pp. 331–369). New York, NY: Guilford Press.

McClure, E. B., Treland, J. E., Snow, J., Schmajuk, M., Dickstein, D. P., Towbin, K. E., et al.
(2005). Deficits in social cognition and response flexibility in pediatric bipolar disorder.
The American Journal of Psychiatry, 162, 1644–1651. doi:10.1176/appi.ajp.162.9.1644.

McCombs, J. S., Ahn, J., Tencer, T., & Shi, L. (2007). The impact of unrecognized bipolar disor-
ders among patients treated for depression with antidepressants in the fee-for-services
California Medicaid (Medi-Cal) program: A 6-year retrospective analysis. *Journal of Affective*
Disorders, 97, 171–179. doi:10.1016/j.jad.2006.06.018.

McConaughy, S. H., & Ritter, D. R. (2008). Best practices in multimethod assessment of emotional
and behavioral disorders. In A. Thomas & J. Grimes (Eds.), *Best practices in school psychology*
V (Vol. 2, pp. 697–715). Bethesda, MD: National Association of School Psychologists.

McElroy, S. L., Kotwal, R., & Keck, P. E. (2006). Comorbidity of eating disorders with bipolar disorder
and treatment implications. *Bipolar Disorders, 8*, 686–695. doi:10.1111/j.1399-5618.2006.00401.x.

McGuffin, P., Rijsdijk, F., Andrew, M., Sham, P., Katz, R., & Cardno, A. (2003). The heritability of bipolar affective disorder and the genetic relationship to unipolar depression. *Archives of General Psychiatry, 60*, 497–502. doi:10.1001/archpsyc.60.5.497.

McIntyre, R. S., Soczynska, J. K., Bottas, A., Bordbar, K., Konarski, J. Z., & Kennedy, S. H. (2006). Anxiety disorders and bipolar disorder: A review. *Bipolar Disorders, 8*, 665–676. doi:10.1111/j.1399-5618.2006.00355.x.

McTavish, S. F., McPherson, M. H., Harmer, C. J., Clark, L., Sharp, T., Goodwin, G. M., et al. (2001). Antidopaminergic effects of dietary tyrosine depletion in healthy subjects and patients with manic illness. *The British Journal of Psychiatry, 179*, 356–360. doi:10.1192/bjp.179.4.356.

Mennuti, R. B., Christner, R. W., & Freeman, A. (Eds.). (2012). *Cognitive-behavioral interventions in educational settings: A handbook for practice—second edition.* New York, NY: Routledge.

Merikangas, K. R., Jin, R., He, J.–. P., Kessler, R. C., Lee, S., Sampson, N. A., et al. (2011). Prevalence and correlates of bipolar spectrum disorder in the World Mental Health survey initiative. *Archives of General Psychiatry, 68*, 241–251. doi:10.1001/archgenpsychiatry.2011.12.

Merikangas, K. R., & Pato, M. (2009). Recent developments in the epidemiology of bipolar disorder in adults and children: Magnitude, correlates, and future directions. *Clinical Psychology: Science and Practice, 16*, 121–133. doi:10.1111/j.1468-2850.2009.01152.x.

Merrell, K. W. (2008). *Behavioral, social, and emotional assessment of children and adolescents* (3rd ed.). New York, NY: Lawrence Erlbaum Associates.

Meyer, S. E., & Carlson, G. A. (2010). Development, age of onset, and phenomenology in bipolar disorder. In D. J. Miklowitz & D. Cicchetti (Eds.), *Understanding bipolar disorder: A developmental psychopathology perspective* (pp. 35–66). New York, NY: Guilford Press.

Mick, E., Biederman, J., Pandina, G., & Faraone, S. V. (2003). A preliminary meta-analysis of the Child Behavior Checklist in pediatric bipolar disorder. *Biological Psychiatry, 53*, 1021–1027. doi:10.1016/S0006-3223(03)00234-8.

Miklowitz, D. J. (2008). *Bipolar disorder: A family-focused treatment approach.* New York, NY: Guilford Press.

Miklowitz, D. J., Axelson, D. A., Birmaher, B., George, E. L., Taylor, D. O., Schneck, C. D., et al. (2008). Family-focused treatment for adolescents with bipolar disorder: Results of a 2-year randomized trial. *Archives of General Psychiatry, 65*, 1053–1061. doi:10.1001/archpsyc.65.9.1053.

Miklowitz, D. J., Chang, K. D., Taylor, D. O., George, E. L., Singh, M. K., Schneck, C. D., et al. (2011). Early psychosocial intervention for youth at risk for bipolar I or II disorder: A one-year treatment development trial. *Bipolar Disorders, 13*, 67–75. doi:10.1111/j.1399-5618.2011.00890.x.

Miklowitz, D. J., George, E. L., Richards, J. A., Simoneau, T. L., & Suddath, R. L. (2003). A randomized study of family-focused psychoeducation and pharmacotherapy in the outpatient management of bipolar disorder. *Archives of General Psychiatry, 60*, 904–912. doi:10.1001/archpsyc.60.9.904.

Miklowitz, D. J., Goodwin, G. M., Bauer, M. S., & Geddes, J. R. (2008). Common and specific elements of psychosocial treatments for bipolar disorder: A survey of clinicians participating in randomized trials. *Journal of Psychiatric Practice, 14*, 77–85. doi:10.1097/01.pra.0000314314.94791.c9.

Miklowitz, D. J., & Johnson, S. L. (2009). Social and familial factors in the course of bipolar disorder: Basic processes and relevant interventions. *Clinical Psychology: Science and Practice, 16*, 281–296. doi:10.1111/j.1468-2850.2009.01166.x.

Miklowitz, D. J., Otto, M. W., Frank, E., Reilly-Harrington, N. A., Wisniewski, S. R., Kogan, J. N., et al. (2007). Psychosocial treatments for bipolar depression: A 1-year randomized trial from the Systematic Treatment Enhancement Program. *Archives of General Psychiatry, 64*, 419–427. doi:10.1001/archpsyc.64.4.419.

Miller, I. W., Uebelacker, L. A., Keitner, G. I., Ryan, C. E., & Solomon, D. A. (2004). Longitudinal course of bipolar I disorder. *Comprehensive Psychiatry, 45*, 431–440. doi:10.1016/j.comppsych.2004.07.005.

Mockenhaupht, M., Viboud, C., Dunant, A., Naldi, L., Halevy, S., Bavinck, J. N. B., et al. (2008). Stevens-Johnson syndrome and toxic epidermal necrolysis: Assessment of medication risks with emphasis on recently marketed drugs. The EuroSCAR-study. *Journal of Investigative Dermatology, 128*, 35–44. doi:10.1038/sj.jiid.5701033.

Mondimore, F. M. (2006). *Bipolar disorder: A guide for patients and families* (2nd ed.). Baltimore, MD: Johns Hopkins Press Health.

Moor, S., Crowe, M., Luty, S., Carter, J., & Joyce, P. R. (2012). Effects of comorbidity and early age of onset in young people with bipolar disorder on self harming behavior and suicide attempts. *Journal of Affective Disorders, 136*, 1212–1215. doi:10.1016/j.jad.2011.10.018.

Moreno, C., Laje, G., Blanco, C., Jiang, H., Schmidt, A. B., & Olfson, M. (2007). National trends in the outpatient diagnosis and treatment of bipolar disorder in youth. *Archives of General Psychiatry, 64*, 1032–1039. doi:10.1001/archpsyc.64.9.1032.

Morgan, V. A., Mitchell, P. B., & Jablensky, A. V. (2005). The epidemiology of bipolar disorder: Sociodemographic, disability and service utilization data from the Australian National Study of Low Prevalence (Psychotic) Disorders. *Bipolar Disorders, 7*, 326–337. doi:10.1111/j.1399-5618.2005.00229.x.

Morris, C. D., Miklowitz, D. J., & Waxmonsky, J. A. (2007). Family-focused treatment for bipolar disorder in adults and youth. *Journal of Clinical Psychology: In Session, 63*, 433–445. doi:10.1002/jclp.20359.

Morris, R. J., & Mather, N. (Eds.). (2008). *Evidence-based interventions for students with learning and behavioral challenges*. Mahwah, NJ: Lawrence Erlbaum and Associates.

Morriss, R., Scott, J., Paykel, E., Bentall, R., Hayhurst, H., & Johnson, T. (2007). Social adjustment based on reported behaviour in bipolar affective disorder. *Bipolar Disorders, 9*, 53–62. doi:10.1111/j.1399-5618.2007.00343.x.

Mortensen, P. B., Pedersen, C. B., Melbye, M., Mors, O., & Ewald, H. (2003). Individual and familial risk factors for bipolar affective disorders in Denmark. *Archives of General Psychiatry, 60*, 1209–1215. doi:10.1001/archpsyc.60.12.1209.

Mundo, E., Cattaneo, E., Russo, M., & Altamura, A. C. (2006). Clinical variables related to antidepressant-induced mania in bipolar disorder. *Journal of Affective Disorders, 92*, 227–230. doi:10.1016/j.jad.2006.01.028.

Narrow, W. E., Rae, D. S., Robins, L. N., & Regier, D. A. (2002). Revised prevalence estimates of mental disorders in the United States: Using a clinical significance criterion to reconcile 2 surveys' estimates. *Archives of General Psychiatry, 59*, 115–123. doi:10.1001/archpsyc.59.2.115.

National Institute of Mental Health. (2001). National Institute of Mental Health research roundtable on prepubertal bipolar disorder. *Journal of the American Academy of Child and Adolescent Psychiatry, 40*, 871–878. doi:10.1097/00004583-200108000-00007.

National Institute of Mental Health. (2008). *Bipolar disorder*. Bethesda, MD: Author. Retrieved April 26, 2009, from http://www.nimh.nih.gov/health/publications/bipolar-disorder/complete-index.shtml#pub15

Nery-Fernandes, F., Quarantini, L. C., Guimarães, J. L., de Oliveira, I. R., Koenen, K. C., Kapczinski, F., et al. (2012). Is there an association between suicide attempt and delay of initiation of mood stabilizers in bipolar I disorder? *Journal of Affective Disorders, 136*, 1082–1087. doi:10.1016/j.jad.2011.10.046.

Nieto, R. G., & Castellanos, F. X. (2011). A meta-analysis of neuropsychological functioning in patients with early onset schizophrenia and pediatric bipolar disorder. *Journal of Clinical Child and Adolescent Psychology, 40*, 266–280. doi:10.1080/15374416.2011.546049.

Nivoli, A. M. A., Colom, F., Murru, A., Pacchiarotti, I., Castro-Loli, P., Gonález-Pinto, A., et al. (2010). New treatment guidelines for acute bipolar depression: A systematic review. *Journal of Affective Disorders, 129*, 14–26. doi:10.1016/j.jad2010.05.018.

Novick, D. M., Swartz, H. A., & Frank, E. (2010). Suicide attempts in bipolar I and bipolar II disorder: A review and meta-analysis of the evidence. *Bipolar Disorders, 12*, 1–9. doi:10.1111/j.1399-5618.2009.00786.x.

O'Neill, R. E., Horner, R. H., Albin, R. W., Sprague, J. R., Storey, K., & Newton, J. S. (1997). *Functional assessment and program development for problem behavior: A practical handbook* (2nd ed.). Pacific Grove, CA: Brooks/Cole.

Öngür, D., Jensen, J. E., Prescot, A. P., Caitlin, S., Lundy, M., Cohen, B. M., et al. (2008). Abnormal glutamatergic neurotransmission and neuronal-glial interactions in acute mania. *Biological Psychiatry, 64*, 718–726. doi:10.1016/j.biopsych.2008.05.014.

Papolos, J., Hatton, M. J., Norelli, S., Garcia, C. E., & Smith, A. M. (2002). *The educational issues of students with bipolar disorder.* Retrieved from www.bipolarchild.com

Papolos, D., Hennen, J., & Cockerham, M. S. (2005). Factors associated with parent-reported suicide threats by children and adolescents with community-diagnosed bipolar disorder. *Journal of Affective Disorders, 86*, 267–275. doi:10.1016/j.jad.2005.02.012.

Papolos, D., Hennen, J., Cockerham, M. S., & Lachman, H. (2007). A strategy for identifying phenotypic subtypes: Concordance of symptom dimensions between sibling pairs who met screening criteria for a genetic linkage study of childhood-onset bipolar disorder using the Child Bipolar Questionnaire. *Journal of Affective Disorders, 99*, 27–36. doi:10.1016/j.jad.2006.08.014.

Papolos, D., Hennen, J., Cockerham, M. S., Thode, H. C., & Youngstrom, E. (2006). The child bipolar questionnaire: A dimensional approach to screening for pediatric bipolar disorder. *Journal of Affective Disorders, 95*, 149–158. doi:10.1016/j.jad.2006.03.026.

Papolos, D., Mattis, S., Golshan, S., & Molay, F. (2009). Fear of harm, a possible phenotype of pediatric bipolar disorder: A dimensional approach to diagnosis for genotyping psychiatric syndromes. *Journal of Affective Disorders, 118*, 28–38. doi:10.1016/j.jad.2009.06.016.

Papolos, D., & Papolos, J. (2006). *The bipolar child: The definitive and reassuring guide to childhood's most misunderstood disorder.* New York, NY: Broadway.

Patel, N. C., DelBello, M. P., Keck, P. E., & Strakowski, S. M. (2006a). Phenomenology associated with age at onset in patients with bipolar disorder at their first psychiatric hospitalization. *Bipolar Disorders, 8*, 91–94. doi:10.1111/j.1399-5618.2006.00247.x.

Patel, N. C., DelBello, M. P., Keck, P. E., & Strakowski, S. M. (2005). Ethnic differences in maintenance antipsychotic prescription among adolescents with bipolar disorder. *Journal of Child and Adolescent Psychopharmacology, 15*, 938–946. doi:10.1089/cap.2005.15.938.

Patel, N. C., DelBello, M. P., Keck, P. E., & Strakowski, S. M. (2006b). Ethnic differences in symptom presentation of youths with bipolar disorder. *Bipolar Disorders, 8*, 95–99. doi:10.1111/j.1399-5618.2006.00279.x.

Pavuluri, M. N. (2008). *What works for bipolar kids: Help and hope for parents.* New York, NY: Guilford Press.

Pavuluri, M. N., Birmaher, B., & Naylor, M. W. (2005). Pediatric bipolar disorder: A review of the past 10 years. *Journal of the American Academy of Child and Adolescent Psychiatry, 44*, 846–871. doi:10.1097/01.chi.0000170554.23422.c1.

Pavuluri, M. N., Graczyk, P. A., Henry, D. B., Carbray, J. A., Heidenreich, J., & Miklowitz, D. J. (2004a). Child- and family-focused cognitive-behavioral therapy for pediatric bipolar disorder: Development and preliminary results. *Journal of the American Academy of Child and Adolescent Psychiatry, 43*, 528–537. doi:10.1097/00004583-200405000-00006.

Pavuluri, M. N., Graczyk, P. A., Henry, D. B., et al. (2004b). RAINBOW: Two programs combined may be better than one for pediatric BD. *The Brown University Child and Adolescent Behavior Letter, 20*(7), 5–7.

Pavuluri, M. N., Henry, D. B., Moss, M., Mohammed, T., Carbray, J. A., & Sweeney, J. A. (2009). Effectiveness of lamotrigine in maintaining symptom control in pediatric bipolar disorder. *Journal of Child and Adolescent Psychopharmacology, 19*, 75–82. doi:10.1089/cap.2008.0107.

Pavuluri, M. N., Henry, D., Devineni, B., Carbray, J., & Birmaher, B. (2006). Child mania rating scale: Development, reliability and validity. *Journal of American Academy of Child and Adolescent Psychiatry, 45*, 550–560. doi:10.1097/01.chi.0000205700.40700.50.

Pavuluri, M. N., Henry, D. B., Nadimpalli, S. S., O'Connor, M. M., & Sweeney, J. A. (2006). Biological risk factors in pediatric bipolar disorder. *Biological Psychiatry, 60*, 936–941. doi:10.1016/j.biopsych.2006.04.002.

Pavuluri, M. N., Herbener, E. S., & Sweeney, J. A. (2004). Psychotic symptoms in pediatric bipolar disorder. *Journal of Affective Disorders, 80*, 19–28. doi:10.1016/S0165-0327(03)00053-3.

Pavuluri, M. N., O'Connor, M. M., Harral, E. M., Moss, M., & Sweeney, J. A. (2006). Impact of neurocognitive function on academic difficulties in pediatric bipolar disorder: A clinical translation. *Biological Psychiatry, 60*, 951–956. doi:10.1016/j.biopsych.2006.03.027.

Pavuluri, M. N., Schenkel, L. S., Aryal, S., Harral, E. M., Hill, S. K., Herbener, E. S., et al. (2006). Neurocognitive function in unmedicated manic and medicated euthymic pediatric bipolar patients. *The American Journal of Psychiatry, 163*, 286–293. doi:10.1176/appi.ajp.163.2.286.

Pavuluri, M. N., West, A., Hill, S. K., Jindal, K., & Sweeney, J. A. (2009). Neurocognitive function in pediatric bipolar disorder: 3-year follow-up shows cognitive development lagging behind healthy youths. *Journal of the American Child and Adolescent Psychiatry, 48*, 299–307. doi:10.1097/CHI.0b013e318196b907.

Pfeifer, J. C., Kowatch, R. A., & DelBello, M. P. (2010). Pharmacotherapy of bipolar disorder in children and adolescents: Recent progress. *CNS Drugs, 24*, 575–593. doi:10.2165/11533110-000000000-00000.

Pfeifer, J. C., Welge, J., Strakowski, S. M., Adler, C. M., & DelBello, M. P. (2008). Meta-analysis of amygdala volumes in children and adolescents with bipolar disorder. *Journal of the American Academy of Child and Adolescent Psychiatry, 47*, 1289–1298. doi:10.1097/CHI.0b013e318185d299.

Pichot, P. (2006). Tracing the origins of bipolar disorder: From Falret to DSM-IV and ICD-10. *Journal of Affective Disorders, 96*, 145–148. doi:10.1016/j.jad.2006.05.031.

Pini, S., de Queiroz, V., Pagnin, D., Pezawas, L., Angst, J., Cassano, G. B., et al. (2005). Prevalence and burden of bipolar disorders in European countries. *European Neuropsychopharmacology, 15*, 425–434. doi:10.1016/j.euroneuro.2005.04.011.

Plante, D. T., & Winkelman, J. W. (2008). Sleep disturbance in bipolar disorder: Therapeutic implications. *The American Journal of Psychiatry, 165*, 830–843. doi:10.1176/appi.ajp.2008.08010077.

Pope, M., Dudley, R., & Scott, J. (2007). Determinants of social functioning in bipolar disorder. *Bipolar Disorders, 9*, 38–44. doi:10.1111/j.1399-5618.2007.00323.x.

Post, R. M.(1992). Transduction of psychosocial stress into the neurobiology of recurrent affective disorder. *The American Journal of Psychiatry, 149*, 999–1010. Retrieved from http://ajp.psychiatryonline.org/.

Post, R. M., & Leverich, G. S. (2006). The role of psychosocial stress in the onset and progression of bipolar disorder and its comorbidities: The need for earlier and alternative modes of therapeutic intervention. *Development and Psychopathology, 18*, 1181–1211. doi:10.1017/S0954579406060573.

Post, R. M., Leverich, G. S., Kupka, R. W., Keck, P. E., McElroy, S., Altshuler, L. L., et al. (2010). Early-onset bipolar disorder and treatment delay are risk factors for poor outcome in adulthood. *The Journal of Clinical Psychiatry, 71*, 864–872. doi:10.4088/JCP.08m04994yel.

Powell, S. B., Young, J. W., Ong, J. C., Caron, M. G., & Geyer, M. A. (2008). Atypical antipsychotics clozapine and quetiapine attenuate prepulse inhibition deficits in dopamine transporter knockout mice. *Behavioural Pharmacology, 19*, 562–565. doi:10.1097/FBP.0b013e32830dc110.

Preston, J., & Johnson, J. (2008). *Clinical psychopharmacology made ridiculously simple* (5th ed.). Miami, FL: MedMaster.

Quanbeck, C. D., Stone, D. C., Scott, C. L., McDermott, B. E., Altshuler, L. L., & Frye, M. A. (2004). Clinical and legal correlates of inmates with bipolar disorder at time of criminal arrest. *The Journal of Clinical Psychiatry, 65*, 198–203. doi:10.4088/JCP.v65n0209.

Raman, R. P. B., Shesadri, S. P., Reddy, Y. C. J., Girimaji, S. C., Srinath, S., & Raghunandan, V. N. G. P. (2007). Is bipolar II disorder misdiagnosed as major depressive disorder in children? *Journal of Affective Disorders, 98*, 263–266. doi:10.1016/j.jad.2006.08.006.

Reichart, C. G., & Nolen, W. A. (2004). Earlier onset of bipolar disorder in children by antidepressants or stimulants? An hypothesis. *Journal of Affective Disorders, 78*, 81–84. doi:10.1016/S0165-0327(02)00180-5.

Reichart, C. G., van der Ende, J., Hillegers, M. H. J., Wals, M., Bongers, I. L., Nolen, W. A., et al. (2007). Perceived parental rearing of bipolar offspring. *Acta Psychiatrica Scandinavica, 115*, 21–28. doi:10.1111/j.1600-0447.2006.00838.x.

Reichart, C. G., van der Ende, J., Wals, M., Hillegers, M. H. J., Nolen, W. A., Ormel, J., et al. (2007). Social functioning of bipolar offspring. *Journal of Affective Disorders, 98*, 207–213. doi:10.1016/j.jad.2006.07.018.

Reikert, K. A., & Drotar, D. (2000). Adherence to medical treatment in pediatric chronic illness: Critical issues and unanswered questions. In D. Drotar (Ed.), *Promoting adherence to treatment in pediatric chronic illness: Concepts, methods, and interventions* (pp. 201–231). Mahwah, NJ: Erlbaum.

Renou, S., Hergueta, T., Flament, M., Mouren-Simeoni, M. C., & Lecrubier, Y. (2004). Diagnostic structured interviews in child and adolescent's psychiatry. *Encephale, 30,* 122–134. doi:10.1016/S0013-7006(04)95422-X.

Rich, B. A., Fromm, S. J., Berghorst, L. H., Dickstein, D. P., Brotman, M. A., Pine, D. S., et al. (2008). Neural connectivity in children with bipolar disorder: Impairment in the face emotion processing circuit. *Journal of Child Psychology and Psychiatry, 49,* 88–96. doi:10.1111/j.1469-7610.2007.01819.x.

Rich, B. A., Vinton, D. T., Roberson-Nay, R., Hommer, R. E., Berghorst, L. H., McClure, E. B., et al. (2006). Limbic hyperactivation during processing of neutral facial expressions in children with bipolar disorder. *PNAS, 103*(23), 8900–8905. doi:10.1073/pnas.0603246103.

Robins, L., & Price, R. (1991). Adult disorders predicted by childhood conduct problems: Results for the NIMH epidemiologic catchment area project. *Psychiatry, 54,* 116–132. http://ajp.psychiatryonline.org/journal.aspx?journalid=13.

Romero, S., Birmaher, B., Axelson, D., Goldstein, T., Goldstein, B. I., Gill, M. K., et al. (2009). Prevalence and correlates of physical and sexual abuse in children and adolescents with bipolar disorder. *Journal of Affective Disorders, 112,* 144–150. doi:10.1016/j.jad.2008.04.005.

Roybal, D. J., Chang, K. D., Chen, M. C., Howe, M. E., Gotlib, I. H., & Singh, M. K. (2011). Characterization and factors associated with sleep quality in adolescents with bipolar I disorder. *Child Psychiatry and Human Development, 42,* 724–740. doi:10.1007/s10578-011-0239-0.

Sachs, G. S., Baldassano, C. F., Truman, C. J., & Guille, C. (2000). Comorbidity of attention deficit hyperactivity disorder with early- and late-onset bipolar disorder. *The American Journal of Psychiatry, 157,* 466–468. doi:10.1176/appi.ajp.157.3.466.

Sakai, T., Oshima, A., Nozaki, Y., Ida, I., Haga, C., Akiyama, H., et al. (2008). Changes in density of calcium-binding-protein-immunoreactive GABAergic neurons in prefrontal cortex in schizophrenia and bipolar disorder. *Neuropathology, 28,* 143–150. doi:10.1111/j.1440-1789.2007.00867.x.

Sala, R., Axelson, D. A., Castro-Fornieles, J., Goldstein, T. R., Ha, W., Liao, F., et al. (2010). Comorbid anxiety in children and adolescents with bipolar spectrum disorders: Prevalence and clinical correlates. *The Journal of Clinical Psychiatry, 71,* 1344–1350. doi:10.4088/JCP.09m05845gre.

Schenkel, L. S., Marlow-O'Connor, M., Moss, M., Sweeney, J. A., & Pavuluri, M. N. (2008). Theory of mind and social inference in children and adolescents with bipolar disorder. *Psychological Medicine, 38,* 791–800. doi:10.1017/S0033291707002541.

Serene, J. A., Ashtari, M., Szeszko, P. R., & Kumra, S. (2007). Neuroimaging studies of children with serious emotional disturbances: A selected review. *The Canadian Journal of Psychiatry/La Revue Canadienne de Psychiatrie, 52,* 135–145. http://publications.cpa-apc.org/browse/sections/0.

Serretti, A., & Mandelli, L. (2008). The genetics of bipolar disorder: Genome 'hot regions,' genes, new potential candidates and future directions. *Molecular Psychiatry, 13,* 742–771. doi:10.1038/mp.2008.29.

Shen, G. H. C., Alloy, L. B., Abramson, L. Y., & Sylvia, L. G. (2008). Social rhythm regularity and the onset of affective episodes in bipolar spectrum individuals *Bipolar Disorders, 10,* 520–529. doi:10.1111/j.1399-5618.2008.00583.x.

Silverstone, T. (1985). Dopamine in manic depressive illness. A pharmacological synthesis. *Journal of Affective Disorders, 8,* 225–231. doi:10.1016/0165-0327(85)90020-5.

Singh, M. K., Pfeifer, J. C., Barzman, D., Kowatch, R. A., & DelBello, M. P. (2007). Pharmacotherapy for child and adolescent mood disorder. *Psychiatric Annals, 37,* 465–476. http://www.healio.com/psychiatry.

Smarty, S., & Findling, R. L. (2007). Psychopharmacology of pediatric bipolar disorder: A review. *Psychopharmacology, 191,* 39–54. doi:10.1007/s00213-006-0569-y.

Somanath, C. P., Jain, S., & Reddy, Y. C. J. (2002). A family study of early-onset bipolar I disorder. *Journal of Affective Disorders, 70,* 91–94. doi:10.1016/S0165-0327(00)00372-4.

Sopko, K. M. (2006). School mental health services in the United States. *InForum*, 1–9. http:// www.projectforum.org

Soutullo, C. A., Chang, K. D., Díez-Suárez, A., Figueroa-Quintana, A., Escamilla-Canales, I., Rapado-Castro, M., et al. (2005). Bipolar disorder in children and adolescents: International perspective on epidemiology and phenomenology. *Bipolar Disorders, 7*, 497–506. doi:10.1111/j.1399-5618.2005.00262.x.

Squires, J. Bricker, D. & Twombly, E. (2002). *Ages and Stages Questionnaires: Social and Emotional*. Baltimore, MD: Brookes Publishing.

Staton, D., Volness, L. J., & Beatty, W. W. (2008). Diagnosis and classification of pediatric bipolar disorder. *Journal of Affective Disorders, 105*, 205–212. doi:10.1016/j.jad.2007.05.015.

Stoddard-Dare, P., Mallett, C. A., & Boitel, C. (2011). Association between mental health disorders and juveniles' detention for a personal crime. *Child and Adolescent Mental Health, 16*, 208–213. doi:10.1111/j.1475-3588.2011.00599.x.

Strawn, J. R., Adler, C. M., Fleck, D. E., Hanseman, D., Maue, D. K., Bitter, S., et al. (2010). Post-traumatic stress symptoms and trauma exposure in youth with first episode bipolar disorder. *Early Intervention in Psychiatry, 4*, 169–173. doi:10.1111/j.1751-7893.2010.00173.x.

Sublette, M. E., Oquendo, M. A., & Mann, J. J. (2006). Rational approaches to neurobiologic study of youth at risk for bipolar disorder and suicide. *Bipolar Disorders, 8*, 526–542. doi:10.1111/j.1399.5618.2006.00372.x.

Sullivan, A. E., & Miklowitz, D. J. (2010). Family functioning among adolescents with bipolar disorder. *Journal of Family Psychology, 24*, 60–67. doi:10.1037/a001813.

Tillman, R., & Geller, B. (2006). Controlled study of switching from attention-deficit/hyperactivity disorder to a prepubertal and early adolescent bipolar I disorder phenotype during 6-year prospective follow-up: Rate, risk, and predictors. *Development and Psychopathology, 18*, 1037–1053. doi:10.1017/S095457940606051.

Townsend, L. D., Demeter, C. A., Youngstrom, E., Drotar, D., & Findling, R. L. (2007). Family conflict moderates response to pharmacological intervention in pediatric bipolar disorder. *Journal of Child and Adolescent Psychopharmacology, 17*, 843–851. doi:10.1089/cap.2007.0046.

Tsuang, M. T., & Faraone, S. V. (1990). *The genetics of mood disorders*. Baltimore, MD: John Hopkins University Press.

U.S. Department of Education. (2006). 34 C. F. R. Parts 300 and 301: Assistance to states for the education of children with disabilities; Final rule. *Federal Register, 71*, 46540–46845. www.federalregister.gov.

Valtonen, H. M., Suominen, K., Mantere, O., Lappämäki, S., Arvilommi, P., & Isometsä, E. (2007). Suicidal behaviour during different phases of bipolar disorder. *Journal of Affective Disorders, 97*, 101–107. doi:10.1016/j.jad.2006.05.033.

Van Meter, A. R., Moreira, A. L. R., & Youngstrom, E. A. (2011). Meta-analysis of epidemiologic studies of pediatric bipolar disorder. *The Journal of Clinical Psychiatry, 72*, 1250–1256. doi:10.4088/JCP.10m06290.

Van Meter, A., Youngstrom, E. A., Youngstrom, J. K., Feeny, N. C., & Findling, R. L. (2011). Examining the validity of cyclothymic disorder in a youth sample. *Journal of Affective Disorders, 132*, 55–63. doi:10.1016/j.jad.2011.02.004.

West, A. E., Henry, D. B., & Pavuluri, M. N. (2007). Maintenance model of integrated psychosocial treatment in pediatric bipolar disorder: A pilot feasibility study. *Journal of the American Academy of Child and Adolescent Psychiatry, 46*, 205–212. doi:10.1097/01. chi.0000246068.85577.d7.

West, A. E., Jacobs, R. H., Westerholm, R., Adabel, L., Carbray, J., Heidenreich, J., et al. (2009). Child and family-focused cognitive-behavioral therapy for pediatric bipolar disorder: Pilot study of group treatment format. *Journal of the Canadian Academy of Child and Adolescent Psychiatry, 18*, 239–246. www.cacap-acpea.org/.

West, A. E., Weinstein, S. M., Celio, C. I., Henry, D., & Pavuluri, M. N. (2011). Co-morbid disruptive behavior disorder and aggression predict functional outcomes and differential response to risperidone versus divalproex in pharmacotherapy for pediatric bipolar disorder. *Journal of Child and Adolescent Psychopharmacology, 21*, 545–553. doi:10.1089/cap.2010.0140.

Wilens, T. E., Biederman, J., Adamson, J. J., Henin, A., Sgambati, S., Gignac, M., et al. (2008). Further evidence of an association between adolescent bipolar disorder with smoking and substance use disorders: A controlled study. *Drug and Alcohol Dependence, 95*, 188–198. doi:10.1016/j.drugalcdep.2007.12.016.

Wiste, A. K., Arango, V., Ellis, S. P., Mann, J. J., & Underwood, M. D. (2008). Norepinephrine and serotonin imbalance in the locus coeruleus in bipolar disorder. *Bipolar Disorders, 10*, 349–359. doi:10.1111/j.1399.5618.2007.00528.x.

World Health Organization. (1992). *The ICD-10 classification of mental health and beahvioural disorders: Diagnostic criteria for research*. Geneva, Switzerland: Author.

World Health Organization. (2001). *The World Health Report 2001. Mental health: New understanding, new hope*. Geneva, Switzerland: Author. http://www.who.int/whr/2001/en/.

Wozniak, J., Biederman, J., Faraone, S. V., Blier, H., & Monuteaux, M. C. (2001). Heterogeneity of childhood conduct disorder: Further evidence of a subtype of conduct disorder linked to bipolar disorder. *Journal of Affective Disorders, 64*, 121–131. doi:10.1016/S0165-0327(00)00217-2.

Wozniak, J., Biederman, J., Mick, E., Waxmonsky, J., Hantsoo, L., Best, C., et al. (2007). Omega-3 fatty acid monotherapy for pediatric bipolar disorder: A prospective open-label trial. *European Neuropsychopharmacology, 17*, 440–447. doi:10.1016/j.euroneuro.2006.11.006.

Wozniak, J., Petty, C. R., Schreck, M., Moses, A., Faraone, S. V., & Biederman, J. (2011). High level of persistence of pediatric bipolar-I disorder from childhood onto adolescent years: A four year prospective longitudinal follow-up study. *Journal of Psychiatric Research, 45*, 1273–1282. doi:10.1016/j.jpsychires.2010.10.006.

Wozniak, J., Spencer, T., Biederman, J., Kwon, A., Monuteaux, M., Rettew, J., et al. (2004). The clinical characteristics of unipolar vs. bipolar major depression in ADHD youth. *Journal of Affective Disorders, 82*(suppl), 59–69. 10.1016/j.jad.2004.05.013.

Yatham, L. N., Liddle, P. F., Lam, R. W., Shiah, I. S., Lane, C., Stoessl, A. J., et al. (2002). PET study of the effects of valproate on dopamine D(2) receptors in neuroleptic- and mood-stabilizer-naive patients with nonpsychotic mania. *The American Journal of Psychiatry, 159*, 1718–1723. doi:10.1176/appi.ajp.159.10.1718.

Yen, C.-F., Chen, C.-S., Ko, C.-H., Yen, J.-Y., & Huang, C.-F. (2007). Changes in insight among patients with bipolar I disorder: A 2-year prospective study. *Bipolar Disorders, 9*, 238–242. doi:10.1111/j.1399-5618.2007.00407.x.

Yerevanian, B., Koek, R. J., & Mintz, J. (2007). Bipolar pharmacotherapy and suicidal behavior part 1: Lithium, divalproex and carbamazepine. *Journal of Affective Disorders, 103*, 5–11. doi:10.1016/j.jad.2007.05.019.

Yerevanian, B., Koek, R. J., Mintz, J., & Akiskal, H. S. (2007). Bipolar pharmacolotherapy and suicidal behavior part 2: The impact of antidepressants. *Journal of Affective Disorders, 103*, 13–21. doi:10.1016/j.jad.2007.05.017.

Young, M. E., & Fristad, M. A. (2007). Evidence based treatments for bipolar disorder in children and adolescents. *Journal of Contemporary Psychotherapy, 37*, 157–164. doi:10.1007/s10879-007-9050-4.

Youngstrom, E. A., Findling, R. L., Danielson, C. K., & Calabrese, J. R. (2001). Discriminative validity of parent report of hypomanic and depressive symtpoms on the General Behavior Inventory. *Psychological Assessment, 13*, 267–276. doi:10.1037/1040-3590.13.2.267.

Youngstrom, E. A., Findling, R. L., Calabrese, J. R., Gracious, B. L., Demeter, C., Bedoya, D. D., et al. (2004). Comparing the diagnostic accuracy of six potential screening instruments for bipolar disorder in youths aged 5 to 17 years. *Journal of the American Academy of Child and Adolescent Psychiatry, 43*, 847–858. doi:10.1097/01.chi.0000125091.35109.1e.

Youngstrom, E. A., Findling, R. L., Youngstrom, J. K., & Calabrese, J. R. (2005). Toward an evidence-based assessment of pediatric bipolar disorder. *Journal of Clinical Child and Adolescent Psychology, 34*, 433–448. doi:10.1207/s15374424jccp3403_4.

Youngstrom, E. A., Birmaher, B., & Findling, R. L. (2008). Pediatric bipolar disorder: Validity, phenomenology, and recommendations for diagnosis. *Bipolar Disorders, 10*, 194–214. doi:10.1111/j.1399-5618.2007.00563.x.

Youngstrom, E. A., Frazier, T. W., Demeter, C., Calabrese, J. R., & Findling, R. L. (2008). Developing a 10-item mania scale from the Parent General Behavior Inventory for Children and Adolescents. *The Journal of Clinical Psychiatry, 69*, 831–839. doi:10.4088/JCP. v69n0517.

Youngstrom, E., Meyers, O., Demeter, C., Youngstrom, J., Morello, L., Piiparinen, R., et al. (2005). Comparing diagnostic checklists for pediatric bipolar disorder in academic and community mental health settings. *Bipolar Disorders, 7*, 507–517. doi:10.1111/j.1399-5618.2005.00269.x.

Youngstrom, E., Youngstrom, J. K., & Starr, M. (2005). Bipolar diagnoses in community mental health: Achenbach Child Behavior Checklist profiles and patterns of comorbidity. *Biological Psychiatry, 58*, 569–575. doi:10.1016/j.biopsych.2005.04.004.

Zito, J. M., Derivan, A. T., Kratochvil, C. J., Safer, D. J., Fegert, J. M., & Greenhill, L. L. (2008). Off-label psychopharmacologic prescribing for children: History supports close clinical monitoring. *Child and Adolescent Psychiatry and Mental Health, 2*, 24–35. doi:10.1186/1753-2000-2-24.

Zuckerman, M. (1999). *Vulnerability to psychopathology: A biosocial model.* Washington, DC: American Psychological Association.

Appendix

Bipolar Disorder in Children: List of Resources for Teachers and Parents

Epidemiology and General Information on Assessment and Treatment

American Academy of Child and Adolescent Psychiatry

http://www.aacap.org/cs/BipolarDisorder.ResourceCenter

AACAP's *Practice Parameters for the Assessment and Treatment of Children and Adolescents with Bipolar Disorder* aids mental health professionals and physicians in their clinical decision making. The *Practice Parameters* shows the best treatment options available to families living with childhood and adolescent mental illness.

Juvenile Bipolar Research Foundation

www.jbrf.org

JBRF is dedicated to researching and advancing understanding, assessment, and treatment of bipolar disorder in children and teens. JBRF's Website includes educational materials for parents, educators, and other professionals.

National Institute of Mental Health

http://www.nimh.nih.gov/health/topics/bipolar-disorder/index.shtmlhttp://www.nimh.nih.gov/health/publications/bipolar-disorder-in-children-and-teens-easy-to-read/index.shtmlhttp://www.nimh.nih.gov/health/publications/bipolar-disorder-in-children-and-teens-a-parents-guide/nimh_bipolar_children_parents_guide.pdf

S.R. Hart et al., *Identifying, Assessing, and Treating Bipolar Disorder at School*,
Developmental Psychopathology at School, DOI 10.1007/978-1-4614-7585-9,
© Springer Science+Business Media New York 2014

The National Institute of Mental Health (NIMH) strives to provide complete and accurate information on mental health and behavioral disorders. The Website provides exhaustive information on symptoms, course, prognosis, treatment options, and outcomes as per latest research in the field. The Website provides "easy-to-read" materials such brochures for parents as well as reports of the latest NIMH investigations.

School Psychiatry Program and the Mood & Anxiety Disorders Institute (MADI) Resource Center

www.schoolpsychiatry.org

The School Psychiatry Program and the Mood & Anxiety Disorders Institute (MADI) Resource Center is committed to enhancing the education and mental health of every student in every school. The Website has resources for parents, educators, and clinicians to ensure that each group is working together to support children and teens with neurological, behavioral, and mood disorders.

Information about Diagnosis, Assessment, Treatment Options, and Advocacy for Parents

The Balanced Mind Foundation

http://www.thebalancedmind.org/

The Balanced Mind Foundation is a parent-led organization that provides information, support, and advocacy for parents of children diagnosed with bipolar disorder. The Website is complete with resources, forums, and multiple links to other resources. This Website is highly ranked by parents.

Depression and Bipolar Support Alliance

www.dbsalliance.orghttp://www.dbsalliance.org/site/PageServer?pagename=help_lifespan

DBSA is the nation's leading patient-directed organization focusing on depression and bipolar disorder, primarily for adults and their families. The organization fosters an understanding about the impact and management of these illnesses by providing up-to-date, scientifically based tools and information written in a language that the general public can understand. DBSA supports research to promote more timely diagnosis, develop more effective and tolerable treatments, and discover a cure. The Website is dedicated to supporting individuals diagnosed with depression and bipolar disorder of all ages. While it does not exclusively focus on children and teens, it provides great resources for mood tracking and management, medication options, as well as personal accounts of individuals and their families as to what worked and did not work for them in managing the condition.

The National Alliance for the Mentally Ill (NAMI)

http://www.nami.org/Template.cfm?Section=Child_and_Adolescent_Action_ Center&template=/ContentManagement/ContentDisplay.cfm&ContentID=23448

The nation's leading grassroots, self-help, and family advocacy organization dedicated to improving the lives of people with brain disorders. NAMI is active in the research and political arenas and campaigns actively against discrimination and for access to treatment.

Bipolar Children

www.bpchildren.com

The Website provides a constellation of resources and links to other organizations that address the issues specific to bipolar disorders in children and youths. Specifically, the Website offers mood charts, posters, a newsletter, and excellent books such as *Intense Minds* and *My Roller Coaster Feelings Book and Work Book.*

Parenting of Children with Mood Dysregulation

Mindsight and Whole Brain Parenting Strategies

http://drdansiegel.com/

Dr. Dan Siegel advocates neurodevelopmental approach to emotional regulation and parenting. His Website is not specific to families with children who suffer from bipolar disorders. However, the information provided on development and advancement of emotional regulation in children via parenting is highly relevant to parents whose children suffer from mood dysregulation and bipolar disorders.

Attachment-Focused Parenting

http://www.danielhughes.org/

Dr. Dan Hughes is a well-known expert practitioner in attachment family therapy that promotes bonding with children with emotional dysregulation of all ages. Given that familial dysregulation often follows the emotional dysregulation of the diagnosed child, his work is essential in understanding how to create and preserve safe, loving environment for child's development.

Treatment Resources

www.semel.ucla.edu/champ

The Child and Adolescent Mood Disorders Program provides diagnostic evaluations, second-opinion consultation, and short-term treatments (medication management and various forms of psychotherapy) for youth who have symptoms of significant and impairing mood disorders and their families.

Residential Treatment

Facilities

The following treatment facilities utilize a multimodal treatment approach with a heavy emphasis on mind–body connection and neurosequential approach in treating mood dysregulation.

The Green Chimney School

http://www.greenchimneys.org/index.php?option=com_content&view=article&id=44&Itemid=140

The Sand Hill Child Development Center

http://www.sandhillcenter.org/

Suicide Prevention

The National Alliance for the Mentally Ill (NAMI)

http://www.nami.org/Template.cfm?Section=By_Illness&Template=/TaggedPage/TaggedPageDisplay.cfm&TPLID=54&ContentID=23041&gclid=CL7nv-i5grMCFdKd4AodSxsAnQ

The alliance provides helpful information on statistics and symptoms of suicidal tendencies and attempts in children and youths.

American Association of Suicidology

www.suicidology.org
   This national organization offers resources for suicide prevention and survivors of suicide (SOS). They provide a newsletter, a directory of resources for suicide prevention, conferences, and referrals to local SOS chapters.

American Foundation for Suicide Prevention (AFSP)

www.afsp.org
   This Website provides information for survivors and a 24/7 National Lifeline: 1-800-273-TALK (8255)

Society for the Prevention of Teen Suicide

www.sptsnj.org
   This Website provides great resources for teens, educators, and parents. A very powerful short film, *"Not My Kid"* is posted on the Website and can be used for parental training. Further, the organization provides the 24/7 National Lifeline: 1-800-273-TALK (8255).

Advocacy and Legal Issues

The National Child Abuse Defense and Resource Center

http://www.falseallegation.org/
   The families of children with bipolar disorders often face great challenges in containing the child's episodes of rage and violence. Sometimes, the parents are falsely accused of abusing the child when they have to physically restrain the child to prevent injury and/or suicide.
   The National Child Abuse Defense and Resource Center is an advocacy organization for parents falsely accused of child abuse.

The Balanced Mind Foundation

http://www.thebalancedmind.org/learn/library/legal-issues-of-pediatric-bipolar-disorder-0
   The Balanced Mind Foundation's "Legal Issues of Pediatric Bipolar Disorder" is a comprehensive guide regarding various legal issues the families of children with bipolar disorders may be facing ranging from insurance-related issues to education related to juvenile criminal system-related issues.

Individuals with Disabilities Education Act (IDEA)

http://idea.ed.gov/explore/home

First signed in 1997 and then reauthorized in 2004, the IDEA aims at bridging the gap between what the learning needs of children with disabilities are and the requirements of the regular curriculum. Parents can help their bipolar children much more effectively by educating themselves about their rights under the law.

The Individualized Education Program is a legal document that delineates how exactly the school will assist the child in learning. Harley Tomey of the Virginia Department of Education has written an excellent, comprehensive article entitled "Individualized Education Program—The Process."http://www.ldonline.org/article/6277

About the Authors

Shelley R. Hart, Ph.D., is currently a postdoctoral fellow at Johns Hopkins University in the Psychiatric Epidemiology Training Program, Department of Mental Health, Bloomberg School of Public Health. Her research at Hopkins has focused on individuals with emotional and behavioral challenges, specifically those with bipolar disorder or with suicidal thoughts and behaviors. Her academic preparation consists of undergraduate and graduate degrees in psychology, with a Master of the Arts in Education from the California State University, Sacramento (school psychology credential) followed by a doctorate from the University of California, Santa Barbara, in the Department of Counseling, Clinical and School Psychology.

Prior to her graduate studies, Dr. Hart spent a number of years in the mental health arena working with severely impaired individuals in psychiatric facilities or transitioning to the community. Her desire to intervene earlier in the progression of mental health challenges led her to school psychology, and she practiced in schools in Northern California for several years. Dr. Hart has focused her career on children and youth with emotional and behavioral challenges, particularly the intersection between mental health and the educational context; that is, promoting successful experiences for this underserved population in the schools. Her scholarly activities include manuscripts, articles, and book chapters, as well as local, state, and national presentations related to these topics.

Stephen E. Brock, Ph.D., is a Professor and the School Psychology Program Coordinator at California State University, Sacramento (CSUS). His professional preparation includes undergraduate and graduate degrees in psychology, and a Ph.D. in education (with an emphasis in psychological studies) from the University of California, Davis, where he researched attention-deficit/hyperactivity disorder.

A Nationally Certified School Psychologists (NCSP) and Licensed Educational Psychologist (LEP), Dr. Brock worked for 18 years as a school psychologist with the Lodi Unified School District (the last six of which included assignment as Lead Psychologist) before joining the CSUS faculty. As a school psychologist he helped to develop the district's school crisis response protocol, served on an autism specialty team, and specialized in functional behavioral assessment.

S.R. Hart et al., *Identifying, Assessing, and Treating Bipolar Disorder at School*,
Developmental Psychopathology at School, DOI 10.1007/978-1-4614-7585-9,
© Springer Science+Business Media New York 2014

A member of the National Association of School Psychologists (NASP) since 1985, Dr. Brock currently serves as the Association's President-Elect, as a Contributing Editor to the *Communiqué* (the NASP newsletter), is on the Editorial Advisory Board of the *School Psychology Review*, is a member of the National Emergency Assistance Team, and is cochair of the PREPaRE Crisis Prevention and Intervention Training Curriculum workgroup. In addition, he previously served as the California representative to the NASP Delegate Assembly, the Western Region Representative to the NASP Executive Council, and Coordinator of the Crisis Management Interest Group. He was the lead editor of the NASP publication *Best Practices in School Crisis Prevention and Intervention* and lead author of *School Crisis Prevention and Intervention: The PREPaRE Model.*

At the state level, Dr. Brock is a past president of the California Association of School Psychologists (CASP). Previously, he served CASP as the Region X representative, the Employment Relations Specialist, the Convention Chairperson, was on the editorial board of *CASP Today* (the CASP newsletter), and was an Associate Editor of *The California School Psychologist.*

Dr. Brock received NASP's Presidential award in 2004 and 2006, NASP's Crisis Management Interest Group's Award of Excellence in 2006 and 2007, CASP's Outstanding School Psychologist award in 1997, the Sandra Goff Memorial Award in 2012; and the CSUS Outstanding Faculty Scholarly and Creative Activity Award in 2013

Dr. Brock's academic work has included study of school-based crisis intervention; system-level school crisis response; suicide prevention, intervention, and postvention; ADHD; functional behavioral assessment; violence prevention; threat assessment; reading; and autism. His curriculum vitae lists over 230 publications (including 15 book titles) and over 150 invited or refereed state/national/international conference presentations. Recently he was the lead author of the books *School Crisis Prevention and Intervention: The PREPaRE Model* and *Identifying, Assessing, and Treating ADHD at School.* Currently in press is the second edition of *Best Practices in School Crisis Prevention and Intervention* (to be published by the National Association of School Psychologists). He is on the editorial board of the *Journal of School Violence,* and along with Dr. Shane R. Jimerson, is editor of a book series for Springer Science+Business Media titled *Developmental Psychopathology Scientist Practitioner at School Series.* Books from this series, which find Dr. Brock also playing an authorship role, include: *Identifying, Assessing, and Treating Autism at School*; *Identifying, Assessing, and Treating Posttraumatic Stress Disorder at School*; *Identifying, Assessing, and Treating Dyslexia at School*; *Identifying, Assessing, and Treating ADHD at School*; and *Identifying, Assessing, and Treating Self-Injury at School.* His books have been translated into Greek, Japanese, and Chinese.

Ida Jeltova, Ph.D., is a licensed psychologist with extensive research and clinical experience working with individuals who are facing challenges with self-regulation. Until recently Dr. Jeltova focused on research and teaching at the Graduate Center, City University of New York. Starting in 2012, Dr. Jeltova is exclusively focusing on clinical work and advocacy for families with children with emotional and behavioral challenges. Her work combines biological and psychological dimensions and focuses on developing psychological interventions to optimize and harmonize child–family and child–environment match. Dr. Jeltova has extensive experience in working with adoptive families, including post-institutionalized and foster care children. She is an active member at the Adoption and Foster Care Therapist Network.

Index

S.R. Hart et al., *Identifying, Assessing, and Treating Bipolar Disorder at School*,
Developmental Psychopathology at School, DOI 10.1007/978-1-4614-7585-9,
© Springer Science+Business Media New York 2014

CPSIA information can be obtained at www.ICGtesting.com
Printed in the USA
LVOW01*2136021113

359753LV00006B/79/P

9 781461 475842